THE PRUDENTIAL CARVE-OUT FOR FINANCIAL SERVICES

The World Trade Organization's (WTO's) General Agreement on Trade in Services (GATS) sets out a framework and rules for the liberalisation of international trade in services. Paragraph 2(a) of the GATS Annex on Financial Services is generally known as the Prudential Carve-Out (PCO). Notwithstanding GATS obligations, it allows WTO Members to pursue prudential regulatory objectives. This book studies the GATS PCO in light of its negotiating history and economic rationale as well as PCOs in all preferential trade agreements notified to the WTO Secretariat up to the summer of 2017. The author clarifies the state of play of international cooperation on financial services regulation, provides a current understanding of the GATS PCO, analyses how PCOs are drafted in preferential trade agreements and, finally, seeks to understand whether alternative approaches to the mainstream understanding of the PCO are possible and suggests options for reform.

CARLO MARIA CANTORE is a lecturer in International Trade and Investment Law at the University of Antwerp.

CAMBRIDGE INTERNATIONAL TRADE AND ECONOMIC LAW

Series Editors

Dr Lorand Bartels, *University of Cambridge*
Professor Thomas Cottier, *University of Berne*
Professor William Davey, *University of Illinois*

As the processes of regionalisation and globalisation have intensified, there have been accompanying increases in the regulations of international trade and economic law at the levels of international, regional and national laws.

The subject matter of this series is international economic law. Its core is the regulation of international trade, investment and cognate areas such as intellectual property and competition policy. The series publishes books on related regulatory areas, in particular human rights, labour, environment and culture, as well as sustainable development. These areas are vertically linked at the international, regional and national level, and the series extends to the implementation of these rules at these different levels. The series also includes works on governance, dealing with the structure and operation of related international organisations in the field of international economic law, and the way they interact with other subjects of international and national law.

Books in the Series

The Prudential Carve-Out for Financial Services: Rationale and Practice in the GATS and Preferential Trade Agreements
Carlo Maria Cantore

Judicial Acts and Investment Treaty Arbitration
Berk Demirkol

Distributive Justice and World Trade Law: A Political Theory of International Trade Regulation
Oisin Suttle

Freedom of Transit and Access to Gas Pipeline Networks under WTO Law
Vitalily Pogoretskyy

Reclaiming Development in the World Trading System, 2nd edition
Yong-Shik Lee

Developing Countries and Preferential Services Trade
Charlotte Sieber-Gasser

WTO Dispute Settlement and the TRIPS Agreement: Applying Intellectual Property Standards in a Trade Law Framework
Matthew Kennedy

Establishing Judicial Authority in International Economic Law
Edited by Joanna Jemielniak, Laura Nielsen and Henrik Palmer Olsen

Trade, Investment, Innovation and their Impact on Access to Medicines: An Asian Perspective
Locknie Hsu

The Law, Economics and Politics of International Standardisation
Panagiotis Delimatsis

The WTO and International Investment Law: Converging Systems
Jürgen Kurtz

Export Restrictions on Critical Minerals and Metals: Testing the Adequacy of WTO Disciplines
Ilaria Espa

Optimal Regulation and the Law of International Trade: The Interface between the Right to Regulate and WTO Law
Boris Rigod

The Social Foundations of World Trade: Norms, Community and Constitution
Sungjoon Cho

Public Participation and Legitimacy in the WTO
Yves Bonzon

The Challenge of Safeguards in the WTO
Fernando Piérola

General Interests of Host States in International Investment Law
Edited by Giorgio Sacerdoti, with Pia Acconci, Mara Valenti and Anna De Luca

The Law of Development Cooperation: A Comparative Analysis of the World Bank, the EU and Germany
Philipp Dann

WTO Disciplines on Subsidies and Countervailing Measures: Balancing Policy Space and Legal Constraints
Dominic Coppens

Domestic Judicial Review of Trade Remedies: Experiences of the Most Active WTO Members
Edited by Müslüm Yilmaz

The Relevant Market in International Economic Law: A Comparative Antitrust and GATT Analysis
Christian A. Melischek

International Organizations in WTO Dispute Settlement: How Much Institutional Sensitivity
Marina Foltea

Public Services and International Trade Liberalization: Human Rights and Gender Implications
Barnali Choudhury

The Law and Politics of WTO Waivers: Stability and Flexibility in Public International Law
Isabel Feichtner

African Regional Trade Agreements as Legal Regimes
James Thuo Gathii

Liberalizing International Trade after Doha: Multilateral, Plurilateral, Regional, and Unilateral Initiatives
David A. Gantz

Processes and Production Methods (PPMs) in WTO Law: Interfacing Trade and Social Goals
Christiane R. Conrad

Non-Discrimination in International Trade in Services: 'Likeness' in WTO/GATS
Nicolas F. Diebold

The Law, Economics and Politics of Retaliation in WTO Dispute Settlement
Edited by Chad P. Bown and Joost Pauwelyn

The Multilateralization of International Investment Law
Stephan W. Schill

Trade Policy Flexibility and Enforcement in the WTO: A Law and Economics Analysis
Simon A.B. Schropp

THE PRUDENTIAL CARVE-OUT FOR FINANCIAL SERVICES

Rationale and Practice in the GATS and Preferential Trade Agreements

CARLO MARIA CANTORE
University of Antwerp

CAMBRIDGE
UNIVERSITY PRESS

University Printing House, Cambridge CB2 8BS, United Kingdom

One Liberty Plaza, 20th Floor, New York, NY 10006, USA

477 Williamstown Road, Port Melbourne, VIC 3207, Australia

314–321, 3rd Floor, Plot 3, Splendor Forum, Jasola District Centre, New Delhi - 110025, India

79 Anson Road, #06-04/06, Singapore 079906

Cambridge University Press is part of the University of Cambridge.

It furthers the University's mission by disseminating knowledge in the pursuit of education, learning, and research at the highest international levels of excellence.

www.cambridge.org
Information on this title: www.cambridge.org/9781108415767
DOI: 10.1017/9781108235136

© Carlo Maria Cantore 2018

This publication is in copyright. Subject to statutory exception and to the provisions of relevant collective licensing agreements, no reproduction of any part may take place without the written permission of Cambridge University Press.

First published 2018

Printed and bound in Great Britain by Clays Ltd, Elcograf S.p.A.

A catalogue record for this publication is available from the British Library

Library of Congress Cataloging-in-Publication data
Names: Cantore, Carlo Maria, 1986–, author.
Title: The prudential carve-out for financial services : rationale and practice in the GATS and preferential trade agreements / Carlo Maria Cantore, University of Antwerp.
Description: New York : Cambridge University Press, 2018. | Includes bibliographical references.
Identifiers: LCCN 2018000410 | ISBN 9781108415767
Subjects: LCSH: General Agreement on Trade in Services (1994 April 15) | Commercial treaties. | Financial services industry – Law and legislation. | Financial institutions – Law and legislation. | Foreign trade regulation. | World Trade Organization.
Classification: LCC K4609.5.C36 2018 | DDC 346/.08215 – dc23
LC record available at https://lccn.loc.gov/2018000410

ISBN 978-1-108-41576-7 Hardback

Cambridge University Press has no responsibility for the persistence or accuracy of URLs for external or third-party internet websites referred to in this publication and does not guarantee that any content on such websites is, or will remain, accurate or appropriate.

A Mamma e Papà

CONTENTS

List of Figures   *page* xi
List of Tables   xii
Acknowledgements   xiii
List of Abbreviations   xvi
List of Cited Panel and Appellate Body Reports   xviii

1 The Subject Matter of the Study   1
   1.1 The Issue   1
   1.2 Presentation of the Rest of the Volume   3

2 International Cooperation on Financial Services and Prudential Measures: WTO and Beyond   5
   2.1 The Multilateral Discipline on Trade in Financial Services: Origins and Negotiations   5
   2.2 International Cooperation on Financial (and Prudential) Regulation   16
   2.3 Explaining the Need for Prudence   33
   2.4 The Evolution of Financial Regulation after the Entry into Force of the GATS   42
   2.5 The Macroprudential Toolbox in the Aftermath of the 2007–8 Financial Crisis   56
   2.6 Conclusion: Do Prudential Concerns Justify More Regulatory Autonomy Than Other Areas?   62

3 The Current Understanding of the GATS PCO   64
   3.1 A Non-Self-Interpreting Provision and the Opinion of Scholars   65
   3.2 Discussions in the WTO Committee on Trade in Financial Services   73
   3.3 The Panel in *Argentina – Financial Services*   84
   3.4 The Appellate Body in *Argentina – Financial Services*   103
   3.5 Conclusion   104

4 Prudential Carve-Outs in Preferential Trade Agreements 106
   4.1 Preferential Trade Agreements under Article V of the GATS 106
   4.2 Prudential Carve-Outs in PTAs 114
   4.3 Ongoing Negotiations 154
   4.4 Conclusion 167

5 A Possible Alternative Approach 168
   5.1 Introduction 168
   5.2 Problems with the Current Mainstream Approach 168
   5.3 The PCO as a Tool to Address Contingencies 191
   5.4 Conclusions on Why Classifying the PCO as an Exception Is Not the Only Permissible Option 194
   5.5 What the Mainstream Approach Overlooks: Negotiating History and Economic Rationale 194
   5.6 An Alternative Approach 211
   5.7 Conclusion 219

6 Suggestions for Reform 225
   6.1 Procedural Innovations 226
   6.2 Substantive Innovations 231
   6.3 Conclusion 237

References 238
Index 247

FIGURES

4.1 Chapters on financial services in preferential trade agreements
(elaboration on data from WTO Regional Trade Agreements Database) *page* 111
4.2 Prudential carve-outs in preferential trade agreements (elaboration on
data from WTO Regional Trade Agreements Database) 114
4.3 Types of prudential carve-outs in preferential trade agreements
(elaboration of data from the WTO Regional Trade Agreements Database) 118
4.4 Trends of categories of preferential prudential carve-outs over time 151
4.5 Frequency of requirements in preferential prudential carve-outs 153

TABLES

2.1	Outcomes of international financial regulation	*page* 21
2.2	Minimum liquidity coverage ratio requirements	26
4.1	Prudential carve-out (PCO) restrictiveness index	152
5.1	Positions of the delegations with regard to the chairperson's proposal for a prudential carve-out	197
5.2	Three formal proposals on prudential measures	200

ACKNOWLEDGEMENTS

Kim Hughes, Abigail Neale, Elizabeth Budd, Bhawna Batra and the staff of Cambridge University Press made the birth of this book possible, and I will be forever grateful for their patience and support.

This book is a revised version of my PhD thesis, which I wrote and defended at the European University Institute (EUI) of Florence. The manuscript was submitted on 30 October 2017, and covers developments that took place at that date. Whilst I am the sole responsible party for any errors and shortcomings the reader might find in it, this book would not have seen the light of day without the precious help and support I received from several people and institutions.

I need to thank the Italian Ministry of Foreign Affairs and the European University Institute for granting me a full PhD scholarship.

Not a single word would have been written without the tireless help of my supervisor Petros Mavroidis. I had the privilege of being his research assistant in Florence over four years and to share with him the most random and hilarious moments. I owe him everything I know about law (which is still much too little), and I hope he will keep forgiving me for the many (many) things that I still do not know after all this time by his side. Although I miss our endless afternoons in his office, discussing law and life, things have not really changed. He has been and will always be my one and only mentor, a role model and one of my best friends.

The core idea of this work took shape in endless discussions with Juan Marchetti, when I was an intern at the Trade in Services Division of the WTO. He is one of the most knowledgeable and generous people I have ever met, and I am glad he accepted the request to serve as jury member for my PhD defence. Bernard Hoekman and Jean-François Bellis (the other two members of the jury) gave me very useful comments, which I tried to fully incorporate in the final version of the manuscript.

Gustavo Luengo Hernàndez de Madrid and Bart De Meester gave me invaluable feedback on my ideas and earlier drafts. Cristiano Cantore, my brother, helped me understand the economics behind what I was writing.

I benefitted enormously from discussions with Alberto Alemanno, Alessandro Aresu, Natasa Athanasiadou, Jonathan Chevry, James Flett, Andrea Garnero, Nicola Limodio, Mislav Mataija, Margherita Melillo, Leonardo Pierdominici, Boris Rigod, Marco Rizzi, Luca Rubini, Ulrich Woelker and Georges Zavvos.

Giuseppe Martinico, as always, has been a great guide and prevented me from making wrong decisions. I owe immense gratitude to him and to Prof. Paolo Carrozza, my supervisor at Sant'Anna School, who supported me even when I chose to leave my first academic nest.

I warmly thank the administrative staff of the institutions that hosted me during the stops of my journey: the EUI (in particular, Eleonora Masella and Laurence Duranel), the WTO and the European Commission.

The personnel of the libraries of the EUI (especially Machteld Nijsten and Alberto Caselli), Sant'Anna, the WTO, the European Commission and Columbia Law School made my path much smoother than it would have otherwise been.

At Van Bael & Bellis, the law firm where I was working at the time of finalising this book, I had the luck of sharing my journey with some of my favourite trade lawyers in the world: Gabriele Coppo, Sidonie Descheemaeker, Kornel Olsthoorn, Francesco Pili, Aldo Scalini, Benoît Servais, Andrea Tel and Isabelle Van Damme. My discussions with them are somewhat reflected in the volume.

I am also indebted to many more people for what they have given me over the years.

James, in addition to being my wingman during my Florentine period, pointed out the many flaws in my arguments. I believe his path towards sanctity has become much shorter since he met me. All I can say is that I am a much more relaxed person since I met him. Together he, Benedita and Luísa have been my Florentine family. They were always there for me, and I will always keep every moment of our long hours in via dei Rustici and Santo Spirito in my heart. Pasquale and Elena were amazing housemates and keep being amazing friends.

Other friends in Potenza, Florence, Pisa, Geneva and Brussels deserve credit as well. It would take too many pages to thank them all one by one, but they clearly know whom I am referring to.

I owe Chiara more than can be expressed in words. I cannot promise her that our post-book life will be more relaxing, but she can rest assured that we will make the best out of it, together.

My debt to all the aforementioned people is enormous, as is the debt to my parents and to my brother. They have done and continue doing anything in their power to support me, and I thank them from the bottom of my heart. This book, like everything else, is for them.

Bruxelles, 30 October 2017

ABBREVIATIONS

AA	Articles of Agreement of the International Monetary Fund
AB	Appellate Body
ALOP	adequate level of protection
ANZCERTA	Australia New Zealand Closer Economic Agreement
ASEAN	Association of South-East Asian Nations
BCBS	Basel Committee on Banking Supervision
BIS	Bank for International Settlement
BRRD	Bank Recovery and Resolution Directive
CA	Agreement on Civil Aircraft
CCP	central counterparty
CETA	EU–Canada Comprehensive Economic and Trade Agreement
CRD	Capital Requirements Directive
CRTA	Committee on Regional Trade Agreements
CSDs	central securities depositories
CSI	Coalition of Services Industry
CTFS	Committee on Trade in Financial Services
EAC	East African Community
EEA	European Economic Area
EFTA	European Free Trade Association
EMIR	European Markets and Infrastructure Regulation
FSB	Financial Stability Board
FSOC	Financial Stability Oversight Council
GATT 1947 and GATT 1994	General Agreement on Tariffs and Trade
GATS	General Agreement on Trade in Services
GDP	gross domestic product
GNS	Group Negotiations on Services
GPA	Agreement on Government Procurement
G-SIBs	Global Systemically Important Banks
G-7	Group of Seven
G-10	Group of Ten
G-20	Group of Twenty
HFT	high-frequency trading

HQLA	high-quality liquid assets
IAIS	International Association of Insurance Supervisors
IBM	International Bovine Meat Agreement
IC	Inuit community
IDA	International Dairy Agreement
IMF	International Monetary Fund
IOSCO	International Organization of Securities Commissions
LCR	liquidity coverage ratio
LoI	Letter of Intent
LTV	loan-to-value
MERCOSUR	Mercado Común del Sur (in Spanish)
MFN	Most Favoured Nation
MiFID	Markets in Financial Instruments Directive
MiFIR	Markets in Financial Instruments Regulation
MoU	Memorandum of Understanding
MRA	mutual recognition agreement
NAFTA	North American Free Trade Agreement
NT	National Treatment
OECD	Organization for Economic Cooperation and Development
OTC	over-the-counter
PCO	prudential carve-out
PTA	preferential trade agreement
RCEP	Regional Comprehensive Economic Partnership
RGFS	Really Good Friends of Services
SEACEN	South East Asian Central Banking and Monetary Authorities
SIFIs	systemically important financial institutions
SPS	Agreement on the Application of Sanitary and Phytosanitary Measures
TBT	Agreement on Technical Barriers to Trade
TED	Turtles Excluder Device
TiSA	Trade in Services Agreement
TNC	Trade Negotiations Committee
TPP	Trans-Pacific Partnership
TPRM	Trade Policy Review Mechanism
TTIP	Trans-Atlantic Trade and Investment Partnership
UN	United Nations
URR	Unremunerated Reserve Requirements
USTR	United States Trade Representative
VCLT	Vienna Convention on the Law of Treaties

CITED PANEL AND APPELLATE BODY REPORTS

Argentina – Financial Services	Appellate Body Report, Argentina – Measures Relating to Trade in Goods and Services, WT/DS453/AB/R and Add.1, adopted 9 May 2016
Argentina – Financial Services	Panel Report, Argentina – Measures Relating to Trade in Goods and Services, WT/DS453/R and Add.1, adopted 9 May 2016, as modified by Appellate Body Report WT/DS453/AB/R
Brazil – Retreaded Tyres	Appellate Body Report, *Brazil – Measures Affecting Imports of Retreaded Tyres*, WT/DS332/AB/R, adopted 17 December 2007, DSR 2007:IV, p. 1527
Brazil – Retreaded Tyres	Panel Report, *Brazil – Measures Affecting Imports of Retreaded Tyres*, WT/DS332/R, adopted 17 December 2007, as modified by Appellate Body Report WT/DS332/AB/R, DSR 2007:V, p. 1649
Canada – Continued Suspension	Appellate Body Report, *Canada – Continued Suspension of Obligations in the EC – Hormones Dispute*, WT/DS321/AB/R, adopted 14 November 2008, DSR 2008:XIV, p. 5373
China – Electronic Payment Services	Panel Report, China – Certain Measures Affecting Electronic Payment Services, WT/DS413/R and Add.1, adopted 31 August 2012, DSR 2012:X, p. 5305
China – Publications and Audiovisual Products	Appellate Body Report, *China – Measures Affecting Trading Rights and Distribution Services for Certain Publications and Audiovisual Entertainment Products*, WT/DS363/AB/R, adopted 19 January 2010, DSR 2010:I, p. 3

LIST OF CITED PANEL AND APPELLATE BODY REPORTS

China – Publications and Audiovisual Products	Panel Report, *China – Measures Affecting Trading Rights and Distribution Services for Certain Publications and Audiovisual Entertainment Products*, WT/DS363/R and Corr.1, adopted 19 January 2010, as modified by Appellate Body Report WT/DS363/AB/R, DSR 2010:II, p. 261
China – Rare Earths	Appellate Body Reports, *China – Measures Related to the Exportation of Rare Earths, Tungsten, and Molybdenum*, WT/DS431/AB/R / WT/DS432/AB/R / WT/DS433/AB/R, adopted 29 August 2014, DSR 2014:III, p. 805
China – Rare Earths	Panel Reports, *China – Measures Related to the Exportation of Rare Earths, Tungsten, and Molybdenum*, WT/DS431/R and Add.1 / WT/DS432/R and Add.1 / WT/DS433/R and Add.1, adopted 29 August 2014, upheld by Appellate Body Reports WT/DS431/AB/R / WT/DS432/AB/R / WT/DS433/AB/R, DSR 2014:IV, p. 1127
China – Raw Materials	Appellate Body Reports, *China – Measures Related to the Exportation of Various Raw Materials*, WT/DS394/AB/R / WT/DS395/AB/R / WT/DS398/AB/R, adopted 22 February 2012, DSR 2012:VII, p. 3295
China – Raw Materials	Panel Reports, *China – Measures Related to the Exportation of Various Raw Materials*, WT/DS394/R, Add.1 and Corr.1 / WT/DS395/R, Add.1 and Corr.1 / WT/DS398/R, Add.1 and Corr.1, adopted 22 February 2012, as modified by Appellate Body Reports WT/DS394/AB/R / WT/DS395/AB/R / WT/DS398/AB/R, DSR 2012:VII, p. 3501
EC – Approval and Marketing of Biotech Products	Panel Reports, *European Communities – Measures Affecting the Approval and Marketing of Biotech Products*, WT/DS291/R, Add.1 to Add.9 and Corr.1 / WT/DS292/R, Add.1 to Add.9 and Corr.1 / WT/DS293/R, Add.1 to Add.9 and Corr.1, adopted 21 November 2006, DSR 2006:III, p. 847
EC – Asbestos	Appellate Body Report, *European Communities – Measures Affecting Asbestos and Asbestos-Containing Products*, WT/DS135/AB/R, adopted 5 April 2001, DSR 2001:VII, p. 3243

LIST OF CITED PANEL AND APPELLATE BODY REPORTS

EC – Sardines	Appellate Body Report, European Communities – Trade Description of Sardines, WT/DS231/AB/R, adopted 23 October 2002, DSR 2002:VIII, p. 3359
EC – Seal Products	Appellate Body Reports, *European Communities – Measures Prohibiting the Importation and Marketing of Seal Products*, WT/DS400/AB/R / WT/DS401/AB/R, adopted 18 June 2014, DSR 2014:I, p. 7
India – Quantitative Restrictions	Appellate Body Report, *India – Quantitative Restrictions on Imports of Agricultural, Textile and Industrial Products*, WT/DS90/AB/R, adopted 22 September 1999, DSR 1999:IV, p. 1763
Mexico – Telecoms	Panel Report, *Mexico – Measures Affecting Telecommunications Services*, WT/DS204/R, adopted 1 June 2004, DSR 2004:IV, p. 1537
Turkey – Textiles	Appellate Body Report, *Turkey – Restrictions on Imports of Textile and Clothing Products*, WT/DS34/AB/R, adopted 19 November 1999, DSR 1999:VI, p. 2345
US – Clove Cigarettes	Appellate Body Report, *United States – Measures Affecting the Production and Sale of Clove Cigarettes*, WT/DS406/AB/R, adopted 24 April 2012, DSR 2012: XI, p. 5751
US – Gambling	Appellate Body Report, *United States – Measures Affecting the Cross-Border Supply of Gambling and Betting Services*, WT/DS285/AB/R, adopted 20 April 2005, DSR 2005:XII, p. 5663 (and Corr.1, DSR 2006:XII, p. 5475)
US – Gambling	Panel Report, *United States – Measures Affecting the Cross-Border Supply of Gambling and Betting Services*, WT/DS285/R, adopted 20 April 2005, as modified by Appellate Body Report WT/DS285/AB/R, DSR 2005:XII, p. 5797
US – Gasoline	Appellate Body Report, United States – Standards for Reformulated and Conventional Gasoline, WT/DS2/AB/R, adopted 20 May 1996, DSR 1996:I, p. 3
US – Offset Act (Byrd Amendment)	Appellate Body Report, United States – Continued Dumping and Subsidy Offset Act of 2000, WT/DS217/AB/R, WT/DS234/AB/R, adopted 27 January 2003, DSR 2003:I, p. 375

US – Shrimp (Article 21.5 – Malaysia)	Appellate Body Report, *United States – Import Prohibition of Certain Shrimp and Shrimp Products – Recourse to Article 21.5 of the DSU by Malaysia*, WT/DS58/AB/RW, adopted 21 November 2001, DSR 2001:XIII, p. 6481
US – Shrimp	Appellate Body Report, United States – Import Prohibition of Certain Shrimp and Shrimp Products, WT/DS58/AB/R, adopted 6 November 1998, DSR 1998:VII, p. 2755

1

The Subject Matter of the Study

1.1 The Issue

The main question this volume aims to provide an answer to is the following: what is the legal function assigned to Paragraph 2(a) of the Annex on Financial Services of the GATS, commonly known as the Prudential Carve-Out (PCO)?

Some authoritative documents, including the 2009 *Report of the Commission of Experts of the President of the United Nations General Assembly on Reforms of the International Monetary and Financial System*, have pointed to trade agreements – both at the multilateral as well as the bilateral level – as being among the drivers for the deregulation that has taken place in many jurisdictions since the mid-1990s.[1] In particular, the claim is that trade liberalisation has limited the possibility for domestic governments to support the stability of their financial systems.

Most trade agreements dealing with financial services include a provision that aims to preserve some regulatory freedom for Members wishing to step in and modify the existing domestic rules on financial services for 'prudential reasons'. The paradigmatic example in this regard is the PCO of the GATS, which allows WTO Members to adopt measures they deem appropriate for prudential reasons when regulating trade in financial services. Due to the importance of the objectives pursued by the provision, it is extremely important to clarify its scope of application and legal function in light of the 2007–8 financial crisis and the worldwide regulatory developments that ensued.

---

[1] See para. 208: 'The framework for financial market liberalization under the Financial Services Agreement of the General Agreement on Trade in Services (GATS) under the WTO and, even more, similar provisions in bilateral trade agreements may restrict the ability of governments to change the regulatory structure in ways which support financial stability, economic growth, and the welfare of vulnerable consumers and investors.' The document is available at www.un.org/ga/econcrisissummit/docs/FinalReport_CoE.pdf. All websites were last accessed on 30 October 2017.

The GATS PCO has been a 'sleeping beauty' for more than twenty years. Recently, the Panel in *Argentina – Financial Services* was confronted with the issue. The Panel immediately classified the provision as an exception and deliberately ignored supplementary means of interpretation in its assessment. This volume argues that there is at least one other permissible interpretation of the provision, which would classify it as a 'provision that excludes the application of other provisions'.

The issue of the classification and the legal function performed by a provision of an international agreement is not a mere academic quandary. Grando[2] has conducted a comprehensive analysis of the way in which WTO case law distinguishes between the various rules that allow Members to be exempted from compliance with more generic rules. The author subdivided the various provisions she analysed into two categories: 'exceptions' and 'provisions that exclude the application of other provisions'.

Such a distinction has implications with regard to the allocation of the burden of proof in the event of a dispute. Depending on the classification the burden of proof should fall on the complainant (for 'provisions that exclude the application of other provisions') or on the respondent or regulating Member (for 'exceptions'). Moreover, it also has an impact with regard to the degree of deference that WTO panels must pay to the regulating Members. In the case of 'provisions that exclude the application of other provisions', panels are typically more deferential towards the policy preferences expressed by Members whose regulations are challenged.

The classification of the PCO as a 'provision that excludes the application of other provisions' implies that, in the event of a dispute, the burden of proof should be allocated to the Member alleging a violation of one or more WTO obligations and not on the regulating Member. Moreover, WTO panels and the Appellate Body should be extremely careful when scrutinising the policy choices made by domestic governments in pursuit of prudential objectives as the text and the rationale of the PCO allow them substantial freedom.

The aim of this volume, moreover, is to provide the first comprehensive overview and analysis of prudential carve-outs in free trade agreements on financial services; such analysis had never been conducted. The relevance of this study is twofold: first, it provides an analysis of the state of the art of the evolution of trade rules at the bilateral level (i.e. the only domain where there has been such evolution in light of the deadlock of the multilateral

---

[2] Michelle T. Grando, *Evidence, Proof and Fact-Finding in WTO Dispute Settlement* (Oxford: Oxford University Press, 2009), p. 152.

1.2 Presentation of the Rest of the Volume

negotiations at the WTO); second, it provides ideas for amendments to the current formulation of the GATS PCO, which is admittedly not drafted in the clearest possible fashion.

1.2 Presentation of the Rest of the Volume

The remainder of this volume is structured as follows. Chapter 2 provides the necessary context to the analysis that is conducted in the book. It first recalls the history of the negotiations of the GATS Annex on Financial Services and the role played by prudential concerns at that time. The chapter then examines the economic rationales for prudential regulation and gives account of the evolution of prudential concerns at the national and international level since the entry into force of the GATS. In particular, the chapter looks at regulatory developments that have taken place in national jurisdictions in the aftermath of financial disruptions and provides an overview of the work done by international standard-setting forums. The chapter also gives an account of the most common prudential measures adopted by domestic legislative authorities.

Chapter 3 describes the current understanding of the GATS PCO. It first examines the way in which the provision has been interpreted by the literature so far, then offers an account of the discussions conducted within the Committee on Trade in Financial Services of the GATS in which several Members have indicated that they are not at ease with the formulation of the provision and have even submitted proposals for reform. The chapter also reviews the way in which the GATS PCO was dealt with in the only WTO dispute so far where it was invoked: *Argentina – Financial Services*.

In Chapter 4, an examination is conducted to establish whether PCOs are included in preferential trade agreements (PTAs) and to identify common patterns as well as the different typologies of provisions that have emerged since the late 1990s. It is noted that the model set up in the GATS is still the most commonly adopted in trade negotiations. It is also shown that Members, when they want to 'lock in' their trade commitments and ensure that the PCO is narrowly interpreted or only available upon satisfaction of one or more requirements (be it a necessity test or a non-discriminatory application of prudential measures), have the necessary tools to do so. It is emphasised that this happens only in a minority of cases, given that the overwhelming majority of preferential PCOs give parties substantial leeway when they regulate financial markets according to prudential concerns. Finally, developments in current negotiations are also examined. Given that the PCO in the GATS is rather obscure in terms of its language and not particularly efficient, an overview of the developments in preferential negotiations is instrumental in understanding whether some already existing features in other trade agreements can be imported at the multilateral stage.

Chapter 5 seeks to illustrate that there are a number of problematic implications of the mainstream interpretation of the PCO. By importing the case law on exceptions into the domain of the PCO, this volume shows how the former cannot easily be reconciled with the wording of the PCO, the intention of the drafters or the economic rationale behind prudential regulation.

The economic analysis, combined with the negotiating history of the PCO, shows that the main desire of the negotiators was to avoid Type I errors (false positives), i.e. situations in which the court finds against a defendant, even though the behaviour of the latter was not unlawful. This outcome can hardly be reconciled with the mainstream interpretation advanced by the few scholars who have attempted to analyse the PCO. The classification of the PCO as an exception would imply a different rationale for the provision, namely that of avoiding Type II errors (false negatives), which are those cases in which the judges find in favour of the defendant even though its behaviour was unlawful. In other words, in the realm of 'exceptions', a legal system considers erring in favour of the complainant a less harmful option than erring in favour of the Member invoking the exception in the event of a dispute. The discussion conducted in Chapter 5 proves that there are solid textual, contextual, historical and economic reasons that permit an alternative interpretation of the PCO.

Chapter 6 concludes the work. It acknowledges that, notwithstanding the various readings that can be made of the PCO, the language of the latter is not sufficiently clear and reveals inefficiencies in its construction. Therefore, the present volume suggests possible paths that can be followed should WTO Members decide to reform the provision, mostly drawing inspiration from preferential PCOs.

2

International Cooperation on Financial Services and Prudential Measures

WTO and Beyond

Before embarking on an analysis and a legal interpretation of the GATS Prudential Carve-Out (PCO), it is necessary to understand the process and the context that led the Members of the World Trade Organization (WTO) to approve an obscure and non-self-explanatory provision in the framework of the Uruguay Round of negotiations for the establishment of the WTO. In so doing, it is of quintessential importance to identify the position of financial services within the framework of the GATS because the PCO is meant to serve this Agreement and, more specifically, its discipline on financial services. Only at the end of this exercise will it be possible to identify the role played by the PCO in such a delicate institutional and legal setting.

2.1 The Multilateral Discipline on Trade in Financial Services: Origins and Negotiations

There is no comprehensive negotiating history of the Annex on Financial Services of the GATS to date. Uruguay Round negotiators usually met informally during the talks on the discipline on financial services, hence the difficulty and the need to put together the pieces of the story.[1]

Moreover, various Members sent to the negotiating tables on financial services officials from both trade and finance (or treasury) departments, hence personnel with a different mind-set compared with that of trade experts. Without indulging in hindsight speculation, it is fair to argue that this is somehow reflected in the way in which the norms were formulated.

---

[1] Juan A. Marchetti, 'The GATS Prudential Carve-Out', in Panagiotis Delimatsis and Nils Herger (eds.), *Financial Regulation at the Crossroads: Implications for Supervision, Institutional Design and Trade* (Alphen aan den Rijn: Kluwer Law International, 2011), 279–95 (p. 280).

2.1.1 Financial Services as the Driving Force for the Negotiation of a Multilateral Agreement on Trade in Services

While the idea of liberalising international trade in goods at the multilateral level became popular right after the end of World War II, it took more time for negotiations on trade in services to take place. The first multilateral agreement on trade, the General Agreement on Tariffs and Trade (GATT), dates back to 1947 and only encompasses disciplines regarding trade in goods.[2]

There is more than one reason for the absence of any meaningful discipline on trade in services in the GATT. First, the share of services produced and consumed within the domestic markets was significantly higher than that traded at the international level. In addition, in the immediate aftermath of World War II, the technological revolution that dominated the second half of the twentieth century was only at its start, and services were still a small percentage of the world gross domestic product (GDP). Moreover, it should also be recalled that the evolution of the services market was unequal: for instance, whilst it represented a small percentage of the GDP of Organization for Economic Cooperation and Development (OECD) countries, it was barely existent in developing countries.

Second, services were traditionally considered as ancillary to trade in merchandise. Francois and Hoekman document that, traditionally, economists had looked at services as 'non-tradables', with very limited exceptions, and that only in the mid-1970s did some scholars begin to study the effects of barriers to transnational trade in services.[3] As of the early 1980s, technological developments increased opportunities for trade in services across borders, and the share of trade in services gradually expanded and eventually overtook that of trade in goods.[4] Actors became increasingly aware of the existing barriers to cross-border trade in services

---

[2] For a detailed account of the negotiation of the GATT, see Douglas A. Irwin, Petros C. Mavroidis and Alan O. Sykes, *The Genesis of the GATT* (American Law Institute Reporters Studies on WTO Law) (Cambridge: Cambridge University Press, 2008).

[3] Joseph Francois and Bernard Hoekman, 'Services Trade and Policy', *Journal of Economic Literature*, 48:3 (2010), 642–92, at 644.

[4] Mario A. Kakabadse, 'Trade in Services and the Uruguay Round', *The Georgia Journal of International and Comparative Law*, 19:2 (1989), 384–91: '[T]he growth of international service transactions exceeded that of world merchandise trade during the last decade. According to IMF figures, fully a third of world trade in 1987 was in services, amounting to a value of some US $960 billion. Ten years earlier this trade represented, at US $282 billion, less than a quarter (23%) of world trade' (p. 384).

and of the interconnectivity of services to many production sites. Against this background, Bhagwati and, later, other scholars, started to discuss situations and mechanisms through which services could be 'disembodied' from goods.[5]

The first voice in favour of a multilateral round of negotiations for the liberalisation of trade in services was the US financial services sector. Ascher, at that time Director of Service Industry Affairs in the Office of the United States Trade Representative (USTR), stated:

> In the 1970s, the growth of the services sector became more pronounced. In the United States, the sector accounted for a larger portion of gross national product and for most of the new jobs created (sixty-seven percent of GNP in 1988 and seventy-five percent of employment). Moreover, the potential for wider distribution of services internationally through new technologies gained greater recognition. At that time, major companies in the services sector... began seeking treatment in international trade equal to goods-producing companies... Many were concerned about restrictions and discriminatory practices in foreign countries which denied them the opportunity of international sales.[6]

The US Congress, through the 1974 Trade Act, expanded the mandate of US trade negotiators to include the goal of reducing barriers to trade in services.[7] Marchetti and Mavroidis reported how important the role played by the Coalition of Services Industry (CSI) was in sensitising the political debate in the United States about the need for a multilateral agreement on trade in services.[8] Within the CSI, the role of financial

---

[5] See, among others: Jagdish Bhagwati, 'Splintering and Disembodiment of Services and Developing Nations', *The World Economy*, 7:1 (1984), 133–44; Joseph Francois, 'Trade in Nontradables: Proximity Requirements and the Pattern of Trade in Services', *Journal of Economic Integration*, 5:1 (1990), 31–46.

[6] Bernard Ascher, 'Multilateral Negotiations on Trade in Services: Concepts, Goals, Issues', *The Georgia Journal of International and Comparative Law*, 19:2 (1989), 392–403, at p. 394.

[7] US Trade Act of 1974, Section 2112, *Barriers to and other distortions of trade*: '(3) the term "international trade" includes (A) trade in both goods and services'.

[8] Juan A. Marchetti and Petros C. Mavroidis, 'The Genesis of the GATS (General Agreement on Trade in Services)', *The European Journal of International Law*, 22:3 (2011b), 689–721. Interestingly, the authors explained why American Express, a leading company in the US financial services sector, lobbied for an agreement on trade in services: 'At the time, the company was specializing in travellers' cheques, charge cards, insurance, and investment services. This business depends on the rapid transmission of large amounts of data across national borders through sophisticated computer and telecommunications networks. Trans-border data flows, essential in fact to international banking and financial services, were threatened by protection, and so was data processing. Clearly, this was of outmost

services companies was prominent. They were actively engaged in public and academic debates, were part of US delegations to various GATT meetings and managed to tighten links with counterparts all over the world, particularly in Europe.

The United States was keen to pursue a landmark agreement, and tensions arose regarding the scepticism of the developing countries. The interests at stake for the United States in the necessity to pursue an international agreement on trade in services were so high that in June 1986, US Trade Representative Clayton Yeutter issued a statement in which he threatened the possibility that the United States would turn to bilateral and plurilateral agreements if trade in services was not included in the Uruguay Round talks that were scheduled to start a few weeks later.[9]

The European Union (EU)[10] at that time did not share the same enthusiasm concerning the inclusion of services on the agenda of the negotiations for three main reasons. First, the EU was unable to speak with one voice on the issue in the negotiations because some Member States were in favour of progressive integration in the domain of trade in services whereas others clearly opposed such. Second the EU itself was facing obstacles to the liberalisation of services in its internal market. Third, developing countries were requesting the EU to make concessions in other market sectors.[11] In particular, as services would become part and parcel of the whole exchange of concessions, EU authorities feared that they would have to relax their protectionist policies in the field of agricultural products in exchange of concessions in the services market, and they were certainly not ready to do so at that point in time.[12]

---

importance to American Express. The rationale for protection varied across countries: privacy reasons, protection of strategic sectors, infant industry and employment. A new agreement regulating trade in services should aim at disciplining the rationale for protection, opening up trade on a worldwide basis' (p. 694).

[9] Marchetti and Mavroidis, 'The Genesis of the GATS': 'In June 1986, the US tabled a concrete proposal for a Ministerial Declaration which included clear terms for a negotiation on trade in services. At the same time, the USTR Clayton Yeutter publicly announced that the US would turn to bilateral and plurilateral arrangements, instead of the GATT, if the trading nations did not agree on including the necessary subjects in the agenda of the Uruguay round in particular services' (p. 702).

[10] Throughout this work, the expression 'European Union' (EU) is used to refer to the European Union and its predecessors (European Communities, European Economic Community and so on) invariantly.

[11] This is reported in Jagdish Bhagwati, 'Departures from Multilateralism: Regionalism and Aggressive Unilateralism', *The Economic Journal*, 100/403 (1990), 1304–17.

[12] Hugo Paemen and Alexandra Bensch, *From the GATT to the WTO – The European Community in the Uruguay Round* (Leuven: Leuven University Press, 1995), p. 293.

The EU was struggling to reach a common position. In particular, then French president François Mitterrand was – on several occasions – very vocal against the requests of the United States.[13] It was only subsequently that the EU slowly began to change its position, turning from a 'reluctant participant' to an 'active player'.[14] According to Marchetti and Mavroidis, three main factors contributed to the shift in the attitude of EU officials. First, the EU wanted to avoid the political costs of blocking a multilateral round of negotiations, which would have meant isolation and fewer opportunities for European services suppliers. Second, services suppliers managed to strengthen their lobbying efforts, following the example of their peers in the United States. Eventually, the EU bureaucracy came to be strongly in favour of the positive conclusion of a negotiating round because international trade represented (and, in reality, still represents to a certain extent) the only area where EU political institutions could play an effective role in external relations.[15] This change of attitude in the EU also bolstered developing countries, which had initially been suspicious with regard to the discussions for a comprehensive agreement on trade in services within the realm of the yet-to-be-born WTO. The EU was the middleman between the assertive position of the United States and the reluctance to commit shown by the G-10.[16]

In addition to the foregoing, most developing countries were hostile to the possibility of negotiating the opening of their markets for trade in services: they feared that they would not be able to obtain concessions in other sectors, and they also wanted to avoid a situation in which their economies would be dominated by foreign companies and investors (and many thought that priority should be given to agricultural trade and textiles in any case).[17] Further, developing countries were concerned that the introduction of a unitary dispute resolution mechanism could lead to

---

[13] Sabrina P. Ramet and Christine Ingebritsen, *Coming in from the Cold War – Changes in the US–European Interaction since 1980* (Lanham, MD: Rowman & Littlefield, 2002) 244 (p. 77).

[14] Juan A. Marchetti and Petros C. Mavroidis, 'From Reluctant Participant to Key Player: EU and the Negotiation of the GATS', in Inge Govaere, Reinhard Quick and Marco Bronckers (eds.), *Trade and Competition Law in the EU and Beyond* (Cheltenham: Edward Elgar, 2011), 48–95.

[15] Ibid.: 'Granted, it was unclear whether the EU had competence on services. This would not, however, stop the EU Commission from pushing the agenda further: adding services in the trade agenda would augment its competences and its relative position towards the Council in their inter-agency game', p. 65.

[16] Argentina, Brazil, Egypt, India, Yugoslavia, Cuba, Nicaragua, Nigeria, Peru and Tanzania.

[17] Marchetti and Mavroidis, 'The Genesis of the GATS', p. 698.

'cross-sanctions' that would affect their strategic markets as a retaliation against barriers in trade in services.[18]

The *Café au Lait* group, composed of both developed and developing countries, managed to act as a 'bridge-building coalition' and was instrumental in helping all parties involved to agree to kick-off the negotiations. India and Brazil, in fact, persuaded the parties at the table to launch the negotiations for an agreement on cross-border trade in services on a separate track in relation to the negotiations on new disciplines on trade in goods.[19]

2.1.2 The Negotiations on Financial Services

Negotiations followed what was already happening in practice: as a result of technological developments, some liberalisation was already taking place de facto. It is worth pointing out that the role played by financial services in the context of the Uruguay Round was twofold. On the one hand, financial services were arguably the major driver behind the will of trading nations to sit around a table and discuss the possibility of an agreement on the liberalisation of cross-border trade in services. On the other hand, because financial services were and still are at the heart of contemporary economies, as soon as Uruguay Round negotiators started discussing the issue, problems emerged with regard to the potential conflict between liberalisation of trade in financial services and the loss of regulatory power for domestic governments in a delicate sector. In light of this, it is fair to argue that they represented a major potential stumbling block for the positive conclusion of the Uruguay Round talks for a multilateral discipline governing trade in services. Therefore, it is not a coincidence that, as the conclusion of the Uruguay Round approached, relatively few commitments on financial services were made and it took more time for Members to strike a deal on the relevant sectoral discipline.

After the initial stage of trade talks during the 1990s, which mostly focused on the general discipline on trade in services, key players slowly

---

[18] J. Steven Jarreau, 'Interpreting the General Agreement on Trade in Services and the WTO Instruments Relevant to the International Trade of Financial Services: The Lawyer's Perspective', *North Carolina Journal of International Law & Commercial Regulation*, 25:2 (1999–2000), 1–74, at p. 23.

[19] Marchetti and Mavroidis argue that because the negotiations on trade in goods and services were both included in the same Ministerial Declaration and had a common institutional link in the Trade Negotiations Committee (TNC), the firewall between the two tracks was de facto removed. See Marchetti and Mavroidis, 'The Genesis of the GATS', p. 703.

changed their attitude towards the conclusion of negotiations in the field of financial services. The EU made it clear that it would not support any agreement that did not include financial services.[20] Moreover, the United States insisted that concessions in the field of financial services should be meaningful. These two trading nations proposed the inclusion of a 'non-application clause' in the GATS. In essence, the non-application clause would have permitted the denial of Most Favoured Nation (MFN) treatment to services and service suppliers from Members that had listed insufficient commitments.[21]

The purpose of the non-application clause was that of addressing tensions that arose in the context of financial services negotiations. Jarreau reports the dissatisfaction of the United States at the time, in particular, with the unwillingness of South American and Asian countries to make substantial commitments.[22] Eventually, the clause was not included in the text of the Agreement, but the very fact that a similar issue was extensively discussed testifies to the scepticism of the major players in the domain of trade in services concerning the possibility of concluding a positive deal.

As negotiations advanced, developing countries started nuancing their positions and began to accept a positive conclusion of negotiations for an agreement dealing with financial services trade liberalisation. Meanwhile, the situation was moving in the opposite direction in the United States. In addition to being afraid of the lack of substantial commitments by its trading partners, US negotiators were under huge pressure from Washington due to concerns about how more open markets could potentially harm rather than benefit domestic business, especially in delicate sectors such as banking, telecommunications and transport.

As a consequence, by 1991 the United States had substantially changed its position in the negotiations, moving from being an active proponent of the introduction of meaningful disciplines on financial services in the GATS to maintaining that the latter could be excluded from the scope of application of the Agreement.[23]

In March 1992, the Group of Negotiations on Services conducted an assessment of initial commitments on market access and National Treatment, and the United States judged the initial offers of sectoral commitments in financial services from Japan and Latin American countries to be unsatisfactory. It is for this reason that the United States decided to play the strategic card of announcing the possibility of including financial

---

[20] Jarreau, 'Interpreting the General Agreement on Trade in Services', p. 23.
[21] Ibid.   [22] Ibid.   [23] Ibid., p. 24.

services disciplines in the list of MFN exemptions[24] to put pressure on its trading partners to commit to more substantial market openness.

The situation became complicated. On the one hand, there was significant distance between the parties as to the degree of concessions they were ready to make. On the other hand, the US administration needed to strike a deal before the expiry of the 'fast-track' authority,[25] which was due to occur on 15 December 1993 – precisely the day when the Uruguay Round came to a close in Punta del Este. During the very last hours of the negotiations, Members agreed to conclude the agreements that are still in force: the GATS, the two Annexes on Financial Services and the Understanding on Commitments in Financial Services. However, because they could not agree on the issue of whether to extend MFN treatment on a conditional or unconditional basis, they extended the negotiating period for financial services.

The extended period was due to expire within six months after the entry into force of the WTO Agreement (30 June 1995). By the end of that period, frictions between the United States on one side and Japan and the Latin American countries on the other were still apparent. The EU definitively took the lead of the negotiations when the United States withdrew its offer of unconditional MFN in financial services. European negotiators obtained a one-month extension and managed to reach an agreement on the Second Protocol to the GATS, which is commonly known as the 'Interim Agreement'.[26] Members agreed that the latter would be temporary and due to be replaced by a permanent agreement on financial services, which was to follow.

In 1996, WTO Members convened in Singapore for the Ministerial Conference. In the Ministerial Declaration that followed Members agreed

---

[24] The Annex on Article II Exemptions allows Members to keep in place measures that are not consistent with the MFN obligation of the GATS on the condition that those measures are specifically indicated in a dedicated list. For instance, the United States has an MFN exemption in place in the insurance services subsector.

[25] 'Fast track' is a procedure under US law under which the Congress agrees in advance that a trade agreement negotiated by the Executive will be either ratified or rejected as it is, but it will not be amended after its conclusion. Such a procedure substantially reduces the political tension at the domestic level and speeds up negotiations. The opponents of this practice argue that it amounts to a reduction of democratic guarantees because democratically elected members of Congress do not have the power to amend trade agreements when they deem those to be detrimental for their own constituencies. For a thorough explanation, see John H. Jackson, William J. Davey and Alan O. Sykes, *Legal Problems of International Economic Relations*, 6th edn. (St. Paul, MN: WEST, 2013) 1338 (pp. 97–100).

[26] *Second Protocol to the General Agreement on Trade in Services*, 24 July 1995, available at www.wto.org/english/tratop_e/serv_e/2prote_e.htm.

to resume financial services negotiations in April 1997.[27] Again, negotiations on the issue proved to be difficult. At that time, the Asian continent was experiencing a dramatic financial crisis. However, Members still managed to sign the Fifth Protocol to the GATS (in WTO terminology the 'Financial Services Agreement') at the end of 1997. The United States joined in, withdrawing the MFN exemptions in banking and securities. Moreover, as Jarreau has stated, almost all Members made efforts to maintain or improve their initial commitments.[28] Rather than the Agreement itself and the norms contained therein, it was an overall more generous approach from the international community in terms of substantial concessions made that tilted the balance towards a deal.[29] The Protocol entered into force in March 1999.

The discipline on financial services at the multilateral level is laid down under different instruments: the GATS framework agreement, the Schedules of Specific Commitments, the Annex on Article II Exemptions as well as the lists on Article II exemptions, the GATS Annex on Financial Services, the Understanding on Commitments in Financial Services, the Interim Agreement and the Financial Services Agreement.

The Annexes complement the discipline of the GATS, in that they address specific concerns that are typical to one particular sector. The provisions incorporated in annexes to the GATS are to be considered as being *lex specialis* and thus, pursuant to a customary principle of international law, they override the general provisions provided for under the GATS.

2.1.3 *The Annex on Financial Services of the GATS*

The Annex on Financial Services is an integral part of the GATS and sets out the relevant discipline on trade in financial services including insurance. The Annex is composed of five paragraphs.

Paragraph 1 (*Scope and Definition*) circumscribes the scope of application of the special discipline on cross-border trade in financial services.

---

[27] WTO Doc. WT/MIN(96)/DEC, Singapore Ministerial Declaration, adopted on 13 December 1996, para. 17, available at www.wto.org/english/thewto_e/minist_e/min96_e/wtodec_e.htm.

[28] The United States kept a broad exemption on insurance services, as a direct response to measures taken by Malaysia to make US companies reduce their holdings in the host country. On this see Jarreau, 'Interpreting the General Agreement on Trade in Services', p. 30.

[29] In this context, it is also worth noting that some countries maintained more protectionist behaviour. Jarreau (ibid., p. 31) refers mainly to India, Malaysia and South Korea.

Paragraph 2 ('Domestic Regulation') is articulated in two subparagraphs. Sub-paragraph (a) incorporates the prudential carve-out, i.e. the provision that constitutes the main focus of this book. The provision reads as follows:

2. Domestic Regulation

(a) Notwithstanding any other provisions of the Agreement, a Member shall not be prevented from taking measures for prudential reasons, including for the protection of investors, depositors, policy holders or persons to whom a fiduciary duty is owed by a financial service supplier, or to ensure the integrity and stability of the financial system. Where such measures do not conform with the provisions of the Agreement, they shall not be used as a means of avoiding the Member's commitments or obligations under the Agreement.

Sub-paragraph (b) allows WTO Members to refrain from disclosing information concerning the affairs and accounts of individual customers or any confidential or proprietary information possessed by public entities.

Paragraph 3 (*Recognition*) allows Members to sign Recognition Agreements (either unilaterally or *sub specie* of mutual recognition agreements [MRAs]) relating to domestic prudential regulations. Should they decide to do so, they must afford adequate opportunity to any other Member in a comparable situation to negotiate its accession to similar agreements. To date the WTO Secretariat has not been notified of a single MRA on financial services.[30]

Pursuant to Paragraph 4 (*Dispute Settlement*), when Panels are established to settle disputes concerning alleged violations of the discipline on cross-border trade in services, they shall be composed of panelists with the necessary expertise relevant to the specific financial service under dispute. In this regard, the WTO Secretariat holds a specific roster of experts to be appointed in the event of disputes.

Finally, Paragraph 5 (*Definitions*) contains, as the heading irrefutably reports, a list of definitions that are useful for the purpose of the application of the Annex.

The Annex on Financial Services is important in the GATS architecture for two main reasons. On the one hand, it excludes social security and central bank operations as well as services provided in the exercise of

---

[30] Juan A. Marchetti and Petros C. Mavroidis, 'I Now Recognize You (and Only You) as Equal: An Anatomy of (Mutual) Recognition Agreements in the GATS', in Ioannis Lianos and Okeoghene Odudu (eds.), *Regulating Trade in Services in the EU and the WTO: Trust, Distrust and Economic Integration* (Cambridge: Cambridge University Press, 2012), 415–44.

governmental authority from the scope of application of the rules on trade in services. On the other hand, it provides a strong restatement of the right for WTO Members to regulate according to prudential concerns, irrespective of any other conflicting WTO obligation. With specific regard to the latter, a correct interpretation of the provision establishing a specific discipline on domestic legislation addressing prudential concerns is fundamental for preserving the balance of the rights and obligations enshrined in the Annex.

2.1.4 The Second Annex on Financial Services

The Second Annex on Financial Services included a transitional regime that was effective for a limited period of time after the entry into force of the WTO Agreement. The Second Annex allowed Members to include measures that were inconsistent with Article II of the GATS (i.e. the provision laying down MFN treatment) in the specific list of exemptions provided for under the Annex on Article II of the GATS. Furthermore, the Second Annex allowed Members to have a limited time window to modify or withdraw their commitments. These provisions are no longer in force.

2.1.5 The Understanding on Commitments on Financial Services

The Understanding on Commitments in Financial Services lays down a pre-defined set of commitments and at the same time ensures that exceptions are still possible for Members that decide to adopt the aforementioned set of commitments. It is not a priori binding on all Members, which have to express their intention to liberalise their trade in financial services according to the rules laid down therein.

The discipline enshrined in the Understanding covers all sectors, including banking and insurance. The aim of the commitments is to ensure market opening and to prevent governments from introducing new conditions that are more restrictive compared with the existing situation at the time when commitments where undertaken.

Particularly relevant for the domain of financial services is the obligation related to market access for 'new financial services'. In this respect, Members adopting the approach provided under the Understanding shall permit 'financial service suppliers of any other Member established in its territory to offer in its territory any new financial service'.

2.2 International Cooperation on Financial (and Prudential) Regulation

The WTO is not the only forum dealing with the regulation of financial services. A plethora of other bodies deals with financial services, and that creates many problems of a different nature in terms of overlap of disciplines. On the one hand, public international law agreements (such as the GATS and its Annexes, for instance) provide a framework discipline for progressive liberalisation of trade in financial services. On the other hand, it is bodies of a hybrid nature (whose measures are effectively implemented at the national level without having binding force) that have largely performed the 'rule-making' task.[31]

The international financial regulation landscape that has taken shape since the 1970s is complex and evolved at different speeds in the various fields. Some areas of financial regulation are 'governed' by detailed recommendations and standards such as capital rules in banking, for instance. In contrast, other fields of financial law have progressed unevenly.

2.2.1 The Rationale for International Cooperation on Financial Regulation (or, More Properly, for the Lack Thereof)

It is useful to start the overview of the state of the art of international cooperation on financial regulation by looking at the rationale for such cooperation and why the path towards harmonisation of financial rules at the international level has been less smooth than in other fields of law, such as trade in goods.

Verdier[32] identifies five possible objectives of international regulatory co-operation in the domain of financial services.

The first objective consists 'securing cross-border coordination of enforcement and supervision'. This objective emerges from the circumstance according to which national authorities are ill placed to effectively monitor and supervise global financial institutions or to prevent or repress fraudulent activities that take place in different jurisdictions simultaneously.

---

[31] See Chris Brummer, *Soft Law and the Global Financial System – Rule Making in the 21st Century* (Cambridge: Cambridge, 2012) 296.

[32] Pierre-Hugues Verdier, 'The Political Economy of International Financial Regulation', *Indiana Law Journal*, 88/4 (2013), 1405–74 (pp. 1439 and ff.).

The second objective identified by Verdier is that of 'liberalising international finance by harmonising regulatory requirements'. This issue affects several domains and is not only typical of banking and finance.[33] The idea behind this concept is simple and boils down to the fact that different competent domestic regulators and supervisors may adopt different legislations and different criteria with regard to essentially the same activities and the same problems. Whilst in some cases dissimilar legislations are justified by genuine specific concerns of domestic origins, in other cases they are unduly burdensome and simply put an obstacle to more efficient economic exchanges.[34]

'Compelling States to improve their financial regulation' is a third objective singled out by Verdier. According to Verdier, certain domestic jurisdictions might maintain inadequate levels of regulation in absence of international coordination. Building on existing literature, Verdier explains that the explanation behind a country's decision to adopt a lax regulatory framework for his financial system could be manifold. On one side of the spectrum, it has been studied that some (smaller) countries have found it convenient to leave their financial markets poorly regulated because other (bigger and wealthier) countries would eventually bear the costs of the recovery. On the other side of the spectrum, it has been convincingly argued that some governments have used shallow financial regulation to attract foreign businesses to invest in their domestic industry. These reasons contribute to explain why, given certain circumstances, it cannot be expected that domestic governments autonomously step in and modify their domestic legislations in light of solid principles of financial regulation and supervision, hence the need for international coordination.

The fourth objective is that of 'securing collective action to raise prudential standards'. In a nutshell, national legislatives might be caught between the need to adopt adequate financial regulations and the necessity not to put their domestic industry at a competitive disadvantage. This problem, in the view of the author, is due to persist over time, when even in presence of international coordination some domestic governments might find it convenient to relax prudential standards to gain competitiveness.

---

[33] See the fascinating discussion in Robert E. Baldwin, *Nontariff Distortions in International Trade* (Brookings Institution: Washington), 1970.
[34] Verdier cites historic GAAP as an example in this respect. See Verdier, 'The Political Economy of International Financial Regulation', p. 1441.

The author argues that even when major events (such as a financial crisis) lead to multilateral coordination, the effects of these efforts are hardly of lasting nature because they are vulnerable to changes in domestic politics and, eventually, to non-compliance.

The final objective identified by Verdier is that of 'making credible commitments to overcome time inconsistency problems'. According to the author, unilateralism is bound to lead to inefficient outcomes, whereas international coordination increases the chances that the agreed-upon instruments are more effective in the attempt to address problems that affect the global financial landscape and not just a single country. This picture is made more complex by the fact that actors may in good faith commit to the implementation or application of particular criteria or policies, but then, when the time for the actual decision arrives, the same actors may be driven by other (political) considerations and opt for the non-implementation of previously agreed principles. Strong(er) international coordination and more stringent rules increase the chances of overcoming time inconsistency problems.

Admittedly – as Verdier[35] argues – international cooperation in financial regulation has been successful over the years in the achievement of just two of the preceding five objectives. Namely, it helped national regulators and supervisors in coordinating their actions and finding reciprocal assistance, and it allowed national governments to liberalise the cross-border flows of capital and financial services between one another by lowering some regulatory barriers through harmonisation and recognition of requirements.

The history of international cooperation in the domain of financial cooperation can hardly be considered successful, especially compared with other domains such as trade, for instance. If this is the case, then why do governments keep following the same strategy rather than abandoning a path dominated by soft law and non-binding international recommendations? The answer can only be partial at this stage, given that the phenomenon is still ongoing. However, there are some explanations and lessons from the recent past that can be reported.

In the view of some authors an explanation can be found using the prism of rational choice theories.[36] The idea is that national governments calculate the costs and benefits of international cooperation and, more

---

[35] Verdier, 'The Political Economy of International Financial Regulation', p. 1456.

[36] *Ex multis*, see Brummer, *Soft Law and the Global Financial System – Rule Making in the 21st Century*.

carefully, of transfers of pieces of sovereignty. According to this view, soft law provides for some incentives for compliance (and there is indeed evidence of high levels of compliance in some sectors), while still preserving the possibility for governments to act (or react) in a fast and flexible way, addressing the specificities of their national markets together with their peculiar problems.[37] The problem with this explanation, however, is that it implies the existence of a deliberate agenda for domestic governments, which is probably far-fetched.

In contrast, others put forward an alternative twofold explanation.[38] One side of the coin has to do with historical path dependence, that is, institutional routes undertaken in the past influencing future choices. The framework of international cooperation on financial regulation emerged gradually in a context in which international flow of capitals and financial services was limited to exceptional circumstances. Financial globalisation took off when the international community was not prepared, and as such the answers to problems were mainly given at the national level. This process started in the mid-1970s when regulators and supervisors became aware of the fact that the negative externalities of the insolvency of a financial institution in one domestic jurisdiction may negatively affect depositors and financial institutions based in other jurisdictions.[39]

In that context, regulators started meeting informally to exchange their views and explore possible solutions, albeit whilst jealously protecting their margin for intervention in the domain of financial services. Today, informal forums dominate the international arena, and several circumstances, including a substantial path dependence, lead one to believe that an evolution of this framework towards an international hard-law setting is highly unlikely.

The other side of the alternative explanation lies the intrinsic political economy of international financial regulation. Essentially, financial regulation and supervision at the domestic level are traditionally delegated to specialised agencies with different degrees of autonomy and independence from political institutions. This peculiarity has an impact at the

---

[37] Although studies reveal how some countries have adopted a strategy of 'mock compliance', that is they formally have complied with standards and recommendations issued at the international level but, in reality, they have ignored them in practice. For a thorough analysis of this phenomenon, please see Andrew Walter, *Governing Finance – East Asia's Adoption of International Standards* (Ithaca, NY: Cornell University Press, 2008), p. 256.
[38] Verdier, 'The Political Economy of International Financial Regulation', pp. 1425 and ff.
[39] In this regard, the history of the birth of the Basel Committee, which is provided *infra*, is illustrative.

international level in the sense that these specialised agencies are those entitled to the setting up of standards and recommendations in most cases. Big corporations and financial institutions enjoy the possibility of moving large amounts of money, and as such they can significantly influence political processes by means of financing electoral campaigns. On another level, however, they also have impressive technical expertise; they are well organised, and it is relatively straightforward for them to gather and promote their interests.[40] Finally, there can be divergent interests between great powers and smaller States in this domain. Whilst great powers such as, for instance, the United States or the EU may well have an agenda to pursue and the incentives to work for stronger standards, some other countries may have the contrary interest to free ride on the situation, leaving the burden to the bigger powers while attracting investors and firms with the promise of a cheaper regulatory environment.[41]

The complexity of the interaction of the actors involved makes it hard for international cooperation in the delicate domain of financial markets to follow a smooth path. Table 2.1, prepared by Verdier, convincingly summarises the different positions that the main actors in financial markets typically hold with regard to the various regulatory objectives that can be pursued by means of international cooperation. It represents a useful graphic tool to understand how hard it is to reconcile the different preferences that the various actors in financial services markets may have.

2.2.2 The Main International Fora Dealing with Financial Regulation

Several international bodies address issues related to trade in financial services.[42] This section gives account of the main international fora dealing with banking and financial services. Such fora saw the light of day because of de facto pre-existing cross-border financial activities and the need to address negative externalities deriving from them.

International fora on financial regulation can be roughly divided into two categories. The first is composed of three sectorial standard-setting organisations that are of particular importance for the sake of the present

---

[40] The most powerful explanation for this kind of phenomenon is still that provided by Mancur Olson, *The Logic of Collective Action – Public Goods and the Theory of Groups* (Cambridge, MA: Harvard University Press, 1965) 178.

[41] See the explanation in John C. Coffee, 'Extraterritorial Financial Regulation: Why E. T. Can't Come Home', *Cornell Law Review*, 99:6 (2014), 1259–302.

[42] For a comprehensive overview of the topic, see David Zaring, 'Finding Legal Principle in Global Financial Regulation', *Virginia Journal of International Law*, 52:3 (2012), 683–722.

Table 2.1 *Outcomes of international financial regulation*

	Regulators	Large firms	Great powers	Outcome
Enforcement/supervisory cooperation	++	~	+	++
Liberalisation	~	++	+	+
Improving regulation in specific countries	~	~	+	~
Adopting stricter prudential standards	~ to ++ (varies)	−	~ to ++ (varies)	−
Committing to cross-border resolution	~	~	~	−

Key: ++ = strongly positive; + = positive; ~ = neutral/indifferent; − = negative; − − = strongly negative.
(Source: Pierre-Hugues Verdier, 'The Political Economy of International Financial Regulation', Indiana Law Journal, 88/4 (2013), at 1457)

work: the Basel Committee on Banking Supervision (BCBS), the International Association of Insurance Supervisors (IAIS) and the International Organization of Securities Commissions (IOSCO). The Joint Forum on Financial Conglomerates, established in 1996, brings the latter three organisations together to facilitate dialogue on issues of common interest.[43]

The second category is composed of those bodies through which political leaders define macrostrategic objectives that are crucial for the stability of the international system. Two are particularly relevant for the current discussion: the Group of 20 (G-20) and the Financial Stability Board. Those fora exist because of the need for supervisors and regulators to address issues deriving from the de facto internationalisation of the operations of their national financial institutions.

2.2.2.1 The Basel Committee on Banking Supervision

Until the 1970s, it was commonplace to consider financial regulation as being something confined within the boundaries of nation States. However, in 1974 a major event shook the financial world. Bankhaus Herstatt, a financial institution based in Cologne, Germany, was declared

---
[43] More information is available at www.bis.org/bcbs/jointforum.htm.

insolvent by the competent domestic agencies after a series of risky foreign exchange exposures. This event represented a turning point because the foreign exchange community started to fear that some international counterparts would not be able to honour their obligations. After a series of other similar (albeit minor) events,[44] the governors of the central banks of the then Group of 10 industrialised countries (G-10) established the Standing Committee on Banking Regulations and Supervisory Practices, housed by the Bank for International Settlements (BIS) in Switzerland.

The BCBS, which is the natural heir of the Standing committee, broadened its membership in 2009 with a view to including all G-20 Members[45] plus Hong Kong and Singapore. However, the BCBS kept the nature and structure of its predecessor in the sense that Members meet informally, with limited records of their meetings and decision-making processes adhering to the rule of consensus. The standards issued by the BCBS are not binding but are in the nature of recommendations. Implementation of the BCBS standards, in fact, takes place on a voluntary basis, as they are effectively transformed into national law also in jurisdictions other than the parties to the BCBS. However, there is expectation that these standards are followed by the membership of the BCBS, and practice reveals that compliance with them is generally high.

Moreover, pressure from international organisations matters. The IMF and the World Bank run the Financial Sector Assessment Program, with the view of analysing the conditions of the financial markets of those countries that agree to voluntarily submit themselves to the scrutiny. Part of the program is devoted to the timely implementation of international standards. In addition, members of the Financial Stability Board have agreed to review the status of the implementation of standards on financial regulation through a peer-review mechanism.[46]

There are two main areas of financial regulation where the BCBS is actively involved: banking supervision and capital adequacy of financial institutions. With regard to banking supervision, the Standing Committee issued its Concordat in 1975 and has proceeded with subsequent revisions

---

[44] For a comprehensive account of the events that preceded the establishment of the BCBS, see D. A. Singer, *Regulating Capital – Setting Standards for the International Financial System* (Ithaca and London: Cornell University Press, 2007) 163 (pp. 38 and ff.).

[45] Argentina, Australia, Brazil, Canada, China, France, Germany, India, Indonesia, Italy, Japan, Republic of Korea, Mexico, Russia, Saudi Arabia, South Africa, Turkey, the United Kingdom and the United States.

[46] See Bart De Meester, *Liberalization of Trade in Banking Services – An International and European Perspective* (Cambridge: Cambridge University Press, 2014) 388, at p. 86.

of the document in the following years. The main idea behind the BCBS's recommendations on banking supervision, known as 'consolidated supervision', was that home country supervisory agencies should be responsible for all the operations conducted by their national financial institutions, both in the domestic market and when they operated abroad.

In 1997, the BCBS released twenty-five Core Principles on best practices on banking supervision, moving from the original idea that mainly consisted of principles for the coordination of national supervisory authorities. In 1999, the BCBS issued a document titled 'Core Principles Methodology' with the aim of avoiding divergent interpretations.

These instruments have undergone successive revisions over the years and, more importantly, since the 2007–8 economic crisis. In 2012, the BCBS revised the Principles and merged them into one document with the Methodology. The new version of the Principles takes into account some lessons learned from the financial crisis and stresses the need for a systemic approach on the micro-supervision of financial institutions and the necessity to invest resources in the supervision of globally systemic important financial institutions. Finally, the Committee also emphasised better corporate governance, transparency and disclosure of information.

The new framework designed by the BCBS is commonly referred to with the name of 'Basel III'. Basel III became necessary in the aftermath of the 2007–8 financial crisis, which revealed a number of fallacies in the global financial system. In particular, the financial meltdown of the end of the 2000s exposed the weaknesses of several financial institutions with regard to their capital composition and to the adequacy of their liquidity coverage. The new set of rules aims to address both problems, as will be examined subsequently.

2.2.2.1.1 Capital[47]   The Basel III discipline on capital consists of three pillars.

Pillar 1 – Capital: The new set of rules focuses on the importance of common equity for the composition of the capital of financial institutions. The minimum common equity that financial institutions are required to hold is increased to 4.5 per cent of the total risk-weighted assets, after deductions. In addition, the new standards on capital require the inclusion of a new clause in the contracts for capital instruments, whereby the competent supervisory authority may, at its discretion, proceed with the

---

[47] BCBS, *Basel III: A Global Regulatory Framework for More Resilient Banks and Banking Systems* (2011), 69, available at www.bis.org/publ/bcbs189.pdf.

writing-off or the conversion in common shares in situations where the contracting bank is declared non-viable. This measure aims to absorb the risks of capital loss and to incentivise a more risk-averse approach by the management of financial institutions, thereby reducing instances of moral hazard.

Besides the strengthening of the microprudential arsenal, the new rules on capital add a macroprudential component, comprising two elements: a capital conservation buffer and a countercyclical buffer. Concerning the former, financial institutions' capital should comprise a buffer common equity for at least 2.5 per cent of the risk-weighted assets. This figure, summed with the new rules on the common equity ration, increases the total equity standard to 7 per cent. Furthermore, banks are required to hold countercyclical buffers of common equity between 0 and 2.5 per cent, when competent authorities determine that credit growth is increasing the possibility of systemic risk.

The second component of the Basel III standards on capital aims to strengthen the risk coverage of the capital framework of financial institutions. In the determination of the capital requirement for counterparty credit risk, banks must determine their capital requirement for counterparty credit risk using stressed inputs. This will address concerns about reserves that become too low during periods of compressed market volatility and help address instances of procyclicality. This approach added to promote a more efficient and integrated management of market and counterparty credit risk. The main features of this new approach include the following:

- the strengthening of the credit analysis for complex securitisations. In particular, financial institutions will be required to conduct independent and more stringent credit analyses with regard to securitisation exposures that are rated by third parties;
- an increase in the capital requirements for activities such as trading and operations involving derivatives. To mitigate the impact of procyclicality, the new rules introduce a stressed value-at-risk framework for the evaluation of these operations. Furthermore, an incremental charge for default and migration risks for non-securitised credit products is foreseen.
- new rules to limit the spreading of counterparty credit risk. In this respect, a more thorough set of rules for the measurement of exposures is foreseen, as well as higher capital requirements for inter-financial sector exposures; and

2.2 INTERNATIONAL COOPERATION ON FINANCIAL REGULATION 25

– incentives to clear over-the-counter (OTC) with qualifying central counterparties (QCCP). Under the new framework established by the BCBS, derivatives cleared with a QCCP will be risk-weighted at 2 per cent.

The third element of the first pillar is represented by the rules aiming to contain excessive leveraging. Leverage is an instrument financial institutions adopt to maximise returns and minimise losses. Typically, it involves risky practices such as using borrowed funds to buy more of an asset at the risk that the borrowing costs may outweigh the returns in income from that asset. New Basel III rules define the leverage ratio as the ratio between the capital measure and the exposure measures and have fixed a minimum requirement of 3 per cent for the ratio so determined for the period 1 January 2013–1 January 2017. Final adjustments to the definition and calibration of the leverage ratio are expected to be carried out by the end of 2017, and a consultative document in this regard was circulated with BCBS Members in April 2016.[48] The declared aim of the BCBS is to complete the migration to a Pillar 1 treatment no later than 1 January 2018, after an appropriate review and calibration.

Pillar 2 – Risk management and supervision: The second pillar of the new rules on capital introduced by the BCBS aims to strengthen the framework for efficient risk management and supervision. On the one hand, financial institutions are required to determine the amounts and types of the internal distribution of capital against the background of their specific risk profile. Furthermore, financial institutions are also required to have a strong internal governance and control arrangements. On the other hand, banks are required to have an effective corporate governance system, which includes an expansion of the role of the board of directors in the supervision of the implementation of effective risk management systems, additional emphasis on the competence of the board and on the necessity for individual members to devote enough time to the fulfilment of their mandates and the adoption of accounting standards for financial instruments.

Pillar 3 – Market discipline: Basel III introduces a revision to the original Pillar 3 disclosure requirements, with specific regard to the exposures on securitisation. Under Pillar 3, banks have additional requirements for a more detailed disclosure on the components of regulatory capital and

---

[48] BCBS, Consultative Document – Revisions to the Basel III leverage ratio framework (2016) 27, available at www.bis.org/bcbs/publ/d365.pdf.

Table 2.2 *Minimum liquidity coverage ratio requirements*

	2015	2016	2017	2018	2019
Minimum LCR requirements	60%	70%	80%	90%	100%

they are required to prove the reconciliation of the disclosed content with the reported accounts.

2.2.2.1.2 Liquidity[49]   The new rules introduced by the BCBS under the Basel III framework also deal with the liquidity requirements for financial institutions. The most relevant innovation introduced in this respect is the reform of the Liquidity Coverage Ratio (LCR), which is the ratio between high-quality liquid assets (specifically assets that can be easily converted in to cash in private markets in a scenario of liquidity stress test lasting more than thirty calendar days, HQLA) and the total net cash outflows of the banks.

Since 2015, financial institutions, to comply with the Basel III requirements, started to progressively increase the amount of HQLA to reach a LCR of 100 per cent or more, according to Table 2.2 published on the website of the Bank for International Settlements.[50]

The aim of this new set of rules is to enhance the short-term resilience of banks' risk profile. It pursues both a micro (short-term resilience of banks' risk profile) and a macroprudential objective (avoidance of the spreading of negative externalities to other financial institutions and other sectors of the economy).

The second element of the discipline on liquidity is the identification of the net stable funding ratio (NSFR), which is a longer-term structural ratio with the aim of identifying and preventing liquidity mismatches. Through the stabilisation of the funding structure, financial institutions are likely to substantially mitigate the risk that disruptions in a regular source of funding lead to the erosion of its liquidity position and trigger a broader systemic domino. The NSFR will ideally limit overreliance on short-term

---

[49] BCBS, Basel III: The Liquidity Coverage Ratio and Liquidity Risk Monitoring Tools (2013) 75, available at www.bis.org/publ/bcbs238.pdf.
[50] More information is available at www.bis.org/publ/bcbs238.htm.

funding and enhance the stability of financial institutions and the financial system as a whole.

The *Principles for Sound Liquidity Risk Management and Supervision*[51] represent the third component of the liquidity pillar. Published in 2008, the document provides with an overview of good practices for the management of liquidity risk in financial institutions. The document lists seventeen principles, classified into a fundamental principle and the following categories: governance of liquidity risk management, measurement and management of liquidity risk and public disclosure and the role of supervisors.

Pillar 2 of Basel III on supervisory monitoring introduces also a common set of metrics for banking supervisors to identify and anticipate trends of liquidity risk both at the micro and macro levels in a timely fashion.

Finally, with a view of avoiding the recurrence of situations in which financial institutions in distress are too big to fail, the BCBS has introduced, in cooperation with the Financial Stability Board (FSB) a specific set of requirements for systemically important financial institutions (SIFIs). Additional information provided subsequently in the context of the assessment of the functions performed by the FSB.

2.2.2.2 The International Organization of Securities Commissions

International cooperation between domestic securities regulators started in the 1970s on the American continent, when a group of securities regulators from North and South America gave birth to an inter-American regional association to share their views on how to best address mutual problems. In 1983, the group decided to open its doors to a larger number of members and evolve into a global forum for securities regulators. At the 1986 meeting in Paris, members decided that the organisation should have a permanent Secretariat. This 1986 conference was a real game-changer for the regulation of securities worldwide.[52]

In 1987, in fact, a group of domestic securities regulators started to discuss the necessity of working towards the harmonisation of capital requirements in the securities industry. The rationale behind this, in

---

[51] BCBS, Principles for Sound Liquidity Risk Management and Supervision, September 2008, available at www.bis.org/publ/bcbs144.pdf.

[52] Details on the history of IOSCO are available on the organisation's website: www.iosco.org/about/?subSection=joint_forum&subSection1=history.

essence, was the same as that which led to the creation of the BCBS, namely that of avoiding a failure in one domestic market spreading its negative effects to the rest of the world and to minimise the inefficiencies and the asymmetries of information deriving from differences in domestic rules.

Today IOSCO includes around 150 Members and is based in Madrid. Given the complexity of securities regulation at the domestic level, particularly in federal States, secondary securities regulators are granted the status of non-voting members. Moreover, the IOSCO has a consultative committee (the Self-Regulatory Organizations Consultative Committee) in which self-regulatory bodies can put forward their perspectives on securities' markets.

IOSCO is responsible for the issuance of the *Objectives and Principles of Securities Regulations*,[53] now in its second edition, which consists of a set of thirty-eight principles based on three main objectives of securities regulation: the protection of investors; ensuring that markets are fair, efficient and transparent; and the reduction of systemic risk.

With regard to the protection of investors, IOSCO's *Objectives and Principles*, for instance, requires issuers to provide accurate and timely disclosure of financial results, risk and other information that might be relevant for the investors to make informed decisions. Concerning the fairness, efficiency and transparency of the markets, the *Objectives and Principles* recommends the attribution of effective and pervasive inspection and surveillance powers to securities regulators.

Finally, in relation to the reduction of systemic risk, the *Objectives and Principles* recommends the adoption of procedures for addressing the failure of market intermediaries to minimise damages and losses to investors to the fullest possible extent and to contain systemic risk. The IOSCO *Objectives and Principles of Securities Regulations* have been endorsed by the G-20 and the FSB.

Another important document is the *Multilateral Memorandum of Understanding Concerning Consultation and Cooperation and the Exchange of Information* (MMoU), last revised in 2012.[54] The document sets out principles for mutual assistance, information sharing and cooperation among securities regulators.

---

[53] IOSCO Objectives and Principles of Securities Regulation, June 2010, available at www.iosco.org/library/pubdocs/pdf/IOSCOPD323.pdf.

[54] IOSCO Multilateral Memorandum of Understanding Concerning Consultation and Cooperation and the Exchange of Information, available at www.iosco.org/library/pubdocs/pdf/IOSCOPD386.pdf.

2.2.2.3 The International Association of Insurance Supervisors

The IAIS, registered as a non-profit organisation under Swiss law, is located in the offices of the BIS in Basel. Established in 1994, this organisation is relatively young compared with its sibling organisations described so far. Membership of IAIS is relatively broad, comprising 180 national and local authorities as well as international organisations. Additionally, 120 (non-voting) insurance professionals participate in the life of the Association in their capacity as 'observers'.

The General Meeting of the IAIS decides on guidelines and technical standards with a qualified majority of two-thirds of the voting members. Singer, however, provides anecdotal evidence according to which members of the IAIS strive for consensus and tend to avoid situations of conflict and tension in which a two-thirds majority vote is required.[55]

Two are the main instruments developed in the context of the IAIS: the Multilateral Memorandum of Understanding (MMoU), adopted in February 2007, which is a framework for cooperation and exchange of information between insurance supervisors,[56] and the *Insurance Core Principles*, last amended in October 2013, which deals, inter alia, with issues of capital adequacy, risk management and corporate governance.[57]

2.2.2.4 The Group of 20

The G-20 is a forum for international cooperation that gathers together nineteen States plus the European Union. The leaders of the G-20 meet annually, whereas finance ministers and governors of central banks meet more often during the year. The forum does not have a permanent staff, and Members rotate on a yearly basis to hold the chair of the G-20 and to provide facilities and a temporary staff dedicated to the meetings and the activities of the Members. It does not have a formal voting system. Rather, it was originally conceived as a discussion forum, and as such the aim of parties is to reach consensus-based compromises for public declarations to be issued at the end of the summits.

---

[55] Singer, *Regulating Capital – Setting Standards for the International Financial System* (p. 97).
[56] IAIS Multilateral Memorandum of Understanding on Cooperation and Information Exchange, available at http://iaisweb.org/index.cfm?event=getPage&nodeId=25287.
[57] IAIS Insurance Core Principles Standards Guidance and Assessment Methodology October 2011 (revised October 2013), available at http://iaisweb.org/index.cfm?event=showPage&nodeId=25224.

The role of this forum has evolved after the 2007–8 financial crisis. In the first three summit meetings (Washington in 2008 and London and Pittsburgh in 2009), the leaders of the G-20 discussed the multilateral response to the financial turmoil and highlighted in their official statements the necessity of an international set of rules for the governance and supervision of financial markets. In particular, in the official statement after the Pittsburgh summit at the end of 2009,[58] the leaders of the G-20 agreed, among other things, to strengthen capital and liquidity requirements (put in place by the BCBS). Moreover, they emphatically decided to '[t]o reform the global architecture to meet the needs of the 21st century' and, to this goal, established the FSB, the structure of which and activities are dealt with in the next subsection.

Years after the declaration at the Pittsburgh meeting, some commentators have tried to test the optimistic tone of the document with a reality check. In addition to the incomplete reforms advocated in the context of the BCBS, a global regulatory and supervisory architecture of financial markets seems as distant a prospect as it ever has.[59]

At the Summit held in Hangzhou in September 2016, G-20 leaders endorsed the *G20 Agenda Towards a More Stable and Resilient International Financial Architecture* and reaffirmed in their communiqué their commitment to the finalisation of the agenda for the reform of the financial sector, including:

– the full implementation of Basel III,
– the development of an insurance capital standard for internationally active insurers and
– the full implementation of the agreed OTC derivatives reform agenda.[60]

2.2.2.5 The Financial Stability Board

The FSB evolved out of the Financial Stability Forum launched by the G-7 in the aftermath of the Asian financial crisis in the late 1990s. It now comprises thirty-six institutions including departments of finance, central banks, domestic supervisory agencies, international organisations and standard-setting bodies.[61] The FSB was established with a view to analysing the causes that led to the financial crisis and to drafting

---

[58] See Leaders' Statement, The Pittsburgh Summit, 24–25 September 2009, available at https://g20.org/wp-content/uploads/2014/12/Pittsburgh_Declaration_0.pdf.
[59] See, in particular, Nicolas Véron, 'The G20 Financial Reform Agenda after Five Years', *Bruegel Working Paper* (2014), 9.
[60] G20 Leaders' Communiqué, *Hangzhou Summit*, 4–5 September 2016, para. 18.
[61] A full list of the Members is available at www.financialstabilityboard.org/about/fsb-members/.

recommendations for the creation of a stronger and more resilient international financial system.

It is a more complex and structured organisation than the G-20 with a permanent secretariat and a secretary general. Members participate in a Plenary, which is assisted by three committees, one dealing with supervision and regulation, another one that discusses issues of cooperation and a third entrusted with the mandate of monitoring the implementation of the FSB agenda. In addition to these bodies, a Standing Committee provides Members with operational guidance between the various sessions of the Plenary.

The FSB does not issue legally binding instruments, nor does it substitute national bodies entrusted with the supervision and policy coordination of financial markets. In other words, the FSB operates as a discussion forum where members, through exchange of information and peer review, agree to set minimum standards to ensure coordination and to mitigate the effects of negative spillovers due to the interconnectedness of financial systems. Although the FSB was entrusted with its mandate by the G-20, and acts in coordination with the latter, it is formally independent and counts on a broader membership.

The FSB provides a 'Compendium of Standards'[62] in which the economic and financial standards that are accepted by the international community as being instrumental for the safety and soundness of financial systems are reported.

There are three the main functions performed by the FSB: vulnerabilities assessment, policy development and coordination and implementation monitoring. Each of these functions are explained in the following subsections.

2.2.2.5.1 Vulnerabilities Assessment
The FSB has a Standing Committee for the Assessment of Vulnerabilities (SCAV), which operates for the identification of macrofinancial vulnerabilities and the prevention of risks connected to the weakness of financial infrastructures. The SCAV, in particular, collects analyses and monitors reports from members and other international financial institutions (IMF, BIS, OECD, World Bank) and, when appropriate, transfers information to other standing committees or to standard-setting bodies and stresses instances of vulnerability. The SCAV reports directly to the FSB Plenary.

---

[62] Available at www.financialstabilityboard.org/what-we-do/about-the-compendium-of-standards/.

In its operations, the SCAV benefits from the support of the Analytical Group on Vulnerabilities, a technical standing sub-committee (a forum for the discussion and analysis of the evolving risks to the global financial system). More importantly, the SCAV conducts early-warning exercises (in cooperation with the IMF) to anticipate the impact of risk scenarios.

2.2.2.5.2 Policy Development and Coordination In the aftermath of the global financial crisis, the FSB played an active role in the definition and implementation of a number of policy reforms deployed to address the main sources of distress that led to the disruption of markets worldwide.

The FSB has focused on several policy initiatives, in coordination with other forums and international financial institutions:

- Enhancing the resilience of financial institutions (The FSB works for the strengthening of risk management practices and monitors the implementation of Basel III standards.)
- Addressing SIFIs (The FSB identified the list of global systemically important insurers – G-SIIs – and a list of global systemically important banks – G-SIBs – that are required to have additional loss absorption capacity, to be subject better and more efficient supervisory mandates and to strict review processes.)
- Effective resolution regimes and policies (The FSB identified the *Key Attributes of Effective Resolution Regimes for Financial Institutions*,[63] which are necessary for an effective resolution regime and to ensure that losses are shouldered by shareholders and creditors of financial institutions and not by the taxpayers. In this framework, the FSB conducts an annual monitoring exercise on the progress made by its member jurisdictions.)
- More effective supervision (The FSB identified elements that are necessary for the promotion of a sound risk culture in financial institutions[64] and key elements for an effective risk appetite framework, with particular attention to the roles and responsibilities of the board of directors and senior management of financial institutions.)[65]

---

[63] FSB, *Key Attributes of Effective Resolution Regimes for Financial Institutions*, 15 October 2014, available at www.fsb.org/wp-content/uploads/r_141015.pdf.

[64] FSB, *Guidance on Supervisory Interaction with Financial Institutions on Risk Culture: A Framework for Assessing Risk Culture*, 7 April 2014, available at www.fsb.org/wp-content/uploads/140407.pdf.

[65] FSB, Principles for an effective risk appetite, 18 November 2013, available at www.fsb.org/wp-content/uploads/r_131118.pdf.

- Derivatives Markets (The FSB is actively engaged in the monitoring of national reforms adopted in line with the G-20 recommendations for a reform of the market for OTC derivatives.)
- Shadow banking (The FSB has adopted recommendations to strengthen the supervision and regulation of shadow banking, which can be described as the activity of credit intermediation conducted by entities that are not part of the traditional banking system.)[66]
- Other policy areas (The FSB is involved in a number of other activities, including the strengthening of accounting standards and the oversight of credit rating agencies, to limit situations of speculation.)

2.2.2.5.3 Implementation Monitoring The Standing Committee on Standards Implementation (SCSI) coordinates the monitoring operations on the implementation of agreed reforms and reports the results of these operations to the G-20.

2.2.3 Conclusion on International Cooperation and Prudential Regulation

The discussion conducted in this section reveals that international cooperation on micro- and macroprudential regulation is far from being complete. Whilst governments are certainly aware that some problems are global in nature and deserve a multilateral framework where they can be discussed and eventually solved, they prefer to adopt non-legally binding recommendations in the context of informal settings. This conclusion is relevant for the purpose of this book because it reveals that, besides the limited level of liberalisation of cross-border trade in financial services under the GATS, governments have also not committed themselves to respect binding rules on financial services in the context of other institutional settings. These elements should be considered when addressing the extent of WTO Members' regulatory autonomy in the domain of prudential regulation.

2.3 Explaining the Need for Prudence

Irrespective of the development in their respective financial systems, all Members that took part in the talks for the negotiation of the sectoral

---

[66] FSB, *Shadow Banking: Strengthening Oversight and Regulation*, 27 October 2011, available at www.fsb.org/wp-content/uploads/r_111027a.pdf.

discipline on cross-border trade in financial services were concerned about the necessity to preserve the autonomy for Members to step in and correct the market failures in a delicate sector that was already at the centre of the economy.

At this stage, it is worthwhile to consider why a trade agreement puts such emphasis on the need to preserve regulatory space for domestic governments and supervisors of financial systems. The analysis in this section thus focuses on the economic rationales behind the adoption of financial regulation and the evolution of the understanding of prudential measures, especially in light of the developments of two economic crises (in the late 1990s and, most recently, in 2007-8). The discussion, besides providing useful theoretical background to the proper understanding of the GATS PCO, also serves the purpose of verifying whether WTO Members have understood their legislative freedom to be somewhat constricted by the discipline on the liberalisation of cross-border trade in financial services.

Moreover, it is only by understanding whether there are solid rationales for prudential regulation that it is possible to carry out meaningful analysis as to whether it is necessary or practically feasible to address these issues exclusively within the framework of the GATS or if considerable margins for different choices by domestic governments should be allowed.

2.3.1 'Prudence Is Never Enough': *The Economics of Prudential Regulation in Financial Services*

The market for financial services is peculiar in many respects and it is a highly regulated environment. While the demand for deregulation in other economic sectors is more widespread, when it comes to banking (and finance in general), positions tend to be more nuanced. The financial sector is at the heart of today's economies, especially in industrialised countries, and the integrity and soundness of financial institutions and the financial system considered as a whole are crucial factors for the stability of the entire economy of a country or a region. As can also be seen in relation to the global financial meltdown of 2007-8, the dust from which is far from settled, 'the social costs of the failure of an institution exceed the private costs'.[67]

---

[67] Charles Goodhart, Philipp Hartmann and David T. Llewellyn, *Financial Regulation – Why, How and Where Now?* (London and New York City: Routledge, 1998), 272 (p. 5).

Financial regulation is fundamentally justified by market failures, both *ex ante* and *ex post*.[68] Left unregulated, the financial sector could produce socially inefficient market outcomes. These inefficiencies can derive from market power, information asymmetries and negative externalities. In particular, financial markets are threatened by specific market failures, namely the existence of multiple equilibriums, pecuniary externalities and moral hazard. These examples are provided with the caveat that many more possible distortions may exist.

2.3.2 Multiple Equilibriums

Multiple equilibriums are the consequence of a coordination problem because banks borrow money on a short-term basis and invest for the long term. This maturity mismatch,[69] which is valuable economically, can fail catastrophically if the mismatch between short-term (liquid) liabilities (bank deposits) and long-term (illiquid) loans gives rise to concerns among bank depositors. Diamond and Dybvig[70] set out the classic theory of bank runs and multiple equilibriums. In a nutshell, they model fractional-reserve banks as intermediaries transforming illiquid assets into liquid liabilities and depict the relationship among depositors as a coordination game with two Nash equilibria: one good and one bad.

A good equilibrium is where, according to Diamond and Dybvig, save for a fraction of depositors in real need of liquidity, bank customers do not withdraw their deposits before the ordinary maturation date. In such a situation, financial institutions are in the position to pay back the

---

[68] Reinhart and Rogoff have identified a number of events that usually precede systemic banking crises (typically, large capital inflows, asset price bubbles and credit booms). They argue that despite the natural and logical differences between major outbursts in financial markets, there are a number of events and indicators that could (or should) help the regulators to understand and prevent major disruptions. See Carmen M. Reinhart and Kenneth S. Rogoff, *This Time Is different: Eight Centuries of Financial Folly* (Princeton: Princeton University Press, 2009), Carmen M. Reinhart and Kenneth S. Rogoff, 'Banking Crises: An Equal Opportunity Menace', *Journal of Banking and Finance*, 37:11 (2013), 4557–73.

[69] Farhi and Tirole convincingly explain that maturity mismatch creates an incentive for collective moral hazard. In fact, when all the actors in the financial business engage in maturity mismatch–based activities, the authorities are basically forced to intervene at a certain point to supply the necessary liquidity. This increases both current and deferred social costs. See Emmanuel Farhi and Jean Tirole, 'Collective Moral Hazard, Maturity Mismatch and Systemic Bailouts', *American Economic Review* (2012), 102:1, 60–93.

[70] Douglas W. Diamond and Philip H. Dybvig, 'Bank Runs, Deposit Insurance and Liability', *The Journal of Political Economy*, 91:3 (1983), 401–19.

funds and the interests that have matured when the depositor decides to withdraw their money. This is a situation in which there is a satisfactory flow of information, and depositors do not panic.

However – and recent news is full of examples – agents in financial markets are sensitive to shocks, and this may lead to a bad equilibrium. Depositors may decide to withdraw their money from banks for fear that many other customers will do the same or because they fear that their deposits may depreciate.[71] This situation may precipitate a 'bank-run' in which banks are forced to liquidate their assets to satisfy depositors before the natural time for the maturity. In this situation, both depositors and financial institutions incur losses. The former may be late in asking for their assets from banks and end up with nothing or a small fraction of the original deposit. The bank faces a loss because it has fewer funds to use in its activities. The final outcome of this problem of coordination, in which it is rational for depositors to withdraw as early as possible, is a scenario in which banks can become bankrupt.

A variety of reasons unrelated to the bank's condition, such as a bad earnings report, a commonly observed run at some other bank or a negative government forecast can trigger a general bank run. Deposit insurance mechanisms (analysed by Diamond and Dybvig), minimum capital requirements, increasing the minimum level of equity within a bank's capital, liquidity requirements and institutions acting as lenders of last resort are examples of regulations that aim to address multiple equilibriums. Although international cooperation has tried to address these issues to a certain extent and recommendations have been issued by relevant organisations,[72] practice reveals that the deterioration of the conditions of the financial market or of a particular financial institution might materialise in unexpected circumstances or forms and thus call for a prompt reaction on the part of domestic regulators or supervisors, who therefore need adequate flexibility to be in the position to effectively intervene when needed.

2.3.3 Pecuniary Externalities

Another rationale for banking regulation is provided by the existence of pecuniary externalities associated with banks' activities. Pecuniary externalities can be described as third-party effects that operate entirely

---

[71] For instance, this occurred in early 2015 in Greece.
[72] See the discussion in Section 2.3 infra.

2.3 EXPLAINING THE NEED FOR PRUDENCE

through the price mechanism. To offer one example from the market for goods, pecuniary externalities emerge when the increased demand for cars by some drives up the price of cars for all. Under complete markets – which basically exist only on textbooks – pecuniary externalities would offset each other. For example, when the prices of cars increase, consumers will be worse off, but producers will be better off and make profits. The loss to consumers is offset by the gain to producers, therefore the resulting equilibrium is Pareto-efficient. Such Pareto-efficient equilibrium, however, will not be superior because evidently some lose out.

However, once there are market imperfections (which are frequent in the domain of finance), such as asymmetric information or incomplete markets, agents facing credit frictions act in a fragmentary fashion and do not internalise market price reactions leading to welfare-reducing pecuniary externalities. These are particularly relevant in credit markets. Banks may be exposed to losses and be constrained to a position in which they have to reduce the funds they are able to lend. This may impede borrowers from accessing the necessary money to make investments or to run their businesses, thus spreading the pecuniary externalities to sectors of the real economy. Depending on the dimension of the problem, pecuniary externalities may constitute a valid reason for regulators to step in.

Pecuniary externalities can also be a problem between banks. The externalities can either take the form of direct financial contagion or indirect financial contagion. The first case is because banks are usually exposed largely to other financial institutions in the interbank market (this situation is commonly known as 'interconnectedness'). In this situation, when a bank is not able to pay its liabilities in full to another bank there arises a situation of contagion.

Contagion, however, can also take place on an indirect basis. A bank on the verge of failure may try to liquidate its assets in the fastest possible way (fire sales). This is likely to lower market prices, thus also affecting other financial institutions in the market. Moreover, there is also another side of pecuniary externalities that must be considered. As Ulltveit-Moe et al. put it:

> There can also be indirect contagion through interbank funding: if one bank incurs unexpected losses, it will tend to reduce its lending and hence reduce the supply of funding through the interbank market. This tightens the funding supply to other banks, and may lead to reduced lending from these banks. If banks expect such tightening to occur, precautionary liquidity hoarding may result, amplifying the tightening... [T]he sum of the risks that the individual banks take into account is less than the sum of all

the risks their activity generates, i.e. systemic risk. This difference is in fact the sum of the pecuniary externalities.[73]

The foregoing points to the fact that regulators should care about more than the robustness of financial institutions taken singularly. Bank regulators, however, should also address a macro-dimension because financial markets are intrinsically vulnerable. De Nicolò et al.[74] explain how links between financial institutions can be 'subtle' and involve, for example, pecuniary externalities propagated as an effect of the liquidation of assets by one financial institution which, in turn, leads to fire sales and negative consequences for the balance sheets of another financial institution. The world has recently experienced similar issues in the context of the 2007-8 financial crisis. As De Nicolò et al. correctly argue, 'the crisis has brought to the fore the idea that the risk in a financial system is not simply the aggregation of individual risks, but is mostly endogenous risk, resulting from the collective behaviour of financial institutions and agents'.[75] These considerations connect this section with the following.

2.3.4 Moral Hazard

There is another market failure that dominates the background of financial markets: moral hazard. Banks typically act in a situation in which neither the depositors nor the shareholders are in the position to effectively control operations. Financial contracts are too complex, and depositors often lack adequate expertise to judge whether an operation is too risky or safe.[76] This lack of efficient control by shareholders and depositors leads bank operators to undertake risky investments.[77] In the end, shareholders will benefit if the risky operation is successful. In an unsuccessful situation, they enjoy limited liability; hence, they may lose only part of their equity. Creditors, however, will be exposed to losses.[78]

---

[73] Karen H. Ulltveit-Moe, Bent Vale, Morten H. Grindaker, Erling Skancke, 'Competitiveness and Regulation of Norwegian Banks', *Staff Memo – Norges Bank* (2013), 93 (p. 47).
[74] Gianni De Nicolò, Giovanni Favara and Lev Ratnovski, 'Externalities and Macroprudential Policy', *IMF Staff Discussion Note* (2012), SDN/12/05, 23, at 6.
[75] Ibid.
[76] Lack of control by shareholders, however, is due to other causes, including the structure of banks, according to which property and governance are usually separated.
[77] Shleifer and Vishny find that profit-maximizing behaviour leads to systemic risk. See Andrei Shleifer and Robert Vishny 'Unstable Banking', *Journal of Financial Economics* (2010), 97:3, 306–18.
[78] Gennaioli et al. contributed to the debate by putting forward a psychological theory to explain moral hazard-driven financial crises. According to their explanation, investors

Among the regulations that aim at reducing moral hazard, Ulltveit-Moe et al. identify risk-based deposit insurance premiums, and regulation of the remuneration schemes of bank managers as means to induce them to behave more prudently.[79] It should be also borne in mind, however, that although such regulations may make investments less risky, they may also make them less remunerative in case of success. This may lead to situations of underinvestment, and therefore the regulator may find itself in a delicate situation.

The recent financial crisis has shown how deleterious these market failures – as well as the absence of adequate prudential regulation – can be in a context of integrated (financial) markets. In particular, the crisis showed how shocks may be transmitted through the financial system, how complicated crisis management and bank resolution may become if coordination among financial regulators is limited and how incentives to monitor and support banks and their foreign affiliates can differ between home and host-country authorities.[80]

2.3.5 Other Rationales for Prudential Regulation

The presence of externalities and moral hazard are not the only economic explanations for financial regulation. As demonstrated by Llewellyn, other rationales, which either occur less frequently or are somehow connected to the main problems discussed earlier, provide reasonable incentives to adopt prudential regulation: market imperfections and failures, economies of scale in monitoring, 'lemons' and confidence, the 'gridlock problem' and the intrinsic difference between financial products and contracts.[81]

Market imperfections and failures: Llewellyn makes a compelling argument that if unregulated financial markets were perfectly competitive, the costs of regulation would be borne by the consumers. Because financial markets are frequently imperfect, as the cyclical financial crises that

---

typically neglect negative signals from the market in boom times. Then, when the situation begins to deteriorate, they tend to overreact. See Nicola Gennaioli, Andrei Shleifer and Robert Vishny, 'Neglected Risks: The Psychology of Financial Crises', *American Economic Review: Papers & Proceedings* (2015), 105:5, 310–14.

[79] Ulltveit-Moe et al., 'Competitiveness and Regulation of Norwegian Banks' (p. 49).
[80] Stijn Claessens and Juan A. Marchetti, 'Global Banking Regroups', *Finance & Development*, 50:4 (2013), 14–17.
[81] David Llewellyn, 'The Economic Rationale for Financial Regulation', *FSA Occasional Paper Series* (1999), 1–58 (pp. 21 and ff.).

the world has experienced so far shows, the benefits of sound financial reforms outweigh the costs to be borne by clients of financial firms. Financial contracts have, among others, two distinctive features: first, they take place between parties that do not have the same ability to access all the necessary information to properly evaluate the risks connected to the investment; second, they are normally long term. As such, financial firms may have the incentive to gamble more or to have a riskier attitude at a later point in time than that of the conclusion of the contract with the client. When regulation of financial markets is sub-optimal, consumers may underinvest because of a reasonable fear of future losses on the capital invested. Alternatively, sub-optimal regulation may provide an incentive to consumers to act as free-riders, assuming that all other investors have adequately collected the necessary information to evaluate the integrity of the financial institutions involved in the transaction. This problem can be seen from two angles: it could be qualified as an instance of moral hazard, or it could well be read through the prism of the logic of collective action.[82]

Economies of scale in monitoring: As stated earlier, financial contracts are typically long-term contracts, and consequently the way in which a financial institution behaves after the conclusion of a contract influences the value of the financial services at the centre of the latter. Consumers lack the instruments and knowledge to effectively monitor the financial firms with which they conclude a contract, regulatory agencies are called to perform this task. Llewellyn argues that effective systems of monitoring and proper supervision can collect information with the appropriate techniques and in an impartial way and have the power to enforce regulation or to authoritatively influence governments to intervene. This could not happen were the task of monitoring left to the customers because it would be too costly for them and highly inefficient.[83]

'Lemons' and confidence: In a seminal paper published in 1970, Akerlof theorised a framework to determine the economic costs of asymmetric information.[84] In so doing, he referred to the used-automobile market as a prototypical example. A customer who wants to buy a used car typically has more difficult access to the relevant information he or she may need for a proper assessment of the quality of the product than that of the seller. Hence, the buyer may not easily distinguish a good car from a 'lemon' (a colloquial term for 'bad cars' in American English) and may

---

[82] Ibid., pp. 21–23. [83] Ibid. pp. 23–24.
[84] George A Akerlof, 'The Market for "Lemons": Quality, Uncertainty and the Market Mechanism', *The Quarterly Journal of Economics*, 84:3 (1970), 488–500.

eventually end up buying a 'lemon' for the price of a good car. Alternatively, it can work in a different way, in the sense that the price of lemons may decrease significantly and the market could eventually collapse. To avoid situations of this kind, consumers may leave the market, leading to its complete breakdown.

Mutatis mutandis, Llewellyn finds that the same problem with asymmetric information and confidence between buyers and sellers arises in the realm of financial services markets. Purchasers, to avoid the costs of buying a product that would reveal its poor quality after some time, may decide to avoid the risk of entering a peculiar market that shares some features with gambling.[85] In such a scenario, regulation plays an important role. By providing the public minimum standards for the tradability of financial products, financial regulatory bodies reduce the costs of a lack of confidence and can play a role in the attempt to take 'lemons' out of the market.[86]

The 'gridlock' problem: Llewelyn[87] describes the situation of 'gridlock' in financial markets as one in which firms know what would be the optimal behaviour to adopt vis-à-vis consumers and yet undertake hazardous operations to gain higher returns. This may lead to two main problems: adverse selection and moral hazard. A firm that decides to behave honestly towards its clients may do so by imposing a higher cost on itself, becoming non-competitive with respect to other players in the market and therefore losing ground (adverse selection). Such a situation may induce 'good firms' to follow the example of the bad ones to avoid being totally cut off from the market (moral hazard). Essentially, this may create 'gridlock' in the financial market, encouraging firms to behave inappropriately. This is yet another reason for sound regulation of financial markets: to ensure fair conditions for competition and sound behaviour by firms when they negotiate contracts with their clients.

Financial markets can be highly volatile, and it is often impossible to make sound forecasts about developments in this sector. In turn, negative consequences deriving from a regulatory or supervisory failure could spread to all other sectors of the economy. This is why, especially in the aftermath of the 2007–8 financial crisis, both international and national authorities stressed the need to revise the financial regulation architecture

---

[85] Ibid., pp. 25 and 26.
[86] It is preferable to use the expression 'can play' instead of 'play' because junk financial products are far from being removed from the market.
[87] Llewelyn, 'The Economic Rationale for Financial Regulation', p. 27.

and to provide supervisory authority with the necessary tools to intervene in a timely manner and limit the negative consequences of financial distress.[88] A collapse in the financial sector is likely to trigger domino effects in (potentially) all other sectors of the economy.

Actors in markets can purchase different kinds of products. These can be classified in many ways but, for the purpose of the current work, it is necessary to differentiate between 'experience goods' (goods whose characteristics and quality can be easily ascertained after the consumption), 'search goods' (goods whose quality can be evaluated before the purchase) and 'credence goods' (goods whose utility and impact is difficult to be evaluated even after consumption). The more information is needed by consumers to assess the quality of a product, the stronger the rationale for regulation is, because information is costly. Financial products, considering what has been written thus far, are clearly 'credence goods'. Information asymmetry is therefore quintessential to financial markets, and as such, there is a strong rationale for regulators to step in and try to correct such imperfections and market failures.

2.3.6 Interim Conclusion on the Economic Rationale for Prudential Regulation

The discussion conducted thus far shows that there are sound reasons for governments to maintain the ability to intervene and regulate financial markets. The reluctance by national governments to cede parts of their sovereignty in the domain of financial services is further proven by the circumstance in which, contrary to the domain of trade in goods, where the global integration of markets has made substantial progress over the years, financial markets are still at the very early stages of international cooperation, mostly due to different sensitivities and fears of 'regulatory chill'.

2.4 The Evolution of Financial Regulation after the Entry into Force of the GATS

The history of financial markets is one of booms and busts. Occasionally governments need to intervene quickly to limit more dramatic consequences of financial turmoil and avoid speculation. Even when international organisations such as the IMF are involved in recovery

---

[88] See Section 2.5, infra.

programs, providing financial aid in exchange of the implementation of reforms in domestic legislation, it is possible that governments deem it necessary to intervene with regulations more than just once because unforeseen circumstances may always arise.

Following the entry into force of the WTO, the world was shocked by the Asian financial market crisis in 1997-8. As mentioned earlier (when discussing the negotiating history of the GATS Annex on Financial Services), Members of the nascent WTO agreed during the 1996 Ministerial Meeting in Singapore that they would resume negotiations on financial services as of April 1997. It comes as no surprise that negotiations in that field, which had already proved to be difficult, became even more so due to the explosion of the financial crisis that hit East Asia in the spring of 1997. Arguably, the context in which WTO Members negotiated the disciplines on financial services helps to explain why they did not move much further in comparison to the Draft text that had already circulated at the Brussels Meeting. In fact, not only the Members hit by the crisis, but also the remainder of the international community were arguably concerned by the introduction of limitations to their regulatory autonomy in a delicate domain such as prudential regulation. The discussion in this section, although short and not exhaustive because it would otherwise not fit within the economy of this book, proves that WTO Members, either on the basis of recommendations of international organisations or autonomously, have substantially modified their financial legislations to address the shortcomings exposed by the crises. This demonstrates, concretely, that the GATS did not bring about a 'regulatory freeze' of the domain of financial services. If situations or regulatory chill have occurred, that is probably due to other factors, including autonomous political decisions deployed by sovereign governments.

The remainder of this chapter gives an account of the main aspects of regulatory changes intervened in key Members hit by financial crises after the entry into force of the GATS. Subsection 2.4.1 recalls the changes in legislation adopted by Indonesia, Korea and Thailand in the aftermath of the East Asia financial crisis of 1997-8. The choice of this sample lies in that those countries were arguably the most severely hit by that financial upheaval and the fact that they requested assistance from the IMF. Subsection 2.4.2 provides a brief sketch of changes in legislation in the EU and the United States after the 2008 financial crisis. It is hoped that this adds to our understanding of how the concept of 'prudential reasons' has evolved over time and to what extent WTO obligations and commitments have represented impediments or obstacles for trading nations dealing with the consequences of financial turmoil. Finally, Subsection 2.4.3 provides a recap of the main instruments that are considered to be part of the macroprudential toolbox available to financial regulators today.

2.4.1 After the 1997 East Asian Financial Crisis

Although the impact of the crisis differed in many aspects in the various countries that were hit and the spread of the contagion did not occur everywhere at the same pace, it is safe to say that broad similarities can be highlighted as regards the financial crisis in Indonesia, Thailand and Korea, and the situation in these countries before and after 'the music stopped'.[89]

The East Asian crisis generally took both national governments and commentators by surprise. Asian countries were growing at a steady pace, with year-on-year growth rates of 5 per cent or more before 1997. Nevertheless, the crisis highlighted the inherent weaknesses that led those economies to economic difficulty. First of all, inadequate regulation and lax supervision were features of all these economies. National governments had put in place implicit safety nets,[90] thus encouraging morally hazardous behaviours of both lenders and borrowers. The latter knew that, eventually, national governments would have bailed out financial institutions experiencing difficulties with regard to their balance sheets. Further, all three countries were exposed to large private short-term foreign currency debt.[91] These countries were exposed to speculative attacks and were eventually forced to allow their currencies, which were pegged to the US dollar, to float.

The IMF coordinated the policy responses in those countries. To quote from a working paper by IMF officials:

> The IMF's support was organized under the Emergency Financing Mechanism. This mechanism, with a shortened period of negotiation, review, and approval by the IMF's Executive Board, permitted the programs to be put in place very quickly in response to immediate and overwhelming market

---

[89] This is the inspired expression used by Alan Blinder in his contribution on the 2007–2008 financial crisis: Alan S. Blinder, *After the Music Stopped: The Financial Crisis, the Response and the Work Ahead* (New Yourk: Penguin, 2013) 476.

[90] Frederic S. Mishkin, 'Lessons from the Asian Crisis', *Journal of International Money and Finance*, 18 (1999), 709–23. Mishkin puts forward a convincing asymmetric information analysis of the Asian financial crisis.

[91] Timothy Lane et al., 'IMF-Supported Programs in Indonesia, Korea and Thailand', *IMF Occasional Paper* (1999), 1–82.

2.4 THE EVOLUTION OF FINANCIAL REGULATION

pressures. At the same time, it forced exceptionally quick analysis by IMF staff and negotiations with country authorities. At times, decisions had to be based on more than usually incomplete information.[92]

In Thailand, where it all began, the government launched a program of privatisation of banks and introduced measures aiming to align its banking sector to internationally agreed best-practice standards.[93] Temporary ceilings on deposit rates were imposed and capital controls, which were put in place when the crisis occurred in May 1997, were lifted as of August 1997.

Between 1997 and 2001, Thailand made attempts to bring about compliance with internationally agreed standards of corporate governance, in accordance with the indications provided by the IMF as to the key reforms to be implemented to restore financial stability in the region. Although key legislation was mostly blocked by domestic opposition, new initiatives were put in place at a sub-legislative level directly by the Stock Exchange of Thailand (SET). In particular, the SET issued a number of recommendations aiming at the resilience of the financial sector. The 1998 'Code of Best Practices for Directors of Listed Companies' introduced recommendations relating to the establishment of audit and nominations committees at the board level, as well as requirements on the independence and accountability of directors. In 1999, SET issued the document entitled 'Best Practice Guidelines for Audit Committees' and, in 2000, new voluntary guidelines on corporate governance that have been revised several times ever since.[94]

Pursuant to a proposal made by the Securities and Exchange Committee (SEC) of Thailand in 2003, listed companies were requested to disclose the identity of their top ten shareholders and to provide audited and verified financial reports. The overall strengthened disclosure requirements had the effect to push a number of Thai companies to voluntarily delist from the stock exchange, preferring to renounce to the benefits of having their shares being traded on the stock-exchange rather than revealing sensitive information and making an effort of transparency.[95]

---

[92] Ibid. (p. 1).
[93] All information on policy responses at the domestic level are taken from the Letters of Intent (LoI) and Memorandums of Understanding (MoU) between national governments and the IMF and publicly accessible on the IMF website (www.imf.org). See, in the case of Thailand: LoI 14.8.1997; LoI 25.11.1997; LoI 24.2.1998; LoI 26.5.1998; LoI 1.12.1998.
[94] Andrew Walter, *Governing Finance – East Asia's Adoption of International Standards* (Ithaca, NY: Cornell University Press), 2008, pp. 80, 81.
[95] Ibid., p. 84.

With regard to financial institutions, going beyond what is required for listed companies by the SET, the Bank of Thailand issued a series of corporate governance requirements in 1999, among which are the recommendations that independent directors are not allowed to own more than 0.5 per cent of the bank's outstanding shares and that their reappointment is subject to the approval of the Bank of Thailand. Later in time (as of 2002), the Bank of Thailand started to require commercial banks to establish various internal committees (on risk, nominations etc.) and audit committees composed, for their majority, of independent members. Furthermore, the Bank of Thailand tightened the rules on related-party lending (50 per cent of a related company's equity, 25 per cent of its total liabilities and 5 per cent of the bank's total Tier I capital, whichever is lowest).[96]

Indonesia, which had high levels of overseas borrowing, experienced a rapid expansion of the financial system, as well as problems concerning non-performing loans and could not sustain the pegging of the Rupiah to the US dollar.[97] Its policy response consisted of: widening the exchange rate band with the Rupiah finally allowed to float in August 1997; fiscal policies implemented to preserve a budget surplus of 1 per cent of GDP; tight monetary policy; amendments in the banking law to encourage private ownership; strengthening of the legal and supervisory framework for banks; and increasing the minimum capital requirements in line with the standards issued by the Basel Committee.

In addition, Indonesia deployed a number of reforms with the aim of ensuring the independence of financial regulators and supervisors. Before the crisis, in fact, the Bank of Indonesia was formally and practically subordinate to the Ministry of Finance and the Government of Indonesia. In 1999, the Central Bank Act was promulgated. Among the novelties introduced, the Central Bank Act established a fixed five-year term for its governor, who had become formally independent from the government. Moreover, it empowered the Bank of Indonesia to impose administrative sanctions vis-à-vis banks violating the regulations. Interestingly, the new rules introduced increasingly intensive forms of bank supervision, depending on the percentage of the capital adequacy ratio of the financial institution concerned (varying from 'normal' for banks with a capital adequacy ratio of 8 per cent or beyond to 'special' for banks with a ratio between 4 and 6 per cent).

Furthermore, Indonesia adopted new rules on capital adequacy, loan classification and provisioning. As of November 1998, capital

[96] Ibid. 86.   [97] MoU 15.1.1998; MoU 10.4.1998; MoU 24.6.1998.

2.4 THE EVOLUTION OF FINANCIAL REGULATION 47

requirements were gradually tightened, and substantial work on their definition was conducted, leading, for instance, to the exclusion of investments in subsidiaries form capital, which in turn reduced substantially the capital adequacy ratio for a number of banks. The Bank of Indonesia introduced new loan classification and provisioning standards in 1998, in accordance with the international standards applied at that time.

Coincident with these reforms, Indonesia tightened the rules on legal lending limits, in accordance with the recommendations of the IMF. As a result of the reforms, legal lending limits for unconnected borrowers were set at a constantly decreasing percentage (from 30 per cent of bank capital until 2001 to 20 per cent as from 2003). Also, the crisis prompted the strengthening of disclosure requirements. As of 2001, the Bank of Indonesia started to require banks to publish periodically detailed financial reports.

Korea, the third country to request assistance from the IMF, focused mainly on restructuring its financial sector.[98] Among the measures adopted were the implementation of Basel standards, the revision of the Bank of Korea Act and the introduction of stricter conditions for support to financial institutions in distress.

The government of Korea established a new financial regulatory authority in 1998, the Financial Supervisory Committee, with the aim of strengthening – at least in theory – the independence of supervisors.[99] Moreover, there was an overall tightening of the capitalisation standards to comply with international standards and the advice of the IMF, with specific regard to the definition and composition of Tier 2 Capital.[100] In addition, the Banking Act and the Regulations on Banking Supervision of 1999 limited the exposure to single and group borrowers substantially (20 per cent for single borrowers, 25 per cent for group borrowers). Limits on foreign currency loans were introduced, requiring that 50 per cent of loans of three years or longer would be financed by foreign currency borrowings of three years or longer. Finally, more stringent standards of corporate governance were introduced, requiring – for instance – that independent directors constitute at least 50 per cent of the board of directors

---

[98] LoI 3.12.1997; LoI 24.12.1997; LoI 7.2.1998; LoI 2.5.1998; LoI 13.11.1998.
[99] Walter reports that concerns were expressed as to the independence of the new body, since they were conceived as being formally part of the President's office and under the supervision of the prime minister. See Andrew Walter, *Governing Finance*, p. 133.
[100] 'From January 1999, banks could no longer include special provisions for substandard loans and below as Tier 2 capital'. See Andrew Walter, *Governing Finance*, p. 135.

and that independent individuals account for at least two-thirds of the components of the audit committees.

Although these considerations fall largely out of the scope of the present study, it should be nevertheless noted that there has been a certain degree of discrepancy between the (official) intentions of Asian legislators and the effective compliance with internationally agreed financial standards on prudential regulation and supervision of financial institutions.[101] While the crisis certainly and undeniably prompted national governments to step in and address some of the most evident shortcomings that had led to the financial distress, the outcome was hijacked by the lukewarm reaction of domestic constituencies, which were neither ready nor willing to renounce to their privileged positions. This largely led to 'mock compliance' with international standards, watering down the response to the financial crisis. It has been suggested that 'there was a trade-off between the extent of formal compliance and the ability of governments to avoid reneging on compliance commitments either through regulatory forbearance or selective enforcement'.[102]

Without indulging in excessive speculation, two conclusions can be made with regard to the evolution of prudential regulation in these countries after the crisis that hit them towards the end of last century: first, domestic legislators did modify their laws and regulations in response to the crisis; second, the main limit towards the building up of solid macroprudential legislative architectures was represented by resistant domestic constituencies.

The WTO rules on the liberalisation of cross-border trade in financial services hardly played any role in the redefinition of the regulatory frameworks for the governance and supervision of the financial sector in the countries concerned.

2.4.2 Financial Regulation in United States and EU after the 2008 Financial Crisis

The United Sates and the EU are the key players in the world market for financial services. Being the main importers and exporters of financial services and the key players in the relevant international forums in which financial regulation is discussed, it is important to see (although

---

[101] See Andrew Walter, *Governing Finance*, quoted by Verdier, *The Political Economy of International Financial Regulation*, p. 1447.
[102] Andrew Walter, *Governing Finance*, p. 167.

only briefly as it is not the core of the present work) how they implement the guidelines, principles and standards that they have contributed to lay down and the main steps that they have taken in the aftermath of the recent financial crisis.

2.4.2.1 Post-Crisis Financial Regulation in the United States

At the time of writing, the world is still recovering from what was in all likelihood the most dramatic economic crisis since 1929. It is complicated to target one factor that triggered the financial meltdown of 2007–8. The origins of the turmoil, however, can probably be traced in the shocks that occurred in the United States, with the collapse of gigantic financial institutions. Two main factors contributed to the outbreak of the crisis: the housing prices bubble and the diffusion of toxic financial products.[103] These events occurred against the background of a process of deregulation that took place in the United States for years before the crisis involving both Republican and Democrat administrations.[104]

Traditionally, US law was strict in forbidding commercial banks from being involved in investment activities (and, vice versa, investment banks were not allowed to receive deposits).[105] This legislation was the object of subsequent reform culminating in the Financial Services Modernization Act of 1999 (commonly known as the Gramm-Leach-Bliley Act), which repealed relevant parts of the Glass-Steagall Act to remove barriers for the activities in which financial institutions could be involved. The Gramm-Leach-Bailey Act has been indicated by various sources as one of the main drivers of the financial crises that originated in the US subprime market and eventually propagated worldwide. By removing the rigid separation between commercial and investment banks, the 1999 reform led to financial conglomerates occupying larger portions of the US financial market, becoming increasingly big and, often, even 'too big to fail'.[106]

---

[103] The literature on the causes of the 2007–8 financial crisis is endless. For an extensive overview, see Alan S. Blinder, *After the Music Stopped: The Financial Crisis, the Response and the Work Ahead* (New York: Penguin, 2013) 476 (pp. 29 and ff.).

[104] See Gretchen Morgenson and Joshua Rosner, *Reckless Endangerments – How Outsized Ambition, Greed and Corruption Led to Economic Armageddon* (New York: Times Books, 2011) 331 (pp. 106 and ff.).

[105] See Sections 16, 20, 21 and 32 of the US Banking Act of 1933, commonly known as the 'Glass-Steagall Act'.

[106] See, for instance, Arthur E. Wilmarth Jr., *The Dodd-Frank Act Does Not Solve the Too-Big-To-Fail Problem*, in Weiss, Friedl and Kammel, Armin J. (eds.) (2015), *The Changing Landscape of Global Financial Governance and the Role of Soft Law* (Leiden/Boston: Brill Nijhoff), p. 125. It should be also pointed out that other authors have criticised

The main legislative act introduced as a response to the financial crisis is the Dodd-Frank Wall Street Reform and Consumer Protection Act (Dodd-Frank Act), signed into law by President Barack Obama in 2010.[107]

The enactment of the Dodd-Frank Act had huge implications for the financial market landscape in the United States. Not only have the rules on financial services activities undergone profound changes, but the number, function and names of the competent agencies have also been substantially modified compared to the pre-crisis situation.

A comprehensive and detailed examination of the innovations introduced by the Dodd-Frank Act falls outside of the scope of the present section. However, certain elements contained in the legislation – and the manner in which they have been approved in their final formulation – are illustrative of how complicated it is to tackle consolidated interests to build a strong and resilient financial system.

Perhaps the most important innovation contained in the Dodd-Frank Act was brought about by the introduction of the so-called Volcker Rule. Named after the former chairman of the Federal Reserve, Paul Volcker, it is designed with the aim of separating traditional banking activities from proprietary trading operations and investments in hedge funds and private equity funds. Cassidy[108] and Silber[109] comprehensively report the various phases of the legislative process and, in particular, how strongly the financial industry was lobbying to weaken the original formulation of the rule, to the extent that Paul Volcker himself was not exactly flattered to have his name paired with the final outcome. First and foremost, financial institutions obtained the concession to invest up to 3 per cent of their capital in hedge funds and private equity funds with the formal approval of their customers. Furthermore, whilst the original formulation of the bill referred to 'tangible common equity' as the basis for the calculation of the 3 per cent quota, banks lobbied to change that expression into 'Tier 1 capital'. In practical terms, Cassidy notes that such change implies that

---

this understanding and argued instead that Gramm-Leach-Bailey did not lead to systemic mergers between commercial and investment banks and that actually those institutions that merged were able to perform better during the crisis. In this sense, see Mark A. Calabria, *Did Deregulation Cause the Financial Crisis?*, Cato Policy Report (2009), available at https://object.cato.org/sites/cato.org/files/serials/files/policy-report/2009/7/cpr31n4.pdf.

[107] Dodd-Frank Wall Street Reform and Consumer Protection Act, Public Law No: 111-203 (21/07/2010).

[108] John Cassidy, 'The Volcker Rule', *The New Yorker* (July 2010), available at www.newyorker.com/magazine/2010/07/26/the-volcker-rule.

[109] William L. Silber, *Volcker – The Triumph of Persistence* (New York: Bloomsbury Press), 2012, pp. 187 and ff.

2.4 THE EVOLUTION OF FINANCIAL REGULATION 51

financial institutions can increase the capital that they could invest in risky activities by no less than 40 per cent.[110]

In addition to the Volcker rule, the Dodd-Frank Act introduced the requirement for riskier derivatives to be cleared through central counter parties (CCPs). Until the entry into force of the new set of rules, the overwhelming majority of the swaps were traded on a bilateral level. After Dodd-Frank, transactions for standardised OTC derivatives are submitted to a CCP, which is bound to respect detailed requirements to mitigate risks.

The explosion of the 2007-8 financial crisis revealed the gaps in the architecture on financial supervision in the United States. The Dodd-Frank Act responded to this situation by creating the Financial Stability Oversight Council (FSOC), with the mandate to identify systemic risks in financial markets and to respond to threats to stability in a timely fashion. However, Kern rightly warns that the FSOC does not have enforcement powers and can only issue recommendations.[111] The Dodd-Frank Act also introduced reforms that affected the Federal Reserve activities. More stringent rules on banking supervision were introduced. New rules for the protection of consumers, particularly in the mortgage market, have seen the light of the day because of the Dodd-Frank Act. Finally, this piece of legislation also introduced changes with regard to the resolution of financial institutions in distress. The United States has also committed to implement the standards set out in Basel with regard to capital adequacy, liquidity coverage and leverage.

It should be noted that some authors, including Coffee, questioned the efficacy of the rules introduced by Dodd-Frank in addressing the causes and mitigating the consequences of the financial crisis. In particular, it is argued that more stringent rules and less delegation to agencies in the implementation would have made the regulatory response to the crisis stronger and more effective.[112]

2.4.2.2 Post-Crisis Financial Regulation in the European Union

The crisis did not start in the EU. However, the Old Continent was severely affected by the negative consequences of the financial meltdown for two main reasons. First of all the high degree of interconnectedness of financial

---

[110] John Cassidy, *The Volcker Rule*.
[111] Steffen Kern, 'US Financial Market Reform – the Economics of the Dodd-Frank Act', *Deutsche Bank Research – EU Monitor* (2010), 23 (p. 4).
[112] John C. Coffee, 'Extraterritorial Financial Regulation: Why E. T. Can't Come Home', *Cornell Law Review*, 99:6 (2014), 1259-302.

markets worldwide also brought instability to Europe. Second, the European Union paid a high price for the lack of common effective legislation among its twenty-eight Member States in financial markets in general and, more specifically, with regard to the resolution of financial institutions in distress.

The European regulators have put in place a strategy for the reform of financial markets that is in the process of being implemented at the time of writing.[113] Essentially, there are four main stated objectives: the promotion of the stability and resilience of the banking sector; the completion and deepening of the European single market for financial services; the enhancement of transparency and disclosure to better protect investors and consumers and making the EU financial system more efficient. The ultimate goal pursued by the institutions of the EU is to realise a Banking Union, which should consist of a singe rulebook for all financial actor across the Member States of the EU. To this end, EU institutions and Member States have agreed to establish a Banking Union based on a single supervisory mechanism and a single resolution mechanism.[114]

The EU has adopted new legal instruments to comply with the international standards issued in the aftermath of the crisis with regard to capital adequacy and loss absorbency. In July 2013, the Capital Requirements Directive (CRD)[115] and Regulation (the CRD IV package)[116] entered into force. Those instruments amend pre-existing rules or introduce new requirements on a number of important issues. For instance, they raised the level and quality of capital that financial institutions must hold,

[113] For a detailed overview of the measures adopted by the EU Commission, together with the other EU Co-legislators, see European Commission, Commission Staff Working Document *Economic Review of the Financial Regulation Agenda* – Accompanying the document 'Communication from the Commission to the European Parliament, the Council, the European Economic and Social Committee and the Committee of the Regions: *A Reformed Financial Sector for Europe*' [COM(2014) 279 final], 15.5.2014, available at http://ec.europa.eu/internal_market/finances/docs/general/20140515-erfra-workingdocument_en.pdf.

[114] More information is available on the European Commission's website: http://ec.europa.eu/finance/general-policy/banking-union/index_en.htm. For more information on the road towards a European Banking Union and the theoretical foundations behind it, see Georges Zavvos, 'Towards a European Banking Union – Legal and Policy Implications', MIMEO, (2013), 23.

[115] Directive 2013/36/EU of the European Parliament and of the Council of 26 June 2013 on access to the activity of credit institutions and the prudential supervision of credit institutions and investment firms, amending Directive 2002/87/EC and repealing Directives 2006/48/EC and 2006/49/EC.

[116] Regulation (EU) No 575/2013 of the European Parliament and of the Council of 26 June 2013 on prudential requirements for credit institutions and investment firms and amending Regulation (EU) No 648/2012.

2.4 THE EVOLUTION OF FINANCIAL REGULATION

introduced systems to better control the increase of leverage in the banking sector; introduced requirements for the improvements of liquidity buffers and requirements for banks to hold capital reserves that they can use in situations of stress (capital conservation buffers); and allowed national regulators to introduce a discretionary buffer up to 2.5 per cent of capital that the bank could be required to collect in periods of high credit growth. Finally, higher requirements have been introduced for systemically important financial institutions.

Another important piece of post-crisis piece of legislation is the Bank Recovery and Resolution Directive (BRRD).[117] This new legal instruments requires all EU Member States to abide by a single rulebook for the resolution of banks and other financial institutions. The main and most revolutionary idea behind this reform is to shift the burden of the resolution of financial institutions in distress from taxpayers to private resources. Moreover, it introduces tools to more effectively deal with the complicated issue of cross-border resolution of banks.

The EU has also sought to strengthen the stability and reliability of the financial market infrastructure. In this regard, Brussels has remarkably adopted three new legal instruments: the Markets in Financial Instruments Directive (MiFID)[118] and the Markets in Financial Instruments Regulation (MiFIR),[119] which together form the 'MiFID II package' (in force from 3 January 2018); the European Markets and Infrastructure Regulation (EMIR)[120] and the regulation on central securities depositories (CSDs).[121]

---

[117] Directive 2014/59/EU of the European Parliament and of the Council of 15 May 2014 establishing a framework for the recovery and resolution of credit institutions and investment firms and amending Council Directive 82/891/EEC, and Directives 2001/24/EC, 2002/47/EC, 2004/25/EC, 2005/56/EC, 2007/36/EC, 2011/35/EU, 2012/30/EU and 2013/36/EU, and Regulations (EU) No 1093/2010 and (EU) No 648/2012, of the European Parliament and of the Council. At the time of writing, Commission's proposals to amend the BRRD are still pending. For an overview of the Commission's proposals, see *Planned actions relating to Directive 2014/59/EU on bank recovery and resolution*, available at: https://ec.europa.eu/info/node/7782/.

[118] Directive 2014/65/EU of the European Parliament and of the Council of 15 May 2014 on markets in financial instruments and amending Directive 2002/92/EC and Directive 2011/61/EU.

[119] Regulation (EU) No 600/2014 of the European Parliament and of the Council of 15 May 2014 on markets in financial instruments and amending Regulation (EU) No 648/2012.

[120] Regulation (EU) No 648/2012 of the European Parliament and of the Council of 4 July 2012 on OTC derivatives, central counterparties and trade repositories.

[121] Regulation (EU) No 909/2014 of the European Parliament and of the Council of 23 July 2014 on improving securities settlement in the European Union and on central securities depositories and amending Directives 98/26/EC and 2014/65/EU and Regulation (EU) No 236/2012.

One of the main lessons from the crisis is that those markets that deal with financial instruments other than equity shares are remarkably opaque. The MiFID II package aims, inter alia, to enhance transparency with new reporting requirements and to mitigate the risks connected to high-frequency trading (HFT).

The EMIR introduced the requirement that standardised derivative contracts have to be cleared through CCPs. It also requires that OTC derivatives are traded in electronic trading platforms and that all data on European trade in derivatives have to be reported to officially recognised trade repositories and is made accessible to supervisory authorities.

The CSD regulation introduces higher standards in line with internationally agreed standards for the safety and the efficiency of securities trade. Remarkably, it introduced for the first time common EU rules on 'short selling'.[122] The new instruments aim to enhance transparency by obliging actors in financial markets to notify net short positions in government debt. Moreover, they imposed restrictions on the possibility of proceeding with naked short-selling instruments.

2.4.3 The Lessons Learned from Post-GATS Regulatory Reforms

As the discussion conducted in the previous subsections reveals, there are strong incentives for governments to establish and maintain sound regulatory frameworks for the supervision and control of financial markets. Moreover, there are solid theoretical arguments behind the necessity of preserving regulatory space for governments to intervene when financial crises hit hard and cause severe contraction of a country's economy by also propagating to other sectors. Finally, recent (and less recent) history reveals that governments can and do intervene in the regulation of financial markets to ensure that they provide responses to the disruption caused by financial instability. With specific regard to the aftermath of the 2007–8 financial crisis, it is impossible to overemphasise the regulatory developments that have ensued worldwide. Empirical studies[123] reveal that prudential regulation has overall been strengthened in response to the

---

[122] 'Short selling' is a transaction in which the seller sells a security that it does not own with the intention of buying it back at a later point in time. 'Naked short selling' is a similar transaction in which the seller has not borrowed the securities, nor has it ensured their borrowing before the main transaction takes place. They are highly risky contracts.

[123] Olivier Denk and Gabriel Gomes, 'Financial Re-regulation since the Global Crisis? – An Index-based Assessment', OECD Economics Department Working Papers, No. 1396,

2.4 THE EVOLUTION OF FINANCIAL REGULATION

financial crisis, with remarkable differences in the degree of intensity of the regulatory changes across the various countries.

Finally, two other elements must be added to the discussion. First, despite the move towards interconnectedness and greater convergence, financial markets are still subject to national legislation. Second, it must be noted that even in those sectors (i.e. capital requirements) where international standards have been agreed upon and have taken account of the lessons from various financial crises, the record of compliance among various jurisdictions is still subject to a large degree of variation. In this respect, Young provides a plausible explanation of the divergence between the EU and the United States in banking reform since the crisis.[124] In his account, Young explains that the EU and the United States substantially diverged in the implementation of the Basel III reform, with the United States in some cases going over and above minimum standards, and the EU being materially incompliant in certain ambits. Young focuses on the reforms of Tier 1 capital and the leverage ratio and links the different responses to the implementation of the Basel III recommendations with the advocacy by the banking industry in shaping the regulatory tools at the domestic level. In a nutshell, the author argues that while US industry was more persuasive in shaping the new recommendations at the international level and is largely behind the definition of the new capital rules that found their way into Basel III, EU industry played a more active role in the definition of the implementation strategy at the EU level. After all, this explanation is in line with the rationale described by Olson in his classic analysis of the logic of collective action, whereby like-minded producers (in this case, financial services suppliers) are often successful in organising the representation of their interests and lobbying their domestic governments in this respect.[125]

If nothing else, the preceding discussion reveals that the GATS has not represented a major deterrent for the re-regulation of financial services markets worldwide. This is coherent with the robust rationale behind the need to preserve the regulatory autonomy of national governments in the domain of financial services.

OECD Publishing, Paris (2017), available at www.oecd-ilibrary.org/docserver/download/0f865772-en.pdf?expires=1507473355&&id=id&accname=guest&checksum=CD5D115E8A652132BBFDCD185B68651C.

[124] Kevin Young, 'Tying Hands and Cutting Ties: Explaining the Divergence between the EU and the US in Global Banking Reform since the Crisis', *Journal of Banking Regulation*, 17:1 (2016), pp. 46–59.

[125] Olson, *The Logic of Collective Action: Public Goods and the Theory of Groups*.

2.5 The Macroprudential Toolbox in the Aftermath of the 2007–8 Financial Crisis

The 2007–8 crisis that shook the financial system on a global scale revealed that the goal of preserving the integrity and stability of the financial system was far from being achieved. Notwithstanding the various attempts by scholars and central banks' services, we still do not have a precise definition of what macroprudential tools are, nor of the very concept of financial stability. The latter in particular, although the subject of extensive research over the years, has never enjoyed a unanimously accepted definition. Schinasi, for instance, borrows the words of thirteen actors – including academics, central bankers and national regulators alike – and sets out with thirteen different definitions of 'financial stability'.[126]

The evolution of the regulations and practices at the national and supranational levels gave birth to a whole new stream of literature on how to better safeguard financial stability and on what are the most valuable tools to predict turmoil, anticipate disruptions and avoid the spread of negative externalities stemming from a failure in the financial system.[127] In particular, as one might expect, a discussion is taking place regarding which tools actually worked, which could have worked better and what new instruments could be adopted to anticipate imbalances, prevent crises and, eventually, provide a timely response to situations of instability.

Despite the natural divergence of opinions in the literature as to how to best target such delicate issues, there seems to be a tendency in the aftermath of the 2007–8 crisis to take into consideration the possibility of differentiating macroprudential tools to a greater extent and to address not only issues dealing with the strengthening of prudential supervision but also other aspects that have an impact on the stability of the financial system (and to reduce the intrinsic risk connected with financial activities).[128]

Recently a number of papers have sought to quantify the impact of new measures as well as the actual diffusion of the tools that are

---

[126] Garry J. Schinasi, *Safeguarding Financial Stability – Theory and Practice* (Washington, DC: International Monetary Fund, 2006) 309 (pp. 286 and ff.).

[127] For a review of the literature, see Gabriele Galati and Richhild Moessner, 'Macroprudential Policy – A Literature Review', *Journal of Economic Surveys*, 27:5 (2012), 846–78.

[128] Olivier Blanchard, Giovanni Dell'Ariccia, and Paolo Mauro, 'Rethinking Macro Policy II: Getting Granular', *IMF Staff Discussion Note* (International Monetary Fund, 2013), 1–25.

commonly deployed.[129] This section attempts to list the most common tools and to briefly describe them to give an account of what measures the international community of regulators and scholars currently consider to be 'prudential' tools in the domain of financial markets regulation.

Capital Requirements (and Sectoral Capital Requirements): This is probably the most common prudential tool under analysis and represents the first pillar of the new standards issued by the BCBS in the aftermath of 2007–8 (Basel III). Essentially, it deals with the amount of capital that banks are required to hold by their financial regulators. The amount of capital to be held is typically expressed in terms of a proportion of common equity capital compared with risk-weighted assets. The aim of such measures is to ensure that financial institutions internalise the externalities deriving from the risky activities in which they participate. Far from being simply a microprudential tool, given the high degree of interconnectedness of financial institutions, raising capital requirements is also useful to avoid domino effects.

Since the crisis, the BCBS has modified and increased the capital requirements that financial institutions of its Members must respect (see the discussion in Section 2.2.2.1). The BCBS conducts a periodical review of how its Members implement the standards, and it appears that all BCBS Members will reasonably comply in a timely fashion with the requirements set to definitively enter into force in 2019.

The epistemic community generally agrees on the classification of capital requirements as instruments for the pursuit of prudential regulatory objectives. Notably, Admati and Hellwig[130] argue that bankers should be forced to finance themselves and their activities like normal firms do and should therefore be required to hold three times or even four times the level of capital that is currently required under the new recommendations issued by the BCBS.

Countercyclical capital buffers: Under this measure, financial institutions are required, in addition to their minimum capital requirements, to build up an additional capital buffer during periods of economic growth. This measure allows financial institutions to have more capital to rely on in

---

[129] Among the others, Cheng Hoon Lim et al., 'The Macroprudential Framework: Policy Responsiveness and Institutional Arrangements' (International Monetary Fund, 2013), 1–38.

[130] Arian Admati and Martin Hellwig, *The Bankers' New Clothes: What's Wrong with Banking and What to Do about It* (Princeton: Princeton University Press, 2013).

times of distress and to avoid situations of credit crunch, which are poisonous for the rest of the economy and exacerbate financial crises. The BCBS set the countercyclical buffer in a range between 0 and 2.5 per cent but governments may well decide to go beyond that threshold, which – it is worth stressing – is only a recommendation.[131]

Maximum leverage ratios: Leverage is an instrument financial institutions adopt to maximise returns and losses. Typically, it involves risky practices such as using borrowed funds to buy more of an asset at the risk that the borrowing costs may outweigh the returns in income from that asset. New Basel III rules define the leverage ratio as the ratio between the capital measure and the exposure measures.

Time-varying/dynamic provisioning: Dynamic provisioning is a tool mostly used by the Spanish regulator (as well as the Bank of India) to measure banks' loan losses. Essentially, it requires banks to build up reserves to cover losses deriving from the concession of loans. Such a buffer will increase during years in which losses are less than expected, whereas it will drop during periods of increased losses.

Restrictions on distributions: Through this measure, the possibility of distributing dividends is limited to maintain a sufficient amount of capital during favourable economic times.

Liquidity coverage ratio: The reform of the LCR represents the second pillar of the innovations introduced by the new 'Basel III' framework. In a nutshell, the recommendation establishes the proportion between HQLA and the banks' total net cash outflows (see the discussion in Section 2.2.2.1).

Loan to value restrictions: A loan-to-value restriction is a tool deployed to limit the amount of money lent to clients. It is expressed in terms of a percentage of the value of the loan that can be awarded compared with the value of the property (typically such loans are instrumental to help clients obtain the necessary money to conclude real estate contracts). New Basel III requirements introduce a ratio of 80 per cent of average issuance. The aim of the instrument is to avoid situations in which borrowers are unable to pay back their loans, which was one of the causes of the crisis from which global financial institutions are slowly recovering.

---

[131] Dewatripont and Tirole find a strong rationale for the introduction of countercyclical capital buffers, as they contribute to the robustness of 'self-defence mechanisms' in the event of financial crises. See Mathias Dewatripont and Jean Tirole, 'Macroeconomic Shocks and Banking Regulation', *Journal of Money, Credit and Banking* (2012), 44 (Supplement S2), 237–54.

2.5 THE MACROPRUDENTIAL TOOLBOX IN THE AFTERMATH 59

Debt-to-income restrictions: Along the same lines (and following the same rationale), some national jurisdictions put in place restrictions on borrowing based on a percentage on the income of the borrower to ensure that they are able to pay back the loan.

Minimum margin requirements for non-centrally cleared derivatives: The BCBS, together with the IOSCO, introduced a framework for margin requirements for non-centrally cleared derivatives. Quoting from the BIS website:

> all financial firms and systemically important non-financial entities that engage in non-centrally cleared derivatives will have to exchange initial and variation margin commensurate with the counterparty risks arising from such transactions. The framework has been designed to reduce systemic risks related to over-the-counter (OTC) derivatives markets, as well as to provide firms with appropriate incentives for central clearing while managing the overall liquidity impact of the requirements.[132]

Use of central counterparties: Among the measures proposed by the G-20, there was one according to which Members committed to ensure that all OTC contracts are cleared through CCPs. These are systemically important because they reduce problems of coordination. However, there are also problems with regard to the concentration of risk within CCPs.

Disclosure requirements: One of the main issues with banking practice is the asymmetry of information between the various actors in the financial market. Disclosure requirements help address the issue and, in theory, make the task of the supervisors easier.[133]

Reserve requirements: Many central banks require financial institutions to hold a fraction of customers' deposits as reserves that they cannot lend (although this is not a universal practice). Such reserves are typically either stored in the banks' vaults or are in the form of deposits made to central banks. They may be considered as performing a prudential function because they force financial institutions to keep part of the deposits and not to use all of them for their operations.

Caps on foreign currency lending: Loans in foreign currency put both the borrower and the lender in a riskier situation. The former is exposed to the risks due to the fluctuations in the foreign exchange rate and, as a consequence, the latter faces higher credit risks.

---

[132] Available at www.bis.org/publ/bcbs261.htm.

[133] For example, the new Basel III framework for the leverage ratio is complemented by disclosure requirements for the banks that have to comply with the standards. Essentially, they must publicly disclose the leverage ratio they apply in a timely fashion.

Limits on net open currency positions or mismatches: Such tools are used to prevent situations in which liabilities exceed assets in a given currency.

SIFIs: One of the main issues during and after the start of the 2007–8 financial crisis has been the so-called 'too-big-to-fail' problem. Essentially, this relates to financial institutions that have grown too big, and, due to their central position in the financial markets, the social costs of their failure may outweigh the costs suffered by the banks themselves.

In late 2011, the FSB, following a methodology developed by the BCBS, issued a list of so-called global systemically important banks (G-SIBs) that are required, among other things, to respect higher loss absorbency requirements. The FSB publishes the list of G-SIBs every year in November.

Capital controls: There is no unanimous definition of capital controls, yet their use has been extensively advocated in the aftermath of the crisis and they are a recurring topic in economic literature. The concept of capital controls refers generally to measures that have the effect of influencing the cross-border movement of capital. For our present purposes, an explanation of what capital controls are and what are the measures typically put in place from a *Staff Discussion Note of the IMF* is useful:

> Capital controls limit the rights of residents or non-residents to enter into capital transactions or to effect the transfers and payments associated with these transactions. Typical measures include taxes on flows from non-residents, unremunerated reserve requirements (URR) on such flows, or special licensing requirements and even outright limits or bans. Measures may be economy-wide, sector-specific (usually the financial sector), or industry specific (for example, 'strategic' industries). Measures may apply to all flows, or may differentiate by type or duration of the flow (debt, equity, direct investment; short-term vs. medium- and long-term). While this taxonomy is analytically useful, it bears emphasising that the classification is not always clear-cut, and often there are only fine distinctions among the measures.[134]

Different forums of international economic law deal with the issue of capital controls and regulate specific facets. Article VI ('Capital Transfers'), Section 3 of the Articles of Agreement (AA) of the IMF reads:

> **Section 3. Controls of capital transfers**
>
> Members may exercise such controls as are necessary to regulate international capital movements, but no member may exercise these controls in

---

[134] Jonathan D. Ostry et al., 'Managing Capital Inflows: What Tools to Use?', *IMF Staff Discussion Note* (2011), 1–41 (p. 11).

a manner which will restrict payments for current transactions or which will unduly delay transfers of funds in settlement of commitments, except as provided in Article VII, Section 3(*b*) and in Article XIV, Section 2.

Another forum of international economic law where the issue is addressed is the Code of Liberalisation of Capital Movements of the Organisation for Economic Co-operation and Development (OECD). A relevant passage of the preamble reads:

> The Code recognises that capital controls can play a role in specific circumstances. But because 'beggar-thy-neighbour' approaches can have negative collective outcomes, countries have agreed under the Code to well-tested principles such as transparency, non-discrimination, proportionality and accountability to guide their recourse to controls.

The GATS itself provides a discipline for the movement of capital. The rationale for the GATS is to establish a forum for the progressive liberalisation of international trade in services, therefore the liberalisation of cross-border capital movement is not an objective in and of itself. However, cross-border movement of capital can either be an essential part of the service itself or may represent the way in which such a service is paid for. Therefore it is not surprising that the GATS provides for a discipline with regard to the limitation of the possibility for its Members to restrict cross-border capital flows.

Article XI of the GATS ('Payments and Transfers') prevents Members from restricting the cross-border movement of financial flows for current account transactions relating to their specific commitments. The same provision, however, makes clear that this cannot compromise the possibility of Members (i) to adopt measures in compliance with their obligations under the IMF AA and with what they negotiate and are requested to do by the Fund; and (ii) to put in place measures to address serious balance of payments and external financial difficulties, as per Article XI of the GATS.

In addition to the two exceptions listed in Article XI of the GATS, it appears that the adoption of capital controls for current account transactions (as well as capital account transactions) could be justified under the general exceptions of Article XIV of the GATS, provided that the conditions set forth therein are satisfied. Moreover, there is increasing awareness that capital controls may serve as a tool to address negative externalities of turmoil in the financial system, and as such they can be considered to be part of the 'prudential' toolbox. This is not straightforward, however, given the concerns raised by some Members in various discussions in the

WTO Committee on Trade in Financial Services, as reported in the following chapter.[135]

2.6 Conclusion: Do Prudential Concerns Justify More Regulatory Autonomy Than Other Areas?

Uruguay Round participants decided to leave to the discretion of financial regulators the adoption of any regulations and policies they deem appropriate to prevent – or limit the effects of – financial instability.

As was shown in the preceding text, at the beginning of the negotiations of a multilateral agreement on trade in services, most trading nations had lukewarm reactions concerning the conclusion of an agreement addressing the liberalisation of cross-border trade in financial services. Along with the intuitive concerns raised by developing countries (which were afraid of a loss in sovereignty in a strategic sector), caution was also expressed by trading nations with different backgrounds and levels of income. Even those Members that, at the time of negotiations, were inclined to deregulate many market sectors and were pushing for tangible liberalisation in international trade in financial services made efforts to find a balance between new market opportunities and clauses for the protection of their domestic financial markets.

The discussion in this chapter reveals that there are strong rationales for the preservation of sufficient regulatory space for governments in the domain of financial services, due to prudential concerns. These concerns might be known *ex ante*, thus leading domestic legislatives and executives to the deployment of sound measures for the correct supervision of financial markets. However, problems in the financial sector often emerge *ex post*, that is, when there is a need to intervene to ease the already critical consequences of a disruption in the financial market. Against this background, two additional elements should be taken into account: on the one hand, financial services are at the centre of today's economies, meaning that the failure by regulators to intervene in order to dam the propagation of negative externalities to other areas of a country's economy is likely to have major repercussions; on the other hand, the record of international cooperation in the domain of financial services is still in its early stages, thus implying that national biases and sensitivities still play an active role

---

[135] For a detailed analysis of these issues, see Gabriel Gari, 'Capital Controls, GATS Disciplines and the Need for a More Coherent Global Economic Governance Structure', *Queen Mary University of London, School of Law, Legal Studies Research Paper* (2014).

in this specific area of law, where international coordination has been less successful than in traditional trade-related areas.

With all of this in mind, it is now time to conduct a legal analysis of the GATS PCO and see whether the current understanding of the provision is in line with the historical and economic rationale for its inclusion in the GATS Annex on Financial Services.

3

The Current Understanding of the GATS PCO

The discussion conducted in the previous chapter revealed the importance of striking an adequate balance between the necessity for WTO Members to respect their GATS obligations and commitments while maintaining sufficient freedom to regulate in order to address micro- and macroprudential concerns. According to the intention of the drafters of the GATS Annex on Financial Services, this function is assigned to Paragraph 2(a) thereof.

The language of the provision is, at least prima facie, not self-interpreting and leaves room for ambiguity and different understandings. The aim of this chapter is to provide readers with the state of the art in the current understanding of the PCO, as interpreted by at least one WTO panel and by the majority of the literature that was called on to interpret it.

As was anticipated in the introduction to this book, there are reasons to believe that the mainstream understanding of the provision is not the only permissible one. To illustrate the possible alternative readings of the GATS PCO, it is first necessary to clarify what the mainstream approach consists of and what are the main concerns that WTO Members expressed over the years before a WTO panel was first called to step in and interpret the provision.

This chapter is structured as follows: Section 3.1 discusses the ambiguous elements that make the provision non-self-explanatory and provides an overview of the way in which the commentators and scholars have understood this provision over the years. Section 3.2 examines the moments in which the provision was debated within the WTO Committee for Trade in Financial Services, the requests for clarifications tabled by national delegations at the WTO and several documents issued by the WTO Secretariat that have discussed the matter. Sections 3.3 and 3.4 are devoted to an analysis of the findings made by the Panel and the Appellate Body in *Argentina – Financial Services*, and Section 3.5 concludes the chapter.

3.1 A Non-Self-Interpreting Provision and the Opinion of Scholars

3.1.1 The Interpretative Problems Connected with the Reading of the GATS PCO

The heading of the provision, 'Domestic Regulation', is also the heading of Article VI of the GATS, which contains distinct sets of obligations. The idea behind Article VI of the GATS is that there may be national measures of regulatory nature that are not on their face discriminatory or market-restrictive – and therefore are not captured by Articles II ('Most-Favoured Nation'), XVII ('National Treatment') and XVI ('Market Access') – but can nonetheless restrict cross-border trade in financial services.[1] Article VI of the GATS contains two separate sets of obligations. On the one hand, Articles VI.1, VI.2, VI.3 and VI.6 contain disciplines of procedural nature, as was correctly pointed out by the Panel in *US – Gambling*.[2] On the other hand, Articles VI.4 and VI.5 specifically refer to the content of the domestic measures and thus can be considered to be of substantive nature. Furthermore, the latter category of disciplines was supposed to be further developed through negotiations in dedicated bodies that the Council for Trade in Services was supposed to establish. Those negotiations were never completed, and a discussion on prudential measures in that context did not even start.

The GATS PCO is peculiar, meaning that it does not fit squarely within either of the two categories. It is not directly related to the administration of the measures, nor does it establish objective criteria for Members to adopt qualification requirements, technical standards and licensing requirements. Rather, its plain language seems to suggest that it provides for an escape clause in case GATS obligations and commitments would not allow domestic governments to adopt measures in pursuance of prudential policy objectives. Yet the question remains as to why the measure falls under such a peculiar heading.

As shown in greater detail in Chapter 5, placing the PCO under the heading 'Domestic Regulation' was a deliberate choice of the drafters of the GATS Annex on Financial Services. In any event, the negotiations did not result in a clear formulation of the provision.

---

[1] For a comprehensive overview of the GATS discipline on domestic regulation, see Markus Krajewski, 'Article VI', in Rüdiger Wolfrum, Peter-Tobias Stoll and Clemens Feinäugle, *WTO – Trade in Services – Max Planck Commentary on World Trade Law* (Leiden/Boston: Martinus Nijhoff), pp. 165–96.

[2] Panel Report, *US – Gambling*, para. 6.432.

Moving on to the wording of the provision, the first expression ('Notwithstanding any other provisions of the Agreement') already certifies that the provision has a broad reach and is capable of overriding the pre-existing obligations that are binding on the WTO Member invoking it. Two interpretative problems nevertheless emerge. On the one hand, as the provision simply refers to 'provisions of the Agreement', it is legitimate to ask whether the carve-out provided by the provision under analysis only applies to general obligations contained in the Annex on Financial Services and to the discipline provided in the text of the GATS or, more broadly, also to any other specific commitment listed by a Member in its schedules. A coherent reading of the provision, however, suggests that the PCO overrides not only all the provisions contained in the Annex on Financial Services but, more in general, each and every single provision of the GATS and all its annexes and protocols (in fact, it refers to the 'Agreement' as a whole, and not to any other instrument more specifically). In addition, in the light of Article XX:3 of the GATS, pursuant to which 'Schedules of specific commitments shall be annexed to this Agreement and shall form an integral part thereof', there is little doubt that the reference to 'any other provision' also encompasses the schedules of specific commitments. Therefore, it is at least clear that the provision has a broad reach.

With regard to the regulatory objectives that WTO Members remain free to pursue, the provision lays down a non-exhaustive list (signalled by the word 'including') of reasons that may lead governments to amend their legislations regardless of pre-existing GATS obligations or commitments. Despite the broad formulation of the provision, divergent interpretations as to its scope of applications cannot be ruled out. In fact, as was clarified in the previous chapter, there is no unanimity as to what measures are, in and of themselves, prudential in nature, as opposed to those with an inherent protectionist aim. Contrary to the Anti-Dumping Agreement, the GATS does not mandate a specific standard of review whereby WTO panels, when they find that a relevant provision of the Agreement allows more than one permissible interpretation, shall find the measures adopted by the Members to conform with their obligations if they fall within one of those permissible interpretations.[3]

The provision, then, ends with a final sentence, the immediate meaning of which is not self-explanatory. The sentence opens with the phrase,

---

[3] See Article 17.6 of the Anti-Dumping Agreement.

'Where such measures do not conform with the provisions of the Agreement', which can hardly be reconciled with the rest of the provision. The GATS PCO, in fact, could be thought of as a purely defensive provision – and, as will be shown in the following section, it has actually been regarded as such by the majority of the commentators. In that regard, it would play a role only after a preliminary finding that a challenged measure is inconsistent with one or more of the GATS obligations or the concerned Member's specific commitments. The use of the term 'when' implies that there may be other ways in which the provision could be interpreted.

Finally, the provision ends with a final clause according to which 'they [meaning the measures] shall not be used as a means of avoiding the Member's commitments or obligations under the Agreement'. The meaning of the second part of the last sentence is, at the very least, obscure and is open to various interpretations. In any event, it is odd to have a provision that, on the one hand, allows for the deviation from obligations and commitments and, on the other hand, affirms that the measures adopted in pursuit of prudential policy concerns shall not be 'used' as a means of avoiding the same obligations under the GATS. Little attention has been paid to the meaning of the last sentence of the provision and its rather circular structure. It is not clear whether it refers to the adoption of the measures themselves or, more specifically, to their administration, in a similar fashion to Article VI:1 of the GATS ('In sectors where specific commitments are undertaken, each Member shall ensure that all measures of general application affecting trade in services are administered in a reasonable, objective and impartial manner') or to Article X:3(a) of the GATT 1994 ('Each contracting party shall administer in a uniform, impartial and reasonable manner all its laws, regulations, decisions and rulings of the kind described in paragraph 1 of this Article').

Admittedly, the provision under analysis provides the interpreter with a heavy task. On the one hand, it seems to allow Members to deviate from their GATS obligations in the presence of prudential policy objectives. On the other hand, the final clause seems to constrain their ability to do so effectively. Its convoluted – and somehow circular – wording leads to various interpretations, as was demonstrated by the various alternative interpretations advanced by the parties (including the third parties) in the only dispute to date that has dealt with the provision (*Argentina – Financial Services*).

Despite the peculiar wording of the provision, however, there has been little disagreement in the academic community concerning its (broad) scope of application and the legal function assigned to it, that is, an exception, with the consequent allocation of the burden of proof on the Member invoking it in the context of a WTO dispute.

3.1.2 The PCO in the Literature

Most likely as a result of the lack of litigation on this issue, the PCO has not been among the most popular topics of research in the field of WTO law. However, a select number of works have tried to shed light on the provision and understand its legal function and scope of application. The aim of this subsection is to provide an overview of the current understanding of the provision.

One of the most frequently cited pieces on the topic is an article by Eric Leroux.[4] The author classifies the provision as a 'rather broad' exception and argues that the PCO covers a priori all measures taken by Members for prudential reasons. With regard to the final clause of the provision, the author describes it as an anti-avoidance clause, which amounts to an obligation of good faith and likens it to the chapeau of Article XX of the GATT 1994.[5] The same approach is shared by subsequent scholarly works[6] (as well as at least one previous contribution[7]).

Other authors agree with the classification of the provision as an 'exception' and explain the consequences of a similar approach in the event of a dispute. Essentially, this classification implies that the burden of proof ought to be allocated to the respondent, following the general principle of law that it is up to the defendant to prove that the conditions required

---

[4] Eric H. Leroux, 'Trade in Financial Services under the World Trade Organisation', *Journal of World Trade*, 36:3 (2002), 413–42 (pp. 430 and ff.).

[5] Ibid. (p. 431).

[6] Joseph Windsor, 'The WTO Committee on Trade in Financial Services: The Exercise of Public Authority within an Informational Forum', *German Law Journal*, 9:11 (2008), 1805–32 (p. 1821); Kern Alexander, 'The GATS and Financial Services: Liberalisation and Regulation in Global Financial Markets', in Kern Alexander and Mads Andenas (eds.), *The World Trade Organization and Trade in Services* (Leiden/Boston: Martinus Nijhoff, 2008), 561–99 (p. 585); Armin Von Bogdandy and Joseph Windsor, 'Annex on Financial Services', in Rüdiger Wolfrum, Peter-Tobias Stoll and Clemens Feinäugle (eds.), *WTO – Trade in Services – Max Planck Commentaries on World Trade Law* (Leiden/Boston: Martinus Nijhoff, 2008), 618–39 (p. 634); Bart De Meester, 'Testing European Prudential Conditions for Banking Mergers in the Light of the Most Favoured Nation in the GATS', *Journal of International Economic Law*, 11:3 (2008), 609–47 (p. 643); Gari, 'Capital Controls, GATS Disciplines and the Need for a More Coherent Global Economic Governance Structure' (p. 21); Bart De Meester, *Liberalization of Trade in Banking Services – An International and European Perspective* (Cambridge: Cambridge University Press, 2014) 388 (pp. 206 and ff.).

[7] Peter Morrison, 'WTO Financial Services Agreement: A Basis for Further Liberalisation in 2000?', *International Trade Law & Regulation*, 4:5 (1998), 188–91 (p. 189).

to benefit from an exception have been met (*quicumque exceptio invokat, ejusdem probari debet*).[8]

Cottier and Krajewski note that the GATS PCO does not oblige WTO Members to adopt prudential measures, and therefore domestic governments cannot bring complaints against each other for the failure by the counterparty on that basis.[9]

Other scholars and practitioners dealing with the PCO insist on highlighting the wide scope of the provision and avoid classifying it according to the legal function it performs[10] or point to the differences between the provision under analysis and other relevant exception-type provisions in the GATS and other WTO agreements.[11] Some scholars have stressed the necessity to defer disputes on prudential matters to experts in the field of financial services, in light of the requirement laid down under Paragraph 4 of the Annex on Financial Services ('Panels for disputes on prudential issues and other financial matters shall have the necessary expertise relevant to the specific financial service under dispute').[12]

Concerning the specific functioning of the final clause, some authors read it in parallel with the requirement laid down under the chapeau of Article XIV of the GATS (or Article XX of the GATT 1994)[13] – that is, a bulwark against disguised discriminatory behaviours by regulating Members – whereas others have argued that it calls for the application of a 'reasonableness' test.[14]

---

[8] Anne Van Aaken and Jürgen Kurtz, 'Prudence or Discrimination?: Emergency Measures, the Global Financial Crisis and International Economic Law', *Journal of International Economic Law*, 12:4 (2009), 859–94 (p. 876); Panagiotis Delimatsis and Pierre Sauvé, 'Financial Services Trade after the Crisis: Policy and Legal Conjectures', *Journal of International Economic Law*, 13:3 (2010), 837–57 (p. 851).

[9] Thomas Cottier and Markus Krajewski, 'What Role for Non-Discrimination and Prudential Standards in International Financial Law', *Journal of International Economic Law*, 13:3, 817–35 (826).

[10] Wei Wang, 'The Prudential Carve-Out', in Kern Alexander and Mads Andenas (eds.), *The World Trade Organization and Trade in Services* (Leiden/Boston: Martinus Nijhoff, 2008), 601–14 (p. 604).

[11] Mamiko Yokoi-Arai, 'GATS Prudential Carve out in Financial Services and Its Relation with Prudential Regulation', *International and Comparative Law Quarterly*, 57 (2008), 613–48.

[12] Samuel Trujillo, 'Demystifying the Prudential Carve-Out: A Proposal', *Revista Contexto*, 43:1 (2015) pp. 157–208.

[13] Amongst others, Bart De Meester, *Liberalization of Trade in Banking Services*, p. 208.

[14] See, for instance, Andrew D. Mitchell, Jennifer K. Hawkins and Neha Mishra, 'Dear Prudence: Allowances under International Trade and Investment Law for Prudential Regulation in the Financial Services Sector', *Journal of International Economic Law*, 19:3 (2016), 787–820, p. 813.

Surprisingly, only a small number of authors have ever paid attention to the heading of the PCO ('Domestic Regulation') and pinpointed the correspondence between the provisions of the GATS and those of the Annex on Financial Services, thus interpreting Paragraph 2(a) of the latter as an addendum to Article VI of the GATS.[15]

Among the scholarly papers that have attempted to study and clarify the scope and function of the PCO, only the paper by McAllister Shepro[16] seeks to develop a legal standard against which domestic measures should be evaluated to assess their compliance with the requirements and the scope of application of the provision under analysis. It is important to clarify the arguments of the author because it is the only comprehensive attempt to develop a legal standard for the PCO in the literature to date.

First of all, McAllister Shepro makes clear at the outset that she understands the PCO to be 'an exception provision, similar to, but distinct from, the GATT XX and the GATS XIV exceptions'.[17] The peculiarity of the PCO, according to the author, is that although it can only be applied when a violation of a GATS obligation or commitment has occurred, the defence must be raised at the very beginning of the panel proceedings or it will not be successful.[18]

Second, after the PCO has been invoked and both parties to the dispute have submitted their views and arguments, the panel should embark on the interpretation of the provision, according to the rules set forth in the Vienna Convention on the Law of Treaties (VCLT). First, the Panel or Appellate Body should evaluate the text of the provision under scrutiny. If the text is 'equivocal or inconclusive', it should seek for 'confirmation of the correctness of the reading' from the 'object and purpose of the treaty as a whole'. Then WTO documents can provide context, and, as a last

---

[15] Roger Kampf, 'Liberalisation of Financial Services in the GATS and Domestic Regulation', *International Trade Law & Regulation*, 5/3 (1997), 155–66; J. Steven Jarreau, 'Interpreting the General Agreement on Trade in Services and the WTO Instruments Relevant to the International Trade of Financial Services: The Lawyer's Perspective' (p. 67).

[16] Mary McAllister Shepro, 'Preserving National Regulatory Autonomy in Financial Services: The GATS' Prudential Carve-Out', MIMEO, available at http://ssrn.com/abstract=2418764, 2013.

[17] Ibid., p. 26.

[18] The author argues that this is the case following the reasoning developed by the Appellate Body in *US – Gambling* (paras. 269 and ff.). However, she also notices that the same report acknowledged the following: 'Whether a defense has been made at a sufficiently early stage of the panel proceedings to provide adequate notice to the opposing party will depend on the particular circumstances of a given dispute (Para. 272)'. See Ibid., fn. 117.

3.1 A NON-SELF-INTERPRETING PROVISION AND THE OPINION   71

resort, the negotiating history of the provision can serve as a supplementary means of interpretation.

Third, McAllister Shepro clarifies how she sees the standard of review in disputes concerning prudential measures in the realm of financial services. According to the author, the Panel or Appellate Body should provide answers to three questions: '[f]irst, did the member state adopt a measure non-conforming with their GATS commitments? Second, was the measure used to avoid said commitments? Lastly, was the measure taken for prudential reasons?'[19]

The first stage of the standard of review is intuitive, because, absent successful claims of GATS obligations or commitments, it is immaterial whether a domestic measure was adopted in pursuance of prudential goals, in accordance with the rights and the limits set out in the Agreements and its qualified defences. There is therefore no need to develop further the explanation of this stage of the standard.

The second stage of the standard of review is arguably a more delicate one. This step, in McAllister Shepro's view, is about whether a measure was used to avoid the Member's obligations or commitments. She recalls a background note from the WTO Secretariat on financial services[20] according to which Members should act in good faith in the implementation of prudential measures in the field of financial services. Good faith is a general principle of international law that does not belong exclusively to the realm fo the WTO but is codified in Article 26 VCLT (the *pacta sunt servanda* rule). On one hand, McAllister Shepro points to the fact that the provision does not make explicit reference to 'good faith'. On the other hand, however, she recalls that WTO case law has already established that 'good faith is a core principle [underlying] the WTO Agreement'.[21] In her view, good faith is the only possible guiding principle for a balance in the standard of review of prudential measures overriding a Member's obligations or commitments. She states that through this guiding principle, it is possible to avoid two opposite and 'extreme' interpretations that were clearly not contemplated in negotiations and that are totally absent from the wording of the provision. However, good faith is not a self-interpretative concept and depends on the time, context and

---

[19] Ibid., pp. 37 and ff.
[20] WTO Doc. S/C/W/312 and S/FIN/W/73, 'Council for Trade in Services – Committee on Trade in Financial Services. "Financial Services" – Background Note by the Secretariat', 3 February 2010.
[21] McAllister Shepro, 'Preserving National Regulatory Autonomy in Financial Services' (p. 40), quoting Appellate Body Report, *US – Gambling*, para. 6.50.

situations in which it is invoked. As such, this approach leaves considerable discretion for panels to make evaluations on a case-by-case basis.

At one end of the spectrum, McAllister Shepro puts what she calls 'the self-executing standard of review' that would in effect lead to a situation whereby no standard of review whatsoever is applied. As Chapter 5 will clarify, during the overview of the negotiating history, the idea to exclude prudential measures from the jurisdictions of WTO Panels and Appellate Body was present during the discussions on how to draft the provisions under analysis. As emerges from the structure of the GATS Annex on Financial Services, which contains a provision specifically addressing the issue of the composition of the Panels in the event of disputes on prudential measures,[22] this possibility was discarded by the Uruguay Round delegates.

At the other end of the spectrum, there would be a 'necessity test' such as that provided for by some of the categories of measures listed in Article XX of the GATT 1994 and Article XIV of the GATS. Furthermore, with regard to this other option, McAllister Shepro casts doubts on the feasibility of its application to the provision at issue. Again, the words 'necessity' or 'necessary' are absent from the text of the provision. Were they present, they would require for a rather stringent link between the measure enacted and the prudential goal pursued, if not for the introduction of the least trade distortive means. The author is aware that the aforementioned chapeau amount, at most, to obligations to perform treaties in good faith, although more stringent ones.

McAllister Shepro therefore argues that this second stage of the standard of review should work as follows. *In primis*, the good faith of WTO Members should be presumed, as she claims was clarified by the Appellate Body in *EC – Sardines*:

> Peru expresses doubts about the usefulness and efficacy of this obligation in the TBT [Agreement on Technical Barriers to Trade] Agreement. Peru argues that a Member may not respond fully or adequately to a request for information under Article 2.5, and that, therefore, it is inappropriate to rely on this obligation to support assigning the burden of proof under Article 2.4 to the complainant. We are not persuaded by this argument. We must assume that Members of the WTO will abide by their treaty obligations in good faith, as required by the principle of *pacta sunt servanda* articulated in Article 26 of the Vienna Convention. And, always in dispute

---

[22] Paragraph 4 of the Annex on Financial Services of the GATS.

settlement, every Member of the WTO must assume the good faith of every other Member.[23]

Therefore, the respondent in a dispute need make only a prima facie case that it had adopted measures in pursuance of prudential goals. After this is established, the burden is rebutted and, again according to McAllister Shepro, it is up to the complainant to provide evidence to the contrary. To rebut the presumption of good faith, she correctly points out that it is necessary to make a case that the regulating Member had acted through abuse of its rights (*abus de droit*).[24]

The last stage of the standard of review designed by McAllister Shepro is devoted to the analysis of whether the challenged measure was adopted for prudential reasons. She confines this assessment to the last phase of the analysis. In her view, as long as the regulating Member is able to provide an explanation according to which the challenged measure is based on a plausible prudential reason, the conditions for it to benefit from the shelter provided by the PCO are satisfied. In her words:

> The purpose of the measure need only meet a subjective, threshold intent requirement of avoiding financial sector danger or risk. This requirement should be considered satisfied unless the contested measure has no plausible objective or reasonable relation to the prudential reason advocated.[25]

McAllister Shepro concludes that the only possible way to successfully overcome the PCO defence would be for the complainant to prove that the former had enacted its regulation acting in bad faith. Intuitively, this does not seem to be an easy task, especially given the disproportionate allocation of information between the parties in a dispute.

In sum, it is a common view among commentators that the PCO should be classified as an 'exception', with a small – if not negligible – number of scholars taking a more nuanced stance.

3.2 Discussions in the WTO Committee on Trade in Financial Services

As mentioned earlier, WTO panels had never been called to settle a dispute concerning the PCO until late 2015. Only in one circumstance had the

---

[23] Appellate Body Report, *EC – Sardines*, para. 278.
[24] Mcallister Shepro, 'Preserving National Regulatory Autonomy in Financial Services' (p. 47).
[25] Ibid. (p. 52).

PCO made an appearance in WTO case law, in an obiter dictum. In the Panel Report on *China – Electronic Payment Services*, Paragraph 2(a) of the GATS Annex on Financial Services is incidentally mentioned in the context of the explanation by the Panel of the right to regulate enjoyed by WTO Members.[26]

In absence of clarification from the adjudicating bodies of the WTO, Members still had the opportunity to share their views on the provision under analysis and to seek clarification from the Secretariat. As the debate that took place in recent years reveals, several Members have in fact struggled with the problematic reading of the GATS PCO.

The following sections are devoted to an overview of the various positions expressed by the Secretariat and WTO Members since the entry into force of the provision to provide a comprehensive assessment of the discussion that took place until the dispute between Panama and Argentina, which was eventually settled in 2016.

3.2.1 The WTO Secretariat

In the first version of the Scheduling Guidelines, which dates back to 1993, Paragraph 2(a) of the Annex on Financial Services is recognised as being an exception, thus belonging to the same family as Article XIV of the GATS. Consequently it was deemed that it was not necessary to schedule prudential measures.[27] The document was meant to represent a *vademecum* for negotiators with the aim of explaining how to make offers and requests and how to clearly write their initial commitments. In 2001, a second version of the Scheduling Guidelines was issued that confirmed the approach adopted in the first one.[28] The Appellate Body of the WTO, however, clarified in the *US – Gambling* case that the Scheduling Guidelines can serve, at most, as supplementary means of interpretation as per

---

[26] Panel Report, *China – Measures Affecting Electronic Payment Services*, para. 7.569: '[P]aragraph 2(a) of the GATS Annex on Financial Services provides that, notwithstanding any other provisions of the GATS, a WTO Member may take measures for prudential reasons, including for the protection of e.g. investors and depositors, or to ensure the integrity and stability of the financial system.'

[27] Uruguay Round Doc. MTN.GNS/W/164, 'Scheduling of Initial Commitments in Trade in Services: Explanatory Note', 3 September 1993, Para. 13.

[28] WTO Doc. S/L/92, 'Guidelines for the Scheduling of Specific Commitments under the General Agreement on Trade in Services (GATS)', adopted by the Council for Trade in Services on 23 March 2001, para. 20.

Article 32 VCLT[29] and are thus not conclusive as far as the attribution of the specific legal function to a provision is concerned.

3.2.1.1 The 2010 Secretariat Background Note on 'Financial Services'

At the request of some Members, the WTO Secretariat released a 'Background Note' on financial services on 3 February 2010.[30] This document classifies the PCO as an exception.[31] In the view of the Secretariat, WTO Members can adopt measures inconsistent with their MFN obligations and specific commitments, as long as they are put in place for 'prudential reasons'. In other words, prudential concerns are considered as overriding in importance all other obligations and commitments of the GATS and its annexes.

The Secretariat stressed the 'non-exhaustiveness' of the indicative list provided for in the first subparagraph of the PCO. It then went even further, assuming the evolutionary nature over time of the perception of 'prudential measures', thus expanding the scope of the provision and enhancing the uncertainty of its boundaries.

The background note sought to explain the meaning of the final clause of the GATS PCO. The Secretariat classified the sentence as an 'anti-abuse' device. In other words, the GATS PCO maintained its large and unclear boundaries, provided measures taken for prudential purposes were not put in place simply as a means to avoid the obligations of a WTO Member under the GATS. The document quoted two scholarly works[32] in an attempt to explain the anti-abuse clause. Indeed both works describe the final clause of the GATS PCO as an 'obligation of good faith' which Members have to comply with when overcoming the GATS obligations and commitments.

The document also deals with the delicate issue of the relationship between the PCO and other relevant exceptions. In the view of the Secretariat, the PCO differs substantially from the general rule for exceptions provided by the GATS. Article XIV of the GATS, although broad in terms,

---

[29] Appellate Body Report, *US – Gambling*, paras. 188–90.
[30] WTO Doc. S/C/W/312 and S/FIN/W/73, 'Council for Trade in Services – Committee on Trade in Financial Services. 'Financial Services' – Background Note by the Secretariat', 3 February 2010.
[31] Ibid. para. 28.
[32] Leroux, 'Trade in Financial Services under the World Trade Organisation'; Von Bogdandy and Windsor, 'Annex on Financial Services'.

only covers violations of members' obligations provided that they are 'necessary' to the achievement of their aim. In contrast, measures adopted for prudential reasons need not meet any 'necessity' test nor any 'least trade restrictive means' test.[33]

The document moreover reviews some of the measures adopted in the aftermath of the financial crisis to conduct a prima facie analysis of their compatibility with GATS rules and, more specifically, whether they are covered by the PCO.[34] According to the Background Note, measures such as capital adequacy measures, stronger supervisory powers and measures addressing 'too-big-to-fail' cases, although potentially altering one Member's commitments, are prima facie genuinely motivated by prudential concerns. Therefore they are able in theory to benefit from the shelter provided by the PCO.

The background note, together with the scholarly works it quoted, represented the mainstream understanding of the provision until the publication of the Panel and the Appellate Body reports in *Argentina – Financial Services*. It is important to bear in mind, however, that background notes issued by the WTO Secretariat are of limited legal value and can, at most, serve as supplementary means of interpretation, as the Panel report in *Mexico-Telecoms*[35] clarified.

3.2.2 The PCO in the Practice of WTO Members

As was anticipated earlier in this text, several Members have indicated their discomfort with the exact boundaries of the PCO. First, as a matter of relevant practice, a close look at the Schedules of Commitments by WTO Members reveals that some decided to introduce horizontal entries into their schedules to reaffirm their right to regulate according to prudential concerns. This practice has been highlighted by Mattoo and Wunsch-Vincent, who state that

> despite the existing right of Members to regulate, the inclusion of the prudential carve-out under this horizontal commitment or at the start of each GATS schedule (see the US initial offer, for example) would help to reassure national regulators that the objective is not to question their judgments but to target only blatantly protectionist measures – which is broadly the role of the prudential carve out in financial services. The advantage of this approach is that by accommodating regulatory precaution, it may make it

---

[33] WTO Doc. S/C/W/312 and S/FIN/W/73, para. 31.   [34] Ibid.
[35] Panel Report, *Mexico – Telecoms*, para. 7.43.

3.2 DISCUSSIONS IN THE WTO COMMITTEE 77

easier for Members to make deeper and wider commitments. The disadvantage is that the value of those commitments will depend on the uncertain interpretation of the scope of the carve-out.[36]

A search of all the Schedules of Commitments on financial services reveals the following: the word 'prudential' appears in the horizontal entries of twenty-one Schedules[37] and reference to Paragraph 2(a) of the GATS Annex on Financial Services is made in twenty-five Schedules.[38] Although it would be presumptious to draw conclusions from a limited number of Schedules, some tentative remarks can be made.

First, one may actually think that such entries are of limited, if any, practical relevance. Adlung et al., for instance, refer to these entries as 'foggy commitments' because they contain simple references to provisions 'that would apply in any event'.[39] However, this practice can be justified, particularly in the field of financial services. Given the intrinsic obscurity

---

[36] Aaditya Mattoo and Sacha Wunsch-Vincent, 'Pre-Empting Protectionism in Services: The GATS and Outsourcing', *Journal of International Economic Law*, 7:4 (2004), 765–800 (p. 795).

[37] Albania, Australia, Austria, Bulgaria, China, Cyprus, EC-12, EC-15, Egypt, El Salvador, Ghana, Japan, Kazakhstan, Korea, Lao PDR, Malaysia, Poland, Romania, Russian Federation, Senegal, Vietnam. To give one example, the following is an excerpt from the Lao PDR's Schedule of Specific Commitments (GATS/SC/150), among the most recent ones to be submitted:

> Access by foreign services suppliers and the provision of new financial services within the scope of the commitments below and that have not yet been provided by the private sector in Lao PDR at the date of accession, may be subject to measures adopted for prudential reasons.
> Direct branching is not allowed. Financial institutions in Lao PDR must adopt a specific legal form.
> All the commitments are subject to entry requirements, domestic laws, rules and regulations and the terms and conditions of the Bank of Lao PDR, the Ministry of Finance and/or any other competent authority in Lao PDR, as the case may be, which are consistent with Article VI of the GATS and paragraph 2 of the Annex on Financial Services and do not impair the commitments undertaken herewith.'

Similarly, the following is taken form the Schedules of Specific Commitments of the European Union (formerly EC) (GATS/SC/31):

> 'The admission to the market of new financial services or products may be subject to the existence of, and consistency with, a regulatory framework aimed at achieving the objectives indicated in Article 2.1 of the Financial Services Annex.'

[38] Austria, Bahrain, Bulgaria, Cyprus, Czech Republic, EC-12, EC-15, Hungary, Israel, Japan, Kazakhstan, Korea, Lao PDR, Mauritius, Montenegro, New Zealand, Nepal, Poland, Russian Federation Senegal, Singapore, Slovak Republic, Slovenia, Sri Lanka, Turkey.

[39] Rudolf Adlung et al., "Fog in GATS Commitments – Why WTO Members Should Care", *World Trade Review*, 12:1 (2013), 1–27 (p. 15).

of the boundaries of the provision, Members may not be confident about the extent to which the PCO covers all prudential policies, especially when they can discriminate between domestic and foreign services suppliers or may have the effect of limiting market access.

Moreover, the GATS is a complex agreement. The issue of opening-up the financial services market of a country involves the participation of a number of players (executives, parliaments, central banks, and so on). Not all such actors may necessarily be familiar with trade negotiations. As such, reaffirming the right to regulate according to prudential purposes in a horizontal entry in the Schedule may limit tensions among different actors in the domestic decision-making process.

Finally, on various occasions both before and after the 2007–8 financial crisis, different WTO Members have brought the issue before the relevant bodies of the Organization to have a discussion and clarify some aspects concerning the interplay between domestic policies and their compatibility with the PCO. This is the focus of the next subsection.

3.2.3 Proposals for Reform by WTO Members and Discussions in the Committee on Trade in Financial Services

The WTO is a living body with an active institutional life. Trading nations share their views on relevant issues and table proposals for amending the existing rules. It is interesting to provide an overview of the state of the art of the debate among WTO Members on the issue and, in particular, the proposals that have been tabled from 2000 onwards with a view of revising the PCO. The following sections give an account of the various proposals put forward by WTO Members.

3.2.4 The Australian Proposal (2000)

During a meeting of the Committee on Trade in Financial Services (CTFS) in April 2000, Australia proposed a discussion among WTO Members to develop a common understanding of the meaning of the expression 'prudential regulation'.[40] To do so, the Australian delegation suggested using the core principles set up by the BCBS for banking and the IAIS for insurance. The aim pursued by the Australian delegation was, explicitly, to

---

[40] WTO Doc. S/FIN/M/25, 'Committee on Trade in Financial Services – Report of the Meeting Held on 13 April 2000', para. 20.

3.2 DISCUSSIONS IN THE WTO COMMITTEE

clarify the scope of the PCO and to understand where to draw the line between prudential and intolerable protectionist measures.

The Australian proposal did not attract much support among the other delegations, with the remarkable exception of Japan. The EU and Switzerland did not oppose a discussion on the issue, whereas Malaysia stood firmly against the usefulness of the Australian proposal. According to the Malaysian delegation: 'The prudential carve-out was the result of a fine balance struck when the GATS was concluded and trying to define prudential regulation could upset that balance.'[41]

In subsequent meetings of the CTFS,[42] parties debated the Australian proposal, but it failed to gain momentum. Members of the US delegation, although affirming that they would further examine the proposal, warned that the conclusion of a positive negotiation on the prudential carve-out was not easy and was the result of a difficult compromise among various exigencies. Moreover, the US delegation added that there was no 'compelling evidence' that the PCO was being abused.[43] However, the United States advanced the possibility of enhancing transparency as acknowledging a lack thereof in the field.

The delegate of the Philippines, backing Malaysia, provided a further explanation of their position. It is worth quoting, for the sake of completeness of the reconstruction of the debate, the relevant passage from the minutes:

> The representative of the Philippines supported the statements made by Malaysia at the previous and present meeting. Looking at the provision contained in the Annex on financial services, his delegation found no need to define what measures for prudential reasons meant. A definition would be required if the phrase sought to be defined was so ambiguous or vague as to require interpretation from Members. However, the language contained in paragraph 2(a) of the Annex was quite clear. The grounds cited in that provision might be broad and comprehensive but it did not at all mean that they were ambiguous. Following the international law on interpretation of provisions in treaty language, where a phrase was not vague or ambiguous, Members should not endeavour to put in their own interpretation. *The fact that the grounds cited in the mentioned provision were general and comprehensive did not translate into vagueness or ambiguity.*

---

[41] Ibid., para. 22.
[42] WTO Doc. S/FIN/M/26, 'Committee on Trade in Financial Services – Report of the Meeting Held on 25 May 2000'; WTO Doc. S/FIN/M/27, 'Committee on Trade in Financial Services – Report of the Meeting Held on 13 July 2000'; WTO Doc. S/FIN/M/28, 'Committee on Trade in Financial Services – Report of the Meeting Held on 9 October 2000'.
[43] WTO Doc. S/FIN/M/26, para. 19.

Even if there was a wide discretion granted to Members in invoking that provision, his delegation believed that it was intentional. *In fact that provision sought to allow Members that discretion in case of certain contingencies, like those experienced by Asian countries in the past two years.* Therefore, his delegation would not want to see deliberations on the proposal taken forward, and hence supported the removal of the proposal from the agenda of subsequent meetings. [Emphasis added][44]

Eventually the discussion came to an end at the November meeting of the CTFS when, among others,[45] the US delegation reaffirmed the importance of the provision and clearly stood against further discussion on the topic.[46]

3.2.5 Switzerland (2001): The 'GATS 2000: Financial Services' Communication

In May 2001, Switzerland issued a communication ('GATS 2000: Financial Services')[47] to the Council for Trade in Services.[48] One section of the document was devoted to prudential regulation of financial services markets. The section started with a strong acknowledgment of the importance of prudential regulation:

> The liberalization of trade in financial services must be accompanied by solid prudential regulation and supervision in order to ensure confidence in the system, and hence its smooth operation. *Members must be given plenty of room for manoeuvre so that they can implement the necessary measures as soon as the problems arise.* [Emphasis added][49]

The Swiss proposal consisted of two main points. First, it encouraged the CTFS to keep abreast of the work of the relevant standard-setting bodies in the field of financial services (BCBS, IAIS and IOSCO and the Joint Forum on Financial Conglomerates). Second, it recommended that the

---

[44] WTO Doc. S/FIN/M/27, para. 19.   [45] WTO Doc. S/FIN/M/28.
[46] Nevertheless Marchetti, 'The GATS Prudential Carve-Out' (p. 283) reports that Japan later promoted the collection of (at least) information from the relevant standard-setting bodies and, in October 2001, BCBS, IAIS and IOSCO held a seminar at the initiative of WTO Members, outside the proceedings of the CTFS.
[47] WTO Doc. S/CSS/W/71, 'Council for Trade in Services Special Session – Communication from Switzerland: "GATS 2000: Financial Services", 4 May 2001'.
[48] Quoting from Marchetti, 'The GATS Prudential Carve-Out' (p. 284, fn. 17): 'It is interesting to note that, unlike the Australian and the Japanese ideas, the Swiss proposal was not discussed in the relevant WTO sectoral committee – the Committee on Trade in Financial Services – but in the group overseeing services negotiations in the DDA – formally called the Council for Trade in Services in Special Session'.
[49] WTO Doc. S/CSS/W/71, para. 18.

CTFS work on a more precise definition of the scope of the PCO of the GATS because this would improve transparency and prevent a disproportionate use of prudential regulatory schemes. The Swiss proposal was no more successful that the previous Australian proposal due to the same kinds of criticisms.

3.2.6 Barbados: Are Domestic Measures Adopted in the Aftermath of the Crisis GATS Compatible?

In February 2011, the delegation of Barbados submitted a Communication titled 'Unintended Consequences of Remedial Measures Taken to Correct the Global Financial Crisis: Possible Implications for WTO Compliance' to the CFTS.[50] The document tabled by Barbados aimed to shed light on the issue of compatibility of some of the measures adopted domestically by many countries across the world in response to the financial crisis with the rules of the GATS and, more specifically, those of the Annex on financial services.

Barbados asked the Members of the CFTS whether the PCO should be reformed. In particular, the delegation expressed doubts as to the correct interpretation of the second part of the PCO. According to the delegate from Barbados, the text of the provision could lead to an interpretation in which all domestic measures incompatible with the GATS could be used as means to avoid a Member's commitments or obligations. The CTFS discussed the issues raised by the document tabled by Barbados in a meeting held in April 2011.[51]

Hong Kong was open to further discussion but firmly disagreed with Barbados about the interpretation of the second part of the PCO. Allowing for such an interpretation – in the view of the Hong Kong delegation – would render the PCO useless.[52] Interestingly, the strongest opposition to the proposal to discuss the issues concerning domestic prudential measures came from developed countries. The representatives of the EU,[53] Norway,[54] the United States,[55] Canada[56] and Japan[57] expressly stated that there had been enough discussion, that it was necessary to keep

---

[50] WTO Doc. JOB/SERV/38, 'Committee on Trade in Financial Services – Communication from Barbados: "Unintended Consequences of Remedial Measures Taken to Correct the Global Financial Crisis: Possible Implications for WTO Compliance", 18 February 2011'.
[51] WTO Doc. S/FIN/M/67, 'Committee on Trade in Financial Services – Report of the Meeting Held on 9 March 2011'.
[52] Ibid., paras. 17–19.   [53] Ibid., para. 21.   [54] Ibid., para. 27.
[55] Ibid., para. 28.   [56] Ibid., para. 30.   [57] Ibid., para. 32.

the provision as broad as it was to allow WTO Members to adopt useful domestic measures and that a discussion on the potential reform of the PCOs was outside the mandate of the Doha Development Round.

The Korean delegation took a more nuanced stance, suggesting that the FSB be invited to brief the CTFS on the latest developments on the issue.[58] In contrast, Turkey[59] and Argentina[60] were eager to discuss the issue further, whereas Brazil,[61] backed by China,[62] warned that the wording of the PCO was unclear and that countries feel uncomfortable when addressing the consequences of financial crises. India took a more skeptical stance on the PCO because, in its view, a broad interpretation of the provision might cover some measures that, in the medium term, could lead to situations of protectionism and moral hazard.[63] Members also discussed the issue at other meetings but, given the significant opposition from developed countries, no concrete steps followed.

3.2.7 Ecuador: 'Proposal for Discussing Progress in Respect of Macroprudential Regulation and Its Relationship with GATS Rules'

In late June 2012, Ecuador submitted a communication to the CTFS to stimulate a discussion on the compatibility of some of the domestic measures adopted in various countries of the world to address the economic crisis.[64] This communication followed the aforementioned debate and the refusal by most developed countries to hold a comprehensive discussion on financial services trade and the economic crisis. However, the issue was a source of significant concern for the Ecuadorian delegation, which decided to insist before the CTFS. Ecuador succeeded in attracting support from associations and trade unions and, as a result, interest in the issue increased outside the institutional context.[65] The main aim for Ecuador was to ensure that all WTO Members had as much regulatory freedom as they needed when addressing macroprudential concerns without running the risk that their regulations were eventually outlawed

---

[58] Ibid., para. 22. [59] Ibid., para. 23. [60] Ibid., para. 29.
[61] Ibid., para. 31. [62] Ibid., para. 33. [63] Ibid., para. 24.
[64] WTO Doc. S/FIN/W/84, Committee on Trade in Financial Services – Communication from Ecuador: 'Proposal for Discussing Progress in Respect of Macro-Prudential Regulation and Its Relationship with GATS Rules', 26 June 2012.
[65] One hundred fourteen associations and networks from around the world signed a 'Statement in Support of Ecuador's Proposal at the October Committee on Trade in Financial Services Meeting'. The text of the statement is available at www.citizen.org/documents/sign-on-statement-in-support-of-ecuador.pdf.

by WTO panels. In particular Ecuador asked to discuss whether measures for capital controls were covered by the PCO, given that other international organisations had softened their positions on similar instruments.

The WTO CTFS held a meeting on 20 March 2013 during which Members debated the basis of the request made by Ecuador.[66] Actually, the topic of the discussion was a bit broader because it encompassed Members' experience at large with macroprudential policies. The aim of the meeting was to allow WTO delegations to exchange their experiences and views on the subject in an informal manner. There was no desire to proceed to an interpretation of the GATS rules or an elaboration of an exhaustive list of measures adopted in the domain of financial services in pursuance of macroprudential policy objectives.

Members discussed the policy options adopted in the aftermath of the 2007–8 financial crisis. The discussion is instructive in the sense that the reader of the minutes can look at how, despite the commonalities and the reference to international regulatory standards, the ideas concerning macroprudential instruments vary substantially from one country to the other.

Interestingly, some delegations took the floor to address the issue of the interplay between domestic rules on prudential measures and the GATS PCO. The minutes report the following when summarising the intervention of the Japanese delegate:

> He further said that the GATS Annex on Financial Services provided each country with the right to take measures for prudential reasons. On the other hand, the Annex also stated that the measures should not be used as a means of avoiding the Member's commitments or obligations under the GATS. This might be interpreted that, when taking prudential measures, Members should take care not to obscure the real purpose of WTO agreements, which was to achieve economic growth through vigorous trade.[67]

A different issue was raised by the delegation of Korea.[68] The representative acknowledged the high degree of flexibility provided by the PCO with regard to *ex ante* macroprudential tools. However, Korea expressed concerns about the extent to which *ex post* (mainly crisis-management) tools were covered by the carve-out and as such he encouraged the Committee to consider a discussion on the topic.

---

[66] WTO Doc. S/FIN/M/76, 'Committee on Trade in Financial Services – Report of the Meeting Held on 20 March 2013'.
[67] Ibid.   [68] Ibid., para. 1.83.

The last delegation to take part to the discussion on the PCO was the United States. The representative of the United States, after briefly recalling the major changes in financial regulation in that country after the 2008 financial crisis, stated:

> The macro-prudential measures taken by the US were non-discriminatory in nature and consistent with its GATS obligations. In the US experience, the GATS had not presented a constraint on its ability to adopt macro-prudential measures in order to address systemic risks.[69]

3.3 The Panel in *Argentina – Financial Services*

After years of silence, in 2015 a WTO Panel was called for the first time to examine the compatibility with the GATS of measures in relation to which the respondent had invoked the PCO.

The dispute originated in a series of measures adopted by Argentina and concerning the regulation of its financial market, with specific regard to transparency and exchange of information with other countries for fiscal purposes. In brief, Argentina sought to impose a series of restrictions or additional requirements for financial service suppliers from countries, which Argentina considered to be 'non cooperating for tax transparency purposes' ('non-cooperative countries'). Panama challenged the regulatory scheme put in place by Argentina, complaining that the measures adopted by Argentina were in violation of the latter's obligations or commitments under Articles II ('Most Favoured Nation'), XVI ('Market Access') and XVII ('National Treatment').

3.3.1 The Measures at Issue

Decree No. 589 of the Federal Public Revenue Administration of Argentina of 27 May 2013 (hereinafter, Decree No. 589/2013) represented the cornerstone of the regulatory scheme challenged by Panama. That measure, in fact, set forth the conditions for Argentina to classify a country or territory as cooperative or non-cooperative as regards the exchange of tax information. In particular, the measure established that countries or territories had to be considered as cooperative when they had signed an agreement with the Argentine Republic on the exchange of tax information or a convention for the avoidance of international double taxation.[70]

---

[69] Ibid., para. 1.88.   [70] Article 1 of Decree No. 589/2013.

Additionally, countries or territories could be deemed as cooperative for tax purposes even if they had only initiated negotiations for the conclusions of such agreements. The Decree further provided that the Federal Public Revenue Administration had to establish the criteria to verify whether there was effective exchange of information.

On the basis of the foregoing, the Federal Public Revenue Administration issued Resolution No. 3.576/2013, according to which cooperative countries could be of three subspecies: (i) countries that had signed an agreement with Argentina and for which there was a positive evaluation as to the effective exchange of information; (ii) countries that had signed an agreement and for which an evaluation as to the effectiveness of the information exchange was not possible; and (iii) countries that had merely started the negotiations of an agreement on exchange of information or a convention on the avoidance of double taxation.

Against this background, Panama challenged eight measures in the dispute, which are reported as follows in the text of the Panel Report:

1. Tax treatment in the collection of gains tax on certain transactions involving non-cooperative countries
2. Tax treatment imposed on entry of funds from non-cooperative countries
3. Valuation of transactions with persons from non-cooperative countries
4. Criteria for applying deductions
5. Measures affecting trade in reinsurance and retrocession services
6. Measures affecting trade in financial instruments
7. Requirements for the registration of companies, branches and shareholders of certain foreign service suppliers
8. Measures affecting the repatriation of investments[71]

All those measures were based on the distinction between cooperative and non-cooperative countries. A detailed examination of all the measures falls outside the scope of the present volume, and thus the present section provides additional information only in relation to those measures (Measures 5 and 6) for the justification of which Argentina had invoked the GATS PCO.

3.3.1.1 Measure 5: Measures Affecting Trade in Retrocession Services

Measure 5 consisted of a series of requirements imposed by Argentina on foreign service suppliers from non-cooperative countries in order

---

[71] Panel Report, *Argentina – Financial Services*, para. 2.9.

for them to be entitled to access the Argentine market for reinsurance services.[72]

First, the challenged measures denied authorisation to provide reinsurance services to branches of suppliers based in countries where the rate of gains was lower than 20 per cent or where domestic law mandated (or at least permitted) secrecy concerning the corporate structure of the supplier, or in countries with low tax rates (so-called tax havens). Second, reinsurance service suppliers based in non-cooperative countries were equally denied authorisation.

In any event, the measure allowed the National Insurance Supervisory Authority to authorise reinsurance contracts with foreign suppliers of the services concerned that conducted their operations from their headquarters, only to the extent that similar contracts could not be provided within the national market, in light of the amount or the characteristics of the risk involved in the transaction. In particular, the measure provided that reinsurance with foreign suppliers could be authorised provided that the individual risks exceeded $50 million and only for the amount exceeding the earlier-mentioned figure.

Those rules were further amended in 2014. The modifications were published on the date that Panama filed its first written submission with the Panel.[73] In light of those additional amendments, to provide reinsurance services in the Argentine market, foreign suppliers either had to demonstrate that they were incorporated or established in cooperative countries (or, in case of branches present on the Argentine territory, that their mother company was established in a cooperative country) or they needed to prove that they were supervised or controlled by an entity fulfilling the same tasks as the National Insurance Supervisory Authority of Argentina and that was cooperating with the latter in terms of information exchange.

3.3.1.2 Measure 6: Requirements for Access to the Argentine Capital Market

The measure at issue consisted of a series of requirements for stock market intermediaries for them to conduct transactions ordered by persons from non-cooperative countries. The requirements were laid down in

---

[72] The measure corresponds to Resolution of the National Insurance Supervisor Authority No.35.611, as amended. Details concerning the amendments of the measure can be found in Panel Report, *Argentina – Financial Services*, para. 2.24.
[73] Panel Report, *Argentina – Financial Services*, para. 2.30.

Title XI ('Prevention of Money Laundering and Financing of Terrorism'), Section III, Article 5 of the Rules of the National Securities Commission.

First, stock market intermediaries could engage in certain transactions (including offering of negotiable securities, forward contracts, futures, options) when they were conducted or ordered by persons domiciled or residing in cooperating countries. Second, stock market intermediaries based in non-cooperating countries or territories could only supply those services upon fulfilment of two conditions: (i) the legal entities providing the services should have been registered as intermediaries wish a body exercising similar functions to those of the Argentine National Securities Commission and (ii) such bodies had signed an agreement on information exchange with the Argentine National Securities Commission.[74]

3.3.2 The Panel's Findings on Most Favoured Nation and Market Access

3.3.2.1 The Panel's Findings on Most Favoured Nation

The Panel found that the two measures violated Article II.1 of the GATS ('Most Favoured Nation') because Argentina failed to accord, immediately and unconditionally, treatment no less favourable to services and service suppliers of Panama than that accorded to like services and service suppliers from other countries.

Having already determined that the measures were covered by the GATS because they affected trade in services,[75] the Panel went on to analyze whether they concerned like services and service suppliers and, if they did, whether Argentina had failed to accord, immediately and unconditionally, treatment no less favourable to Panama's services and service suppliers than that accorded to like services and service suppliers of different origins.

Concerning the first step of this analysis, Panama argued that there was no need for the Panel to make 'casuistic determinations' that the services and service suppliers at issue were like or to examine in detail the conditions of competition of the like services and service suppliers of different origin in the Argentine market, because the measures before the Panel, in the opinion of the claimant, were exclusively based on the origin of the services or service suppliers.[76] In response, Argentina

---

[74] Panel Report, *Argentina – Financial Services*, para. 2.36.
[75] Panel Report, *Argentina – Financial Services*, para. 7.113.
[76] Panel Report, *Argentina – Financial Services*, para. 7.153.

maintained that there were important regulatory differences between the service suppliers, which made it impossible to qualify them as like for the purpose of the application of the Most Favoured Nation clause, as they greatly affected the way in which those service providers operate on the market.[77]

The Panel started its analysis recalling the case law on 'likeness' under the GATS. In particular, emphasis was put on two precedents. In *China – Audiovisuals*, where the parties had not contested the likeness of the services and service suppliers at issue, the Panel found that when origin is the 'only factor' on which a differential treatment is grounded, the conditions for the fulfilment of the 'like service suppliers' test are met.[78] It follows that when the difference in treatment is not exclusively linked to the origin of the service suppliers, a more detailed analysis of the characteristics and the competitive relationship between the service and service suppliers at issue is required to determine whether they can be qualified as being like.

Because the gist of the contested measures relied on the distinction between cooperative and non-cooperative countries for the purpose of applying additional conditions and requirements for the supply of services, the Panel was satisfied that the differential treatment accorded to services and service suppliers was closely linked to origin. However, given that Argentina had operated a distinction between cooperative and non-cooperative countries with regard to the exchange of tax information, the Panel affirmed that it had to determine the extent to which the different regulatory framework played a role in the distinction operated by the measures at issue, or whether it was only and simply the origin to lead to different treatment.[79] Put differently, the issue before the Panel was the extent to which service suppliers based in different regulatory environments – and thus subject to different requirements to lawfully operate – can be considered to be 'like' service suppliers for the purpose of the application of the Most Favoured Nation clause. In this respect, it should be noted that the Panel was moving in a largely uncharted territory, based on the limited reliability of the case law on likeness under the GATT 1994, in light of the structural differences between goods and services, being key amongst all the intangibility of the latter.

---

[77] Panel Report, *Argentina – Financial Services*, para. 7.154.
[78] Panel Report, *China – Publications and Audiovisuals*, para. 7.975, cited in Panel Report, *Argentina – Financial Services*, para. 7.156.
[79] Panel Report, *Argentina – Financial Services*, para. 7.166.

3.3 THE PANEL IN *ARGENTINA – FINANCIAL SERVICES*

Furthermore, previous case law did not add much to the text of Article II.1 of the GATS. For instance, the Panel in *China – Electronic Payment Systems* basically stated that service suppliers are presumed to be like when they provide like services, although the enquiry as to the likeness of the service suppliers must necessarily be made on a case-by-case basis to evaluate whether other factors, different from a mere link to the origin of the suppliers, played a role in the accordance of differential treatment.[80]

Argentina argued that it adopted the measures at issue due to a regulatory concern that impeded classifying the service suppliers at issue as being like, and thus the Panel found it useful to refer to two precedents in which factors of regulatory nature had played a role in the WTO adjudicating bodies' determination of likeness.[81] According to the Panel, the possibility for Argentina to access to tax information on foreign suppliers could reasonably be considered to be an 'other factor' to be taken into account in the context of the likeness analysis.[82] Argentina, in fact, had argued that whether a supplier was based in a jurisdiction subject to an effective exchange of information for tax purposes was a characteristic directly linked to the conditions of competition.

However, the Panel noted that the list of cooperative countries included some that had not signed agreements for the exchange of information with Argentina. Quoting directly from the Panel:

> In looking at how Decree No. 589/2013 has been implemented in practice, we note that the current list of cooperative countries includes countries that have not signed a double taxation convention or an information exchange agreement and with which there is no exchange of tax information, as well as countries which have in fact concluded such conventions or agreements and which, therefore, exchange tax information. Let us take, for example, the cases of Panama and Germany. These two countries belong to the category of cooperative countries. Argentina has signed a double taxation agreement with Germany, which has been in force since 25 November 1979, giving it access to tax information. In the case of Panama, however, Argentina has no access to tax information as it has not signed any agreement on exchange of tax information with Panama. We also note that various countries which have initiated negotiations have a different status. For example, both Panama and Hong Kong (China) have initiated negotiations but neither of the two exchanges tax information with Argentina as there is no agreement or convention in force to cover such exchange.

---

[80] Panel Report, *China – Electronic Payment Services*, para. 7.705.
[81] Appellate Body Report, *EC – Asbestos*, para. 115; Appellate Body Report, *US – Clove Cigarettes*, paras. 116–17.
[82] Panel Report, *Argentina – Financial Services*, para. 7.179.

While Panama has the status of cooperative country, however, Hong Kong (China) is still considered a non-cooperative country.[83]

In light of the ambiguity of the factual situation, the Panel considered that the circumstances made it impossible for it to compare services and service suppliers to verify the role played by factors other than origin in the determination of the likeness of services and service suppliers.[84] On the basis of the foregoing, the Panel found that Panama had demonstrated that the services and service suppliers were like for the purpose of the application of Article II.1 of the GATS.[85]

Having established likeness, the Panel then proceeded with the determination of whether each of the contested measures accorded different treatment to services and service suppliers from non-cooperative countries compared with the treatment of like services and service suppliers based in cooperative countries.

Concerning Measure 5, Argentina accorded different treatment based on whether providers of reinsurance services were incorporated and registered in cooperative or non-cooperative countries. The foregoing emerged clearly from the text of the measure. Pursuant to Measure 6, stock-market intermediaries were treated differently depending on whether they originated in cooperative or non-cooperative countries.[86]

The Panel was then called to determine whether service suppliers from non-cooperative countries were treated less favourably compared with like service suppliers from cooperative countries. Again, the Panel conducted the analysis for each of the contested measures. Measure 5, as described earlier, introduced additional requirements for suppliers of reinsurance services based in non-cooperative jurisdictions. In particular, they had to show that they were placed under the supervision of a body performing functions similar to those of the Argentine National Insurance Supervisory Authority and that had signed a memorandum of understanding with the competent authorities in Argentina. Moreover, the measure required that service suppliers based in non-cooperative countries should be subject to enhanced due diligence.[87]

The Panel found that the imposition of market access conditions on service suppliers originating in a subset of countries modified the

---

[83] Panel Report, *Argentina – Financial Services*, para. 7.183.
[84] Panel Report, *Argentina – Financial Services*, para. 7.184.
[85] Panel Report, *Argentina – Financial Services*, para. 7.186.
[86] Panel Report, *Argentina – Financial Services*, paras. 7.253–58.
[87] Panel Report, *Argentina – Financial Services*, para. 7.323.

3.3 THE PANEL IN *ARGENTINA – FINANCIAL SERVICES*

condition of competition in favour of all other service suppliers, to the detriment of the former.[88] Against this background, the Panel further casted doubts as to the manner in which Argentina kept and updated the lists of cooperative and non-cooperative countries, which led to arbitrary and unpredictable results and failed to demonstrate a coherent link between the effective exchange of information and the classification of the jurisdictions.[89] In this light, the Panel concluded that the measure accorded service suppliers from non-cooperative countries treatment less favourable compared with that granted to service suppliers from cooperative countries.[90]

Concerning Measure 6 (*Measures Affecting Trade in Financial Instruments*), the Panel found that Panama was right in arguing that the imposition of additional conditions could discourage the conclusion of contracts for the supply of services by suppliers based in non-cooperative countries, thus creating a competitive advantage for like service suppliers established in cooperative countries.[91] Moreover, as was the case for Measure 5, the Panel stressed again that the unclear terms in which the distinction between cooperative and non-cooperative countries was made further contributed to the distortion of the condition of competition, thus leading to a situation in which service suppliers from non-cooperative countries were accorded treatment less favourable compared with that granted to service suppliers from cooperative countries.[92]

3.3.2.2 The Panel's Findings on Market Access

Panama also challenged the compatibility of Measure 5 with Articles XVI:1 and XVI:2 of the GATS. In the claimant's view, Argentina was restricting the number of foreign service suppliers allowed to operate in its territory and was according them treatment less favourable than what it had specified in its Schedule of Commitments.[93]

Argentina undertook market access commitments under mode 1 (cross-border supply of services) and mode 3 (commercial presence) with regard to the reinsurance and retrocession sector. In particular, Argentina's schedule reads 'None' in the market access column concerning limitations on cross-border supply of reinsurance and retrocession

---

[88] Panel Report, *Argentina – Financial Services*, para. 7.328.
[89] Panel Report, *Argentina – Financial Services*, para. 7.329.
[90] Panel Report, *Argentina – Financial Services*, para. 7.330.
[91] Panel Report, *Argentina – Financial Services*, para. 7.337.
[92] Panel Report, *Argentina – Financial Services*, paras. 7.339–40.
[93] Panel Report, *Argentina – Financial Services*, para. 7.368.

services, meaning that it had agreed upon full liberalisation of mode 1 market access in that specific subsector. Concerning mode 3, the relevant entry in the market access column reads 'Authorization of the establishment of new entities is suspended'.

Panama contested that, pursuant to Measure 5, service suppliers from non-cooperative countries were prohibited from providing reinsurance services under mode 1 in the Argentine market. In the view of the claimant, the effect of that prohibition boiled down to a 'zero quota', which Argentina was not allowed to impose in light of its full commitment on mode 1 market access in the relevant subsector. Furthermore, Panama argued that the same did not apply to providers of reinsurance and retrocession services from cooperative countries.[94]

The Panel dismissed Panama's claims. In fact, it noted that Measure 5 aimed at the regulation of certain reinsurance operations and individual risks and thus did not specifically regulate suppliers as such. As a result, the Panel concluded that the measure at issue did not fall within the scope of Article XVI:2(a) of the GATS.[95] Because Panama only brought forward a consequential claim of violation of Article XVI:1 of the GATS, the Panel concluded that the prima facie threshold to prove a violation thereof was not met and, as a result, also dismissed that other claim.[96]

3.3.2.3 The Panel's Findings on the GATS PCO

Argentina did not raise any defence under Article XIV of the GATS ('General Exceptions') to justify the alleged violation of its GATS obligations or commitments through Measures 5 and 6. With regard to the latter, in fact, the only justification advanced by the respondent was the GATS PCO. Because this was the first time in history when a party to a WTO dispute invoked the provision, it is important to provide a detailed overview of the positions of the parties as well as the Panel's findings.

3.3.2.3.1 The Positions of the Parties Argentina invoked the PCO already in its first written submission before the Panel.[97] Concerning the qualification of the PCO, Argentina noted that Paragraph 2(a) of the GATS provides an 'exception for GATS-inconsistent measures that are taken for prudential or precautionary purposes'.[98] With regard to the scope of

---

[94] Panel Report, *Argentina – Financial Services*, paras. 7.370 and 7.371.
[95] Panel Report, *Argentina – Financial Services*, paras. 7.428 and 7.429.
[96] Panel Report, *Argentina – Financial Services*, paras. 7.432–7.434.
[97] Panel Report, *Argentina – Financial Services*, para. 7.781, fn. 951.
[98] Panel Report, *Argentina – Financial Services*, para. 7.782.

application of the PCO, Argentina argued that the words 'notwithstanding any other provisions of the Agreement' clearly indicate that the provision can override any violation of the GATS, provided that the measures in justification of which the PCO is invoked affects trade in financial services, as per Article I of the GATS and Paragraph 1 of the Annex on Financial Services of the GATS.[99]

Moving to the legal standard, Argentina described it as being composed of three steps that the Panel had to fulfil: '(i) establish whether the measure in question is a measure 'affecting the supply of financial services' within the meaning of paragraph 1(a) of the GATS Annex on Financial Services; (ii) determine whether the measure has been taken 'for prudential reasons' – Argentina considers that 'this question requires the existence of a 'rational relationship' between the measure and its prudential objective'; and (iii) determine whether the measure is being 'used as a means of avoiding the Member's commitments or obligations under the Agreement'.[100]

Concerning the last step of the legal standard, Argentina argued that the last sentence of the PCO serves the same function as the chapeau of Article XX of the GATT 1994 or Article XIV if the GATS, meaning that it should be read as a bulwark against any abuse in resorting to Paragraph 2(a) of the GATS Annex on Financial Services.[101] Overall, in the view of the respondent in the dispute under analysis, the GATS PCO aims to determine whether a domestic measure has been genuinely adopted with a view to addressing a prudential or precautionary concern and not purely for protectionist purposes.

With specific regard to the second step of the test suggested by Argentina, it is important to recall that it also specified, in its submissions, that the PCO was clearly left open-ended and that the list of objectives included therein is purely illustrative, meaning that other concerns, not expressly listed in Paragraph 2(a) of the Annex on Financial Services, could still rightly be qualified as prudential and thus justify any alleged violation of obligations or commitments under the GATS.[102] With specific regard to the measures at issue, Argentina claimed that it sought 'to protect the insured and the consumers of financial services from risks that could undermine public confidence and affect the functioning of Argentina's financial markets'.[103]

---

[99] Panel Report, *Argentina – Financial Services*, para. 7.782.
[100] Panel Report, *Argentina – Financial Services*, para. 7.783.
[101] Panel Report, *Argentina – Financial Services*, para. 7.783.
[102] Panel Report, *Argentina – Financial Services*, para. 7.785.
[103] Panel Report, *Argentina – Financial Services*, para. 7.785.

Going into more detail as regards the objectives justifying the adoption of Measure 5, the aim behind the restrictions imposed on service suppliers from non-cooperative countries was that of avoiding situations in which, in the event of insolvency or failure of an insurance companies, Argentine policy holders could still be able to collect their claims by the insurers. In cases where the insurer was located in non-cooperative jurisdictions – so the argument put forward by Argentina went – it would have been extremely complicated, if not impossible, for Argentine authorities to acquire sufficient information concerning the ownership of the insurance company and the adequacy of its capitalisation. In turn, similar transactions increase the chances of the propagation of systemic risk.[104] In light of this, Argentina claimed that Measure 5 genuinely pursued a microprudential (the protection of policy holders) as well as a macroprudential regulatory objective (the stability of the financial system as a whole).[105]

Concerning Measure 6, Argentina claimed that the rationale behind the adoption of the latter was the aim of protecting investors and the integrity of the Argentine capital market.[106] In particular, Argentina maintained that 'securities transactions with entities located in non-cooperative jurisdictions pose risks that may not be present in transactions with entities located in cooperative jurisdictions, including risks of money laundering, tax evasion and non-payment of securities transactions'.[107]

With regard to the final step of the proposed standard, Argentina insisted on the genuineness of the measures adopted as well as on the proportionality thereof in relation to the objectives pursued, consistent with the requirements enshrined in the final sentence of the GATS PCO.[108]

Panama, for its part, proposed a radically alternative view on the scope of application of the provision as well as with regard to the specific measures adopted by Argentina. At the outset, Panama acknowledged that the measure was in the nature of an exception, meaning that the burden of proof was on Argentina. In this regard, Panama claimed that Argentina failed to discharge its burden to prove that Measures 5 and 6 fulfil all the requirements of Paragraph 2(a) of the GATS Annex on Financial Services.[109]

---

[104] Panel Report, *Argentina – Financial Services*, para. 7.787.
[105] Panel Report, *Argentina – Financial Services*, para. 7.787.
[106] Panel Report, *Argentina – Financial Services*, para. 7.789.
[107] Panel Report, *Argentina – Financial Services*, para. 7.789.
[108] Panel Report, *Argentina – Financial Services*, paras. 7.791 and 7.792.
[109] Panel Report, *Argentina – Financial Services*, para. 7.794.

3.3 THE PANEL IN *ARGENTINA – FINANCIAL SERVICES*

Despite agreeing with Argentina on the qualification of the PCO as an exception, Panama proposed an alternative four-tier legal standard, pursuant to which four elements had to be verified: (i) the measure at issue affects the supply of financial services; (ii) the measure constitutes a 'domestic regulation'; (iii) the measure was adopted for 'prudential reasons'; and (iv) the measure was not used as a means of avoiding the regulating Member's obligations or commitments under the GATS.[110]

With specific regard to the second element, Panama – in light of the heading of the provision under discussion – affirmed that it should be up to the respondent in a dispute to demonstrate that the measure at issue amounts to a 'domestic regulation', meaning that it has to belong to the type of measures envisaged by Article VI of the GATS ('Domestic Regulation'). In particular, Panama argued that the discipline laid down under Article VI of the GATS relates to domestic regulations concerning qualifications, licenses and technical standards. By the same token, the coverage of the PCO should also be confined to the same type of measures to avoid giving divergent meanings with provisions carrying the same title. In sum, Panama believed that for measures to fall within the scope of the GATS PCO, they had to qualify as domestic regulation. By contrast, measures failing to qualify as domestic regulation could benefit from other exceptions but not from the PCO.[111]

Concerning the third element of the proposed test, Panama again put forward a substantially divergent view. In particular, Panama maintained that, even if the PCO provides a non-exhaustive list of objectives that might justify the violation of GATS obligations or commitments, the reasons for the adoption of the measures must be, in any event, prudential or precautionary.[112] Moving from the Spanish text of the provision[113] – which refers to *medidas por motivos cautelares* – Panama proposed equating the expression 'measures for prudential reasons' with 'provisional measures',[114] that is, a more common concept in public international law.[115]

---

[110] Panel Report, *Argentina – Financial Services*, para. 7.794.
[111] Panel Report, *Argentina – Financial Services*, para. 7.796.
[112] Panel Report, *Argentina – Financial Services*, para. 7.797.
[113] It should be noted that the proceedings took place in Spanish, the official language of both parties.
[114] Panel Report, *Argentina – Financial Services*, para. 7.798.
[115] Panama, in fact, referred to Article 41.1 of the Statute of the International Court of Justice, pursuant to which the Court can indicate any provisional measures that must be adopted to preserve the rights of any of the parties.

Against this background, Panama maintained that – as is the case for other areas of domestic and international law – a measure can be usefully deemed to be adopted in pursuance of a prudential objective if two conditions are met. The first, *fumus boni iuris* (translated by the Panel as 'likelihood of success on the merit of the case'[116]), requires claims to have a sufficient degree of plausibility, that a risk concretely exists and that there are realistic possibilities that it could materialise and entail detrimental consequences for the regulating Member. The second, *periculum in mora* (translated by the Panel as 'danger in delay'[117]), concerns the circumstance that the risk in pursuance of which a Member can regulate in divergence from GATS obligations must be imminent and require the adoption of urgent protective measures. Moreover, Panama derives a systemic implication from this reading of the provision because the risk of imminent danger calls for the adoption of transitional and temporary measures, which should remain in place only as long as the circumstances that led to their adoption persist.[118]

Consequent with the foregoing, Panama's understanding of the scope of application of the provision was also remarkably narrow. With specific regard to the reference made in the PCO to measures adopted to 'ensure the integrity and stability of the financial system', Panama argued that the expression would only encompass measures with the aim of preventing the 'imminent disintegration and destabilization of the financial system'.[119]

Concerning the fourth step of the legal standard, Panama claimed that the last sentence of the provision calls for a rational relationship between the means deployed and the ends pursued, thus boiling down to a good faith obligation.[120]

3.3.2.3.2 The Panel's Findings
The Panel began its analysis by noting that both parties, as well as a number of third parties in the dispute, agreed to qualify the provision as an 'exception'.[121] The Panel took the same view, also in light of the characterisation of the provision as an exception in the Scheduling Guidelines.[122] As was noted earlier in this chapter (see

---

[116] Panel Report, *Argentina – Financial Services*, para. 7.798.
[117] Panel Report, *Argentina – Financial Services*, para. 7.798.
[118] Panel Report, *Argentina – Financial Services*, para. 7.799.
[119] Panel Report, *Argentina – Financial Services*, para. 7.801.
[120] Panel Report, *Argentina – Financial Services*, para. 7.803.
[121] Panel Report, *Argentina – Financial Services*, para. 7.813.
[122] Panel Report, *Argentina – Financial Services*, para. 7.815.

3.3 THE PANEL IN ARGENTINA – FINANCIAL SERVICES

Section 3.3.1), that document recognised that all prudential measures taken in accordance with the GATS PCO constitute exceptions to the Agreement. As a consequence of the classification of the provision as an 'exception', the Panel allocated the burden of proving that Measures 5 and 6 are covered by the PCO on Argentina.[123]

Before examining the merits of the defense invoked by Argentina, the Panel took the opportunity to evaluate the arguments brought forward by Panama in relation to its understanding of the provision as only covering 'domestic regulations' of the type disciplined in Article VI of the GATS.

At the outset, the Panel qualified Panama's characterisation of 'domestic regulation' under Article VI of the GATS as erroneous.[124] In fact, the Panel clarified that the discipline of Article VI of the GATS is not limited to qualifications, technical standards and licensing (which are actually listed in paragraphs 4 and 5 thereof and subject to disciplines that WTO Members still have not agreed upon),[125] but it also covers other 'domestic regulations' including 'measures of general application affecting trade in services' (Article VI:1 of the GATS), 'administrative decisions' (Article VI:2 of the GATS) and 'authorization ... for the supply of a service'.[126] In light of the foregoing, the Panel concluded that the domain of domestic regulations governed by Article VI of the GATS is much broader than what was suggested by Panama.[127]

Additionally, the Panel was not persuaded that Paragraph 2(a) of the GATS Annex on Financial Services only covers measures classifiable as domestic regulations in accordance with Article VI of the GATS. Referring to established case law of the Appellate Body,[128] the Panel warned against a simplistic reading of the provision that would not give meaning to all the terms of a provision so as to make it redundant or inutile.[129]

In particular, the Panel noted that limiting the scope of the PCO to domestic regulations would be in direct contrast with the wording of the provision, which opens with the phrase, 'Notwithstanding any other provisions of the Agreement', thus clearly referring to all obligations and

---

[123] Panel Report, *Argentina – Financial Services*, para. 7.816.
[124] Panel Report, *Argentina – Financial Services*, para. 7.839.
[125] Panel Report, *Argentina – Financial Services*, para. 7.837.
[126] Panel Report, *Argentina – Financial Services*, para. 7.838.
[127] Panel Report, *Argentina – Financial Services*, para. 7.838.
[128] Appellate Body Report, *US – Gasoline*, p. 23; Appellate Body Report, *US – Offset Act (Byrd Amendment)*, para. 271.
[129] Panel Report, *Argentina – Financial Services*, para. 7.840.

commitments under the GATS and not limited to the discipline of Article VI thereof.[130] Quoting from the Panel Report:

> We would also like to express our concern with regard to the serious systemic implications of the narrow interpretation proposed by Panama. Indeed, such an interpretation would drastically reduce the scope of the prudential exception, since it would provide an escape valve only for those 'domestic regulations' which do not conform with Article VI of the GATS and not for those measures which may be covered by other provisions of the GATS (such as those relating to market access, National Treatment or MFN treatment).
>
> We agree with the concern expressed by some third parties in this dispute which also stress the broad policy space which this provision reflects. In particular, we find relevant the comment by the United States to the effect that Members' broad conception of the prudential exception informed the scope of the commitments and limitations that they negotiated and inscribed in their schedules of specific commitments and MFN exemptions lists. Likewise, the European Union has stressed that this provision seems to have been left intentionally broad and notes that it is the result of a delicate compromise. Therefore, a narrow interpretation of the scope of application of the provision or of the conditions under which the prudential exception can successfully be invoked would go against the balance of rights and obligations of the Agreement. [footnotes omitted][131]

After having provided those clarifications, the Panel set forth the legal standard of the provision as being composed of three steps: (i) measures must affect the supply of financial services; (ii) measures must have been taken for prudential reasons; and (iii) measures must have not been used as a means of avoiding the regulating Member's commitments or obligations under the GATS.

Concerning the first step, the Panel recalled its previous conclusions that all the contested measures affected trade in services, as per Article I:1 of the GATS.[132] In addition, the Panel was also satisfied that the services identified by Panama in its Panel request in relation to Measures 5 and 6 were reinsurance services and portfolio management services, both of them financial in nature.[133] Thus, the first step of the legal standard was considered to be met.

The Panel further proceeded with a detailed analysis concerning the second step, which requires that measures be taken for prudential

---

[130] Panel Report, *Argentina – Financial Services*, para. 7.841.
[131] Panel Report, *Argentina – Financial Services*, paras. 7.848–9.
[132] Panel Report, *Argentina – Financial Services*, para. 7.856.
[133] Panel Report, *Argentina – Financial Services*, para. 7.857.

reasons to benefit from the prudential defense of Paragraph 2(a) of the GATS.

To begin with, the Panel provided its analysis of the meaning of 'prudential reasons' (*motivos cautelares* in the Spanish version of the Annex on Financial Services of the GATS). In the view of the Panel, the notion of 'prudential reasons' is directly linked with that of 'preventive or precautionary reasons'.[134] The Panel derived such reading from the text of the provision, which provides an indicative – and by no means exhaustive – list of prudential reasons in accordance to which any potential violation of the GATS could be justified. Additionally, the Panel emphasised that the meaning and importance of prudential objectives may vary over time, depending on the evolution of the social and political preferences of a society, which are inherently subject to change.[135] In this respect, such reading of the PCO is germane to the reading of the 'public order' and 'public morals' clauses put forward by the Panel in *US – Gambling*, according to which Members are free to determine and set the level of protection that they consider appropriate, in accordance with their own systems and scales of values.[136] Moreover, the Panel considered this reading to be consistent and respectful of the preamble of the GATS, which expressly recognises the Members' rights to regulate in accordance with their national policy objectives.[137]

In this respect, the Panel found itself in agreement with the interpretation of the provision put forward by several third parties, which pinpointed the 'intrinsically evolutionary nature' of prudential objectives and measures to achieve them, as well as the paucity of efficient and predictive tools to anticipate financial meltdowns.[138] Moreover, the Panel found further support to its reading of the provision in the concerns expressed by the international community as regards the impact of financial crises and the necessity to ensure that national governments have enough flexibility in the determination of the prudential objectives to be pursued and the tools that they may deploy in that respect.[139]

---

[134] Panel Report, *Argentina – Financial Services*, para. 7.868.
[135] Panel Report, *Argentina – Financial Services*, para. 7.870.
[136] Panel Report, *US – Gambling*, para. 6.461, cited in Panel Report, *Argentina – Financial Services*, para. 7.870.
[137] Panel Report, *Argentina – Financial Services*, para. 7.872.
[138] Panel Report, *Argentina – Financial Services*, para. 7.873, referring to the third parties' submissions and responses to the Panel's questions of the EU, the United States and Brazil.
[139] Panel Report, *Argentina – Financial Services*, para. 7.875.

Against this background, the Panel dismissed Panama's arguments suggesting that the PCO only justifies the adoption of measures in presence of risks of an imminent nature, recognising that systemic risks might simmer for a long time before rapidly erupting, and the dramatic consequences of a financial outburst require that governments could quickly react without the risk of being trapped in a situation of regulatory freeze.[140]

Next, the Panel turned to the specification of its understanding of when a given measure might be considered to have been taken 'for' a prudential reason. The Panel began its analysis in that respect noting that the PCO, unlike several letters of Articles XX of the GATT 1994 and XIV of the GATS, does not require measures to be 'necessary' to achieve a particular aim for them to be justified.[141] Moreover, and perhaps less straightforwardly, the Panel was not persuaded that it could simply transpose the understanding of the expression 'relating to' appearing in Article XX(g) of the GATT 1994.[142] The Panel agreed with Argentina that the word 'for' in the expression 'measures for prudential reasons' calls for a rational relationship of cause and effect between the measure adopted and the objective pursued. In particular, a panel should enquire into the degree of contribution of the measure (through its design, structure and architecture) to achieve its stated aim. Such enquiry, inevitably, can only be conducted on a case-by-case basis.[143]

Having clarified its understanding of the second step of the legal standard, the Panel proceeded with the determination as to whether Measures 5 and 6 were actually taken 'for' prudential reasons. The Panel broke down the analysis into two substeps, aiming at the assessment of whether (i) the reasons adduced for the enactment of the measures were 'prudential' and (ii) whether the measures contributed to achieve the stated aim.

Concerning Measure 5, it should be recalled that Argentina affirmed that the reasons in pursuance of which it was adopted were those of protecting policy holders, to ensure the solvency of insurers and reinsurers and to avoid the spread of negative externalities of insolvency of insurance companies, which could lead to systemic risk.[144] The Panel acknowledged that the stated aims for the adoption of the measure were also expressed in the legal instruments constituting the measure at issue.[145] Furthermore,

---

[140] Panel Report, *Argentina – Financial Services*, para. 7.878.
[141] Panel Report, *Argentina – Financial Services*, para. 7.884.
[142] Panel Report, *Argentina – Financial Services*, para. 7.885.
[143] Panel Report, *Argentina – Financial Services*, para. 7.891.
[144] Panel Report, *Argentina – Financial Services*, para. 7.899.
[145] Panel Report, *Argentina – Financial Services*, para. 7.900.

the Panel noted that the importance of the sound and smooth functioning of the reinsurance services sector had been reaffirmed in several documents approved by regional and international bodies, including the Association of Latin American Insurance Supervisors and the International Association of Insurance Supervisors, which indicated in a 2009 document titled 'Systemic Risk and the Insurance Sector' how the failure of one insurance company could contribute to creating a crisis of systemic dimensions.[146] In light of the arguments and evidence brought forward by Argentina, the Panel was satisfied that the stated objective was prudential and thus eligible to fall within the scope of the PCO.

As a next step, the Panel had to determine whether the measure itself was fit for purpose, in light of the declared prudential objective. Bearing in mind that the measure implied additional requirements for non-cooperative countries' insurance service suppliers to access the Argentine market, the way in which Argentina operated the distinction between cooperative and non-cooperative countries played a relevant role in the determination of whether Measure 5 was actually adopted 'for' a prudential reason.

The Panel recalled that Argentina had established two criteria for a country to be considered cooperative. Pursuant to the first criterion, a country would be considered 'cooperative' if it had either signed an agreement with Argentina concerning the exchange of tax information or an international double taxation convention, which incorporated clauses for the effective exchange of information. According to the second criterion, Argentina could recognise a country as 'cooperative' even if it had only started negotiations of an agreement of the kind discussed earlier.[147] To illustrate the consequences of the approach adopted by Argentina, the Panel referred to the peculiar relationship between the two parties of the dispute:

> The situation between Panama and Argentina illustrates the consequences of using this criterion. As Argentina explains, Panama was included 'as from 1 January 2014 as a 'cooperative country for tax transparency purposes' under Decree No. 589/2013 and AFIP Resolution No. [3576]/2013, after negotiations to conclude an agreement on the exchange of information for tax purposes had been initiated as from November 2013...'. That is to say that, up until 31 December 2013, Argentina regarded Panama as a 'non-cooperative' country. From 25 March 2014, by virtue of Panama's

---

[146] Panel Report, *Argentina – Financial Services*, paras. 7.901 and 7.902.
[147] Panel Report, *Argentina – Financial Services*, para. 7.916.

inclusion in the list of cooperative countries from 1 January 2014, simply because Argentina considered that negotiations had been initiated, reinsurance companies established and registered in Panama were considered to be in compliance with the first of the requirements laid down by points 18(a) and 20(f) I) of Annex I to SSN Resolution No. 35.615/2011. In both cases, that is, both before 31 December 2013 and after 31 December 2013, Panama did not exchange any kind of tax information with Argentina, as follows from Panama's constant refusal during these proceedings to consider that it had initiated negotiations or that it intended to open negotiations with Argentina for the purposes of signing a tax information exchange agreement. [footnotes omitted][148]

Moreover, the Panel found it problematic that countries in the same situation as Panama were not included in the list of cooperative countries, thus implying a certain degree of arbitrariness in the manner in which that list was kept. On the basis of the highlighted problems, the Panel found that Measure 5 did not have a rational relationship with the prudential objectives it was presumed to pursue.[149]

With regard to Measure 6, Argentina claimed that it intended to protect investors from the distortions created by those situations in which the beneficial owner of the securities is unknown and that it aimed at preserving the integrity of the Argentine financial system.[150] In particular, Argentina claimed that the similar recommendations were made by the Financial Action Task Force, which issued a recommendation in 2013 stating that transactions should not be performed when the customer or the beneficial owner could not be identified.[151] Moreover, Argentina insisted that information exchange mechanisms are recognised as important by IOSCO as well.[152]

Similarly to the case of Measure 5, the Panel recognised that the stated regulatory objectives behind Measure 6 could rightly be classified as being 'prudential'. In particular, the Panel referred to a statement of the International Monetary Fund that linked money laundering with concerns relating to the stability of the financial system.[153] However, the Panel was not persuaded that the measure effectively contributed to the realisation of its declared objectives. Again, the Panel was of the view that the mechanism envisaged by Argentina for the classification of countries as cooperative

---

[148] Panel Report, *Argentina – Financial Services*, para. 7.917.
[149] Panel Report, *Argentina – Financial Services*, paras. 7.919 and 7.920.
[150] Panel Report, *Argentina – Financial Services*, para. 7.921.
[151] Panel Report, *Argentina – Financial Services*, para. 7.925.
[152] Panel Report, *Argentina – Financial Services*, para. 7.926.
[153] Panel Report, *Argentina – Financial Services*, para. 7.935.

or non-cooperative for the exchange of tax information was arbitrary and thus would irremediably undermine the effective contribution of the measures to the achievement of its stated aim.[154]

Because the Panel was not satisfied that the measures at issue were taken 'for' prudential reasons, it exercised judicial economy with regard to whether they were used 'as a means of avoiding' Argentina's GATS obligations.[155] The Panel thus dismissed Argentina's defense under the PCO.

3.4 The Appellate Body in *Argentina – Financial Services*

The Appellate Body reversed the Panel report and, most notably, the Panel's findings on likeness. Whilst the Appellate Body was convinced that it is possible to transpose the 'presumption approach' developed under GATT case law – whereby two goods are presumed to be like if a Member has operated a distinction between them that is *exclusively* based on origin[156] – it also held that the Panel had not found that the distinction was only made on grounds of origin.[157] In absence of a finding in which two services or service suppliers were distinguished for reasons exclusively linked to origin, the Panel – in the view of the Appellate Body – should have enquired into the specific characteristics and the competitive relationship between services and service suppliers from cooperative and non-cooperative countries, to establish whether they were like service or service suppliers.[158] Because the Panel did not do so, the Appellate Body reversed its findings on likeness.[159]

Then, instead of declaring all other claims moot and refraining from proceeding with the analysis, the Appellate Body addressed all other claims brought forward by the parties in their appeals, including Panama's challenge of the Panel's characterisation of the scope of application of the PCO. Panama contested the failure of the Panel to give meaning to the heading 'Domestic Regulation' of Paragraph 2(a) of the GATS Annex on Financial Services.[160] The Appellate Body thus reviewed the interpretation of the provision provided by the Panel.

---

[154] Panel Report, *Argentina – Financial Services*, para. 7.943.
[155] Panel Report, *Argentina – Financial Services*, para. 7.945.
[156] Appellate Body Report, *Argentina – Financial Services*, para. 6.52.
[157] Appellate Body Report, *Argentina – Financial Services*, para. 6.56.
[158] Appellate Body Report, *Argentina – Financial Services*, para. 6.61.
[159] Appellate Body Report, *Argentina – Financial Services*, para. 6.70.
[160] Appellate Body Report, *Argentina – Financial Services*, para. 6.247.

First, the Appellate Body clarified that the word 'measures' in the expression 'measures for prudential reasons' should be interpreted in light of the same word appearing in Paragraph 1(a) of the GATS Annex on Financial Services, which establishes the scope of all the provisions falling within the same document. In the view of the Appellate Body, neither of the two provisions imposes specific restrictions on the measure that they cover.[161] Such reading was further reinforced by the introductory sentence of the provision ('Notwithstanding any other provisions of the Agreement'), which permits the PCO to override potential violation of any obligation or commitment under GATS.[162]

Moreover, the Appellate Body was convinced that the expression 'Domestic Regulation' in the heading of the GATS PCO was not meant to circumscribe the scope of application of the provision. Rather, the Appellate Body found that the broad range of measures covered by Article VI of the GATS suggest the opposite of a restrictive reading as to the coverage of the GATS PCO.[163] Such broad reading, in turn, is also consistent with the preamble of the GATS, which reaffirms the Members' right to regulate in pursuance of national policy objectives.[164] Therefore, the Appellate Body upheld the Panel's findings on the GATS PCO.[165]

3.5 Conclusion

The current understanding of the GATS PCO classifies it as an exception with a rather broad coverage. In the first case in which it was examined, the party that invoked it was not able to discharge its burden of proof to show that the measures adopted effectively contributed to the achievement of the stated prudential aim. Nevertheless, the Appellate Body reversed the Panel's findings on Most Favoured Nation, and therefore the result of the dispute was not that of compelling the regulating Member to modify its regulations.

In any event, all the uncertainty surrounding the provision has not yet dissipated. In particular, it is still unclear what kind of scrutiny WTO Members can expect under the final sentence of the provision. More generally, the discussion regarding the legal function of the PCO does not

---

[161] Appellate Body Report, *Argentina – Financial Services*, para. 6.253.
[162] Appellate Body Report, *Argentina – Financial Services*, para. 6.254.
[163] Appellate Body Report, *Argentina – Financial Services*, para. 6.259.
[164] Appellate Body Report, *Argentina – Financial Services*, para. 6.260.
[165] Appellate Body Report, *Argentina – Financial Services*, para. 6.262.

3.5 CONCLUSION

seem to be over. Interestingly, in fact, the Appellate Body stated in a footnote the following:

> The participants refer to paragraph 2(a) of the Annex on Financial Services as either the 'prudential exception' or the 'prudential carve-out'. In its Report, the Panel used the term 'prudential exception'. When referring to the participants' submissions and the Panel's findings, we use the terminology that they employed, without adopting either of the terminologies ourselves.[166]

Therefore, because the discussion concerning the legal function performed by the PCO continues, it remains to be seen whether other interpretations of the provision are permitted.

---

[166] Appellate Body Report, *Argentina – Financial Services*, fn. 592.

4

Prudential Carve-Outs in Preferential Trade Agreements

4.1 Preferential Trade Agreements under Article V of the GATS

Article V of the GATS ('Economic Integration') allows WTO Members to negotiate and take part in agreements with their trading partners with the aim of further liberalising trade in services between them based on more favourable conditions compared with those set out in the context of the GATS and its Schedules. Similar to the corresponding provision in the GATT 1994 – Article XXIV – Article V of the GATS imposes conditions that preferential trade agreements (PTAs)[1] must observe to be compatible with WTO law. Essentially the requirements are the following: (i) the agreement must have 'substantial sectoral coverage' and (ii) it must eliminate 'substantially all discrimination' between the parties.

Both requisites are vaguely drafted.[2] In addition to the 'substantial sectoral coverage' condition, Footnote 1 of Article V of the GATS simply adds the following:

> This condition is understood in terms of number of sectors, volume of trade affected and modes of supply. In order to meet this condition, agreements should not provide for the a priori exclusion of any mode of supply.

As such, as long as a PTA does not exclude from its coverage one specific mode of supply, the first condition is satisfied. However the footnote does not really add much in terms of legal certainty. For instance, nobody knows the percentage of the volume of trade in services that must be affected in order for the 'substantial sectoral coverage' condition to be met.

---

[1] Despite the fact that Article V of the GATS classifies those agreements as 'Economic Integration Agreements' because the agreements at issue, for the most part, cover both goods and services (and other trade-related domains), this study resorts to the more neutral acronym 'PTAs'.

[2] It should also be recalled that WTO panels have never been called to interpret Article V of the GATS, therefore one cannot rely on case law in the quest for an explanation.

With regard to the requirement to eliminate 'substantially all discrimination', paragraph 1 of Article V of the GATS adds that Members should address it through the elimination of previously existing discriminatory measures and that they should abstain from introducing new ones. In sum, it is a 'standstill provision'.

Typically, recent PTAs contain disciplines for the regulation of trade in both goods and services. Interestingly, looking at the notifications of PTAs under Article V of the GATS together with those under Article XXIV of the GATT 1994, one finds that each and every Member of the WTO has in place at least one PTA with a trading partner. This contributes to explaining the lack of litigation on the conditions for the setting up of PTAs. Arguably, Members do not have the incentive to challenge each other's agreements for fear of cross complaints.[3]

Mavroidis put forward convincing explanations with regard to the lack of WTO disputes on the legality of PTAs.[4] Amongst the reasons proposed by the author, one of the most significant is that agents may be risk-averse. For instance panelists, who are normally diplomats or trade delegates in the Geneva missions of other WTO Members, may not want to limit the possibilities for their countries' future preferential trade policy unless the evidence is clear. Furthermore, WTO litigation may be costly, and not all WTO Members may have the capacity to bear the costs. It should also be always borne in mind that trade is part and parcel of international relations, and consequently we cannot exclude the possibility that PTAs are not challenged because of concessions made on other squares of the international chessboard (for instance, at the United Nations).

Additionally, it should be also noted that in December 2006, the General Council of the WTO adopted a decision on the 'Transparency

---

[3] Panels seldom dealt with the consistency of PTAs with the requirements set out in Article XXIV of the GATT 1994 (Article V of the GATS was never the benchmark for a report). In the GATT years, two non-adopted panel reports did so: GATT Panel Report, European Community – Tariff Treatment on Imports of Citrus Products from Certain Countries in the Mediterranean Region, L/5776, 7 February 1985, unadopted (*EC – Citrus*); GATT Panel Report, EEC – Import Regime for Bananas, DS38/R, 11 February 1994, unadopted (*EEC – Bananas II*). There is only one genuine WTO dispute dealing with the issue under analysis: *Turkey – Textiles*. In the latter case, the Appellate Body found that the adoption of quantitative restrictions were not necessary for the formation of a customs union between Turkey and the European Union, hence such violations were not justified under Article XXIV of the GATT 1994. See Appellate Body Report, *Turkey – Textiles*, paras. 42–63.

[4] Petros C. Mavroidis, 'If I Don't Do It, Somebody Else Will (or Won't)', *Journal of World Trade*, 40:1 (2006), 187–214.

Mechanism for Regional Trade Agreements'.[5] The new transparency mechanism has de facto substituted the review mechanism for PTAs in the WTO Committee on Regional Trade Agreements (CRTA). The new rules require that PTAs are notified to the WTO Secretariat. Other WTO Members may ask questions, and the relevant responses must be circulated at least three days before the meeting of the CRTA (a written record of the questions and answers is kept at the WTO Secretariat and uploaded on the Regional Trade Agreements Database of the WTO website).[6] This new system has the potential to enhance the transparency with regard to PTAs in a world in which WTO Members may have more disincentives than incentives to challenge the WTO consistency of PTAs. In any event, it should be stressed that the transparency mechanism does not amount to a review of the legality of the PTAs.

4.1.1 PTAs in Services: Are They Really the 'Exception'?

PTAs were originally conceived as exceptions to the multilateral disciplines governing trade in services. However, over the years, PTAs have rather become the norm in the context of international trade. The 2011 *World Trade Report*, the annual publication prepared by the Economic Research Division of the WTO, shows a constant increase of intra-PTA trade over the years.[7]

Since the entry into force of the WTO (1 January 1995), the number of PTAs notified to the WTO Secretariat under Article V GATS has constantly increased, reaching the number of 139 agreements as of August 2017.[8] In particular, there has been a boom in the number of notifications

---

[5] WTO Doc. WT/L/671, 18 December 2006.   [6] Available at http://rtais.wto.org.
[7] 'We find that the dollar value of trade between members of preferential trade agreements has indeed grown faster than the world average since 1990, and as a result the share of intra-PTA trade in world trade has increased from 18 per cent in 1990 to 35 per cent in 2008.' See World Trade Organization, *World Trade Report 2011 – The WTO and Preferential Trade Agreements: From Co-Existence to Coherence* (Geneva: WTO, 2011) (p. 64).
[8] The European Union and its subsequent enlargements, notified to the WTO Secretariat under Article V of the GATS, are not comprised in these figures. The EU, in fact, is a sui generis organisation, much different from traditional PTAs. Rather than just addressing barriers to trade, it aims to create a single market. Balassa, in 1961, pointed to different stages of economic integration, with free trade agreements and customs unions being the shallowest and a complete economic integration being, on the contrary, the strongest. See Bela Balassa, *The Theory of Economic Integration* (Homewood, IL: Richard D. Irwin, 1961). More recently, André Sapir, on the occasion of the fiftieth anniversary of Balassa's seminal work, published an interesting review essay. See André Sapir, 'European Integration at the Crossroads: A Review Essay on the 50th Anniversary of Bela Balassa's "Theory of Economic Integration"', *Journal of Economic Literature* 49:4 (2011), 1200–29.

4.1 PREFERENTIAL TRADE AGREEMENTS UNDER ARTICLE V

since 2000. WTO Members continue to negotiate preferential trade deals, despite protectionist arguments becoming increasingly popular.

Part of the explanation for the popularity of services PTAs lies in the fact that the GATS is as an 'incomplete' agreement. Several provisions thereof make explicit reference to future negotiations on delicate issues, such as subsidies and domestic regulations to name only two. Moreover, services were a key ingredient in the negotiating recipe of the talks launched in Doha in 2001 for the first multilateral round of negotiations to take place within the WTO.[9] The promise of progressive liberalisation under the GATS, however, was soon broken or, at least, ran into more difficulties than expected. After a first stage in which preferential agreements mainly took place on a regional basis (that is, between neighbouring countries), at the turn of the new century, the system experienced a boom in such agreements as shown by the record of notifications. At the same time, plurilateral initiatives for the negotiations of additional disciplines on trade in services have not been so successful, as the cumbersome path of the negotiations for the Trade in Services Agreement (TiSA) among a group of like-minded countries reveals (additional information concerning the TiSA negotiations is provided in Section 4.3.1).

Why have services PTAs been successful? Although there is robust literature with regard to the rationale for the signing of PTAs in general,[10] research dealing specifically with services PTAs is slightly less popular. However, some efforts have been made.

---

[9] See Doha WTO Ministerial Declaration, WTO Doc. WT/MIN(01)/DEC/1, adopted on 14 November 2001, para. 15: 'The negotiations on trade in services shall be conducted with a view to promoting the economic growth of all trading partners and the development of developing and least-developed countries. We recognise the work already undertaken in the negotiations, initiated in January 2000 under Article XIX of the General Agreement on Trade in Services, and the large number of proposals submitted by members on a wide range of sectors and several horizontal issues, as well as on movement of natural persons. We reaffirm the Guidelines and Procedures for the Negotiations adopted by the Council for Trade in Services on 28 March 2001 as the basis for continuing the negotiations, with a view to achieving the objectives of the General Agreement on Trade in Services, as stipulated in the Preamble, Article IV and Article XIX of that Agreement. Participants shall submit initial requests for specific commitments by 30 June 2002 and initial offers by 31 March 2003.'

[10] For an overview of the debate on the economic rationales for PTAs, see Petros C. Mavroidis, *Trade in Goods* (2 edn.; Oxford: Oxford University Press, 2012) (pp. 194 and ff.). See also Juan A. Marchetti and Martin Roy, 'Services Liberalization in the WTO and in PTAs', in Juan A. Marchetti and Martin Roy (eds.), *Opening Markets for Trade in Services: Countries and Sectors in Bilateral and WTO Negotiations* (Cambridge: Cambridge University Press, 2009), pp. 61 and ff.

Various factors contribute to explain the constant increase in the number of notifications of PTAs. First of all, quantitative studies demonstrate that, on average, Members did not commit to opening up their markets to foreign services and foreign service suppliers to any significant extent before the entry into force of the GATS.[11] Second, because the market for services is traditionally highly regulated, it can be more natural to open markets for trade on a bilateral basis vis-à-vis commercial partners with a comparable level of regulation as opposed to granting National Treatment and Market Access to all other WTO Members in given sectors. Third, services are only one part of the commercial balance of a country. A trading nation might therefore find itself in the position to make concessions on services to obtain additional market access for its goods in one country.[12]

In addition, it cannot be neglected that 'trust' plays an important role and cultural similarities may incentivise countries that share linguistic or historical roots to negotiate trade agreements.[13] As a consequence, it is not surprising that Members are more willing to make more concessions to commercial partners they deem more trustworthy, on a bilateral basis, rather than expanding the scope of their multilateral commitments to all other WTO participants.

There are of course idiosyncratic approaches. The European Union, in particular, does not negotiate PTAs solely to increase opportunities for trade for its suppliers. The 2014 agreement with Ukraine (as well as others) was clearly not concluded solely for commercial purposes but was also conceived as a tool for the pursuit of political and strategic objectives in the region. On a similar note, it is fair to say that Mexico joined the negotiations of the North American Free Trade Agreement (NAFTA) not only for economic reasons but also as a means to signal to the rest of the world that it was able to sit at the same table with its traditionally

---

[11] Juan A. Marchetti, 'Financial Services Liberalization in the WTO and PTAs', in Juan A. Marchetti and Martin Roy (eds.), *Opening Markets for Trade in Services* (Cambridge: Cambridge, 2008), 300–39 (p. 323).

[12] Conconi and Perroni, for instance, argue that negotiating parties are more likely to conclude a trade agreements when as many items as possible are on the table. See Paola Conconi and Carlo Perroni, 'Conditional versus unconditional trade concessions for developing countries', *Canadian Journal of Economics*, 45:2 (2012), 613–31.

[13] On this notion see Luigi Guiso, Paola Sapienza, and Luigi Zingales, 'Cultural Biases in Economic Exchange?', *The Quarterly Journal of Economics*, 124:3 (2009), 1095–131. For an application of this concept to the domain of trade in services, see Juan A. Marchetti and Petros C Mavroidis, 'I Now Recognize You (and Only You) as Equal: An Anatomy of (Mutual) Recognition Agreements in the GATS'.

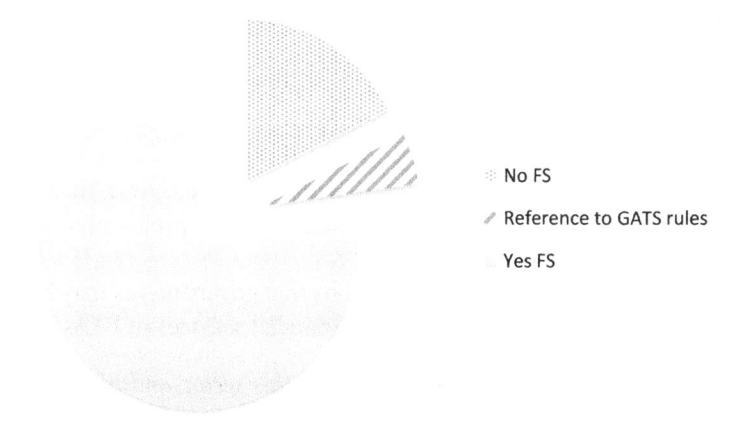

Figure 4.1 Chapters on financial services in preferential trade agreements (elaboration on data from WTO Regional Trade Agreements Database)

more stable North American partners. By the same token, political reasons may also explain why countries do not negotiate trade agreements with others.

4.1.2 *Financial Services in PTAs*

In Chapter 2, we saw how financial services were both a driver for the launch of the talks for a multilateral agreement on trade in services as well as a source of political conflict both within domestic jurisdictions (due to conflicts of competences between trade officials on one side and treasury and central banks representatives on the other) as well as between negotiating teams because not all countries that were participating in the Uruguay Round talks were willing or ready to open up their markets for financial services.

Although it is impossible to provide a suitable explanation for all the PTAs in services as to the inclusion (or the exclusion) of disciplines on financial services, it is perhaps useful to provide some figures and to identify some recurring patterns. Of the 139 PTAs notified under Article V of the GATS until August 2017,[14] 32 do not set out disciplines on financial services, 9 incorporate the GATS rules on financial services and 98 provide for a specific chapter or annex on financial services (Figure 4.1).

---

[14] WTO Regional Trade Agreements Information System: http://rtais.wto.org/UI/PublicMaintainRTAHome.aspx

The relevant percentages are as follows: 70.5 per cent of the notified PTAs contain specific disciplines on financial services, 6.47 per cent make reference to the existing discipline in the GATS and 23.02 per cent of the agreements do not cover financial services.

Because the overwhelming majority of the PTAs provide for specific disciplines on financial services, it is worth understanding the reasons trading nations liberalise trade in that sector at the preferential level, at an arguably deeper level than the GATS.[15]

Stephanou[16] cites the following reasons that governments may have for the inclusion of specific disciplines on financial services in PTAs.

i) *[T]he existence of offensive interests in this sector and of asymmetric bargaining powers between the negotiating counterparts'*. Typically, it is in the interest of the more developed party in the negotiation to secure market access for its suppliers of financial services in the counterpart's jurisdiction. Sometimes financial services are used as a negotiating chip: either financial services are part of the negotiating package or no agreement will see the light of the day. However, liberalisation of trade in financial services may also be in the interest of less advanced parties to the negotiations, as it can serve as a tool to import technology and knowhow.

ii) *Trade agreements as a tool to 'lock in' unilateral concessions or to advance the government's agenda.* Among the theories that contribute towards explaining why governments sign trade agreements, the so-called 'commitment theory' is certainly popular. Essentially, the theory explains why governments may want to use international trade agreements in order as a deterrent against domestic pressure from lobbies, so as to lock in their trade liberalisation agenda.[17] However, it must be borne in mind that various scholars and commentators have expressed scepticism with regard to this explanation for trade agreements.[18] For instance, Mavroidis argues that the commitment

---

[15] Research suggests that this is not always the case. See Marchetti, 'Financial Services Liberalization in the WTO and PTAs' (p. 332).

[16] Constantinos Stephanou, 'Including Financial Services in Preferential Trade Agreements – Lessons of International Experience for China', World Bank Policy Research Working Paper, (April 2009), p. 8.

[17] For an application of this theory to PTAs, see Kyle Bagwell and Robert W. Staiger, *The Economics of the World Trading System* (Cambridge, MA: MIT Press, 2002) (pp. 121–2).

[18] Srinivasan, in particular, is not persuaded that the 'commitment theory' provides a reasonable justification for trade agreements. In fact, he considers the logic behind addressing a domestic distortion with an international obligation to be weak. See Thirukodikaval N.

4.1 PREFERENTIAL TRADE AGREEMENTS UNDER ARTICLE V

theory is more relevant in the attempt to explain why trading nations may be in favour of the building up of legal institutions such as the WTO or the NAFTA.[19] Moreover, for some trading nations, further liberalisation of financial services may be the price to pay to enter such clubs.

iii) *Strategic or political reasons*: There can be also other explanations that do not pertain to the domain of economics. A trading nation may negotiate agreements on financial services because of the will to prove that it is a solid economy that can sit at the same table with wealthy partners, or for other political considerations. It can be argued, for instance, that Mexico decided to join the NAFTA not only for economic reasons, but also in order to send the world a strong message that its market was open to foreign investors.

Alongside Stephanou's attempt, other considerations may assist those in search of a reason for trade agreements on financial services. One explanation derives directly from the text of Article V of the GATS. The provision, as we saw before, requires that PTAs have substantial sectoral coverage without specifying how deep the commitments in each sector have to be. Therefore the introduction of specific disciplines on trade in financial services is of limited stand-alone value because they have to be read together with the limitations listed in the schedules of specific commitments. From a 'black letter law' perspective, Members have a strong incentive to include financial services in their PTAs, hiding strong limitations in their schedules.

In addition, it should be noted that multilateral concessions have been meaningful in some areas (particularly with regard to Mode 3 trade) but not so much in other fields. Consequently Members may find it attractive to pursue a more proactive trade policy agenda at the bilateral or regional level.[20]

Third, despite the deregulation that took place in the banking sector in the 1990s and that, together with other factors, played a role in causing the 2007–8 financial crisis, financial services still remain a heavily regulated market and are undergoing a process of 're-regulation', as shown earlier. As a result, PTAs may help to tackle a series of barriers that financial service suppliers face in the attempt to access other markets.

Srinivasan, 'Nondiscrimination in GATT/WTO: Was There Anything to Begin with and Is There Anything Left?', *World Trade Review*, 4/01 (2005), 69–95.
[19] Mavroidis, *Trade in Goods* (pp. 16 and ff.).
[20] See Marchetti, 'Financial Services Liberalization in the WTO and PTAs' (p. 317).

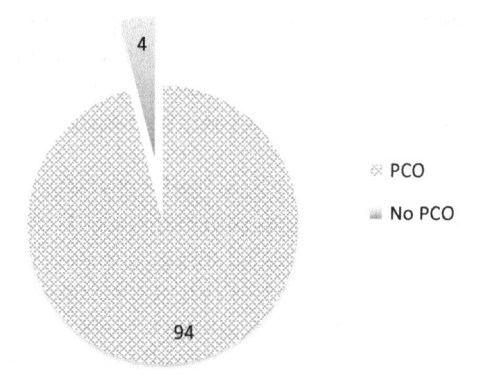

Figure 4.2 Prudential carve-outs (PCOs) in preferential trade agreements (elaboration on data from WTO Regional Trade Agreements Database)

4.2 Prudential Carve-Outs in PTAs

Of the ninety-eight PTAs with relevant disciplines on financial services, ninety-four contain a PCO or specific provisions dealing with prudential measures. This means that 95.91 per cent of the PTAs on financial services (and close to 65 per cent of all PTAs) have a prudential carve-out or a similar provision, a figure that is revealing of the importance of the matter in and of itself (Figure 4.2).

The only four PTAs without a PCO are the European Economic Area (EEA),[21] China–Hong Kong, China–Macao and Iceland–Faroe Islands. An intuitive explanation for the absence of PCOs in the latter four agreements probably lies in their depth. The EEA, for instance, concerns the expansion of the EU single market to the European Free Trade Association (EFTA) countries. It is a case in which the domestic law of a trading nation is made applicable to the preferential trading partners. This may also explain the lack of PCOs in two agreements that involve China and two of its 'satellite-States' and the agreement between Iceland and Faroe Islands. There is no official explanation or existing literature to date that could shed light on the foregoing.

An analysis of the PCOs in all PTAs in services notified to the WTO Secretariat allows identification of recurring patterns. Before looking at

---

[21] The EEA is an international agreement, entered into force on 1 January 1994, that constitutes a single market between the Member States of the European Union and the Members of the EFTA.

the figures, some clarifications must be made with regard to the methodology applied in the study.

4.2.1 Classifying the Data on PCOs

There are distinctive patterns that permit differentiation between the various versions of the provision at the preferential level. Eight elements are considered in the present study.

1) *Scope of application.* PCOs are classified according to their declared scope of application. An analysis of the wording of the various PCOs reveals that they present four options:

(i) they put forward a carve-out for all obligations contained in the whole Agreement;
(ii) they only refer to the provisions of the Chapter or Annex on Financial Services;
(iii) they apply to the obligations laid down in a defined list of Chapters (e.g., financial services, telecoms, insurance); or
(iv) they do not specify their scope of application.

This element, however, should not be overestimated. The disciplines set up in Chapters or Annexes on financial services only apply when the measures adopted by a government 'affect' trade in financial services, thus the broadness of the scope of application is of limited added value in reinforcing the actual right to regulate for the Parties to the relevant agreements.

2) *Content.* Most preferential PCOs provide a non-exhaustive list of prudential objectives, similar to the prototype that can be found in the GATS Annex on Financial Services. They can be subdivided into two groups: those that list two groups of measures, similar to the GATS PCO ('the protection of investors, depositors, policy holders or persons to whom a fiduciary duty is owed by a financial service supplier' and 'to ensure the integrity and the stability of the financial system as a whole'); and those that list three groups of measures, the main example in this regard being Article 1410 of NAFTA (*'(a) The protection of investors, depositors, financial market participants, policyholders, policy claimants, or persons to whom a fiduciary duty is owed by a financial institution or cross-border financial service provider; (b) the maintenance of the safety, soundness, integrity or financial responsibility of financial institutions or cross-border financial service providers; and (c) ensuring the integrity and stability of a party's financial system'*). This volume also identifies PCOs that

merely refer to 'prudential measures' without providing with an indicative list.

The following elements are more important because they actually amount to requisites that Parties to the agreements have to meet to avail themselves of the PCO.

3) *Reasonableness.* PCOs are subdivided according to whether they require measures adopted for prudential purposes to be 'reasonable'. This requisite first appeared in Article 1410 of NAFTA. This study distinguishes between PCOs that contain a 'reasonableness test' and those that do not. This element is a peculiar one because it might have a different meaning depending on the context and the reader that is called to interpret it.

4) *Necessity test.* Necessity tests are common in international economic law. Essentially, they require Members to enact measures that are 'no more burdensome than necessary' to achieve their stated aim. The requirement, in the WTO legal system, is typical of some of the exceptions listed in Article XX of the GATT 1994 or Article XIV of the GATS. This study distinguishes between those PCOs that have a 'necessity test' and those that do not.

5) *National Treatment.* National Treatment is one of the two legs of the principle of non-discrimination in international trade law (the other being Most Favoured Nation). It requires the regulating Member to accord foreign services or foreign service suppliers treatment no less favourable than that granted to like services and service suppliers of national origin. In the case preferential PCOs, the concept of National Treatment is used to refer to those provisions that require Members to provide the same treatment to like domestic and foreign services and service suppliers as regards measures adopted for prudential reasons. This volume distinguishes between PCOs that include a National Treatment clause and those that do not.

6) *'Chapeau' language.* Many commentators have drawn a parallel between the final clause of the GATS PCO and the language of the *chapeau* of the general exceptions provisions of the GATT 1994 and the GATS. The chapeau of Article XIV of the GATS reads as follows:

> Subject to the requirement that such measures are not applied in a manner which would constitute a means of arbitrary or unjustifiable discrimination between countries where like conditions prevail, or a disguised restriction on trade in services, nothing in this Agreement shall be construed to prevent the adoption or enforcement by any Member of measures:...

This study verifies whether similar language is contained in PCOs and to what extent this is a recurring feature in provisions for prudential measures in PTAs.

7) *GATS PCO Final clause.* Another feature for the differentiation of PCOs is whether they provide language similar (or identical) to that adopted in the final clause of the PCO (*'Where such measures do not conform with the provisions of the Agreement, they shall not be used as a means of avoiding the Member's commitments or obligations under the Agreement'*). As ambiguous and vague as it may be, it is nonetheless a recurring feature in PTAs. This is, *en passant*, also revealing of the importance that a coherent interpretation of the GATS PCO may have regarding the interpretation of preferential PCOs. The present volume analyses whether a similar clause is provided by preferential PCOs.

8) *Standards.* This study verifies how many PCOs refer to internationally agreed standards as benchmarks for the lawfulness of prudential measures. Moreover, it identifies the standard-setting bodies to which the PCOs refer.

This book classifies PCOs according to the legal function that their respective treaties assign to them. In this respect, PCOs are classified as follows: 'Exceptions' if they are drafted in a way similar to the relevant exceptions in international trade treaties (in other words, if they include a necessity test, a National Treatment requirement or language similar to that of the chapeau of the General Exceptions provisions in the GATT 1994 and the GATS); 'Provisions that exclude the application of other provisions' (or 'Scope' provisions), if they are designed as tools preserving the parties' right to regulate or 'Unclear' if the language of the provision does not allow to detect the function assigned to the provision.

4.2.2 The Taxonomy

This volume considers those PCOs whose distinctive patterns could be identified as a category in more than two agreements. The categories that were identified are the following: GATS-like, NAFTA-like, US post-2004–like, EFTA third party–like, and EU 2014, plus a residual one ('other'). Figure 4.3 illustrates the distribution of the various types of preferential PCOs.

4.2.2.1 GATS-Like

This volume identifies PCOs that follow the pattern of Paragraph 2(a) of the Annex on Financial Services of the GATS as 'GATS-like'. The text is reported again here for ease of reference:

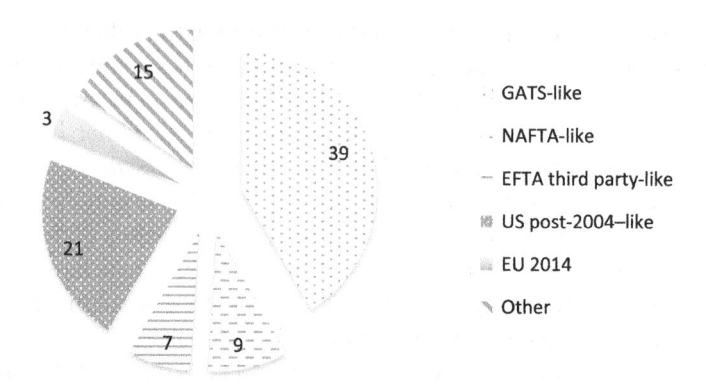

Figure 4.3 Types of prudential carve-outs in preferential trade agreements (elaboration of data from the WTO Regional Trade Agreements Database)

2. Domestic Regulation

(a) Notwithstanding any other provisions of the Agreement, a Member shall not be prevented from taking measures for prudential reasons, including for the protection of investors, depositors, policy holders or persons to whom a fiduciary duty is owed by a financial service supplier, or to ensure the integrity and stability of the financial system. Where such measures do not conform with the provisions of the Agreement, they shall not be used as a means of avoiding the Member's commitments or obligations under the Agreement.

The PCOs that fall under this category are those appearing in the following agreements:

Southern Common Market (MERCOSUR); New Zealand – Singapore; EU – Former Yugoslav Republic of Macedonia; Japan – Singapore; EU – Chile; Thailand – Australia; Thailand – New Zealand; India – Singapore; Korea – Republic of Singapore; Japan – Malaysia; EU – Albania; Chile – Japan; EU – Montenegro; Pakistan – Malaysia; Japan – Indonesia; Brunei Darussalam – Japan; China – New Zealand; Japan – Philippines; Japan – Switzerland; Japan – Vietnam; Korea – India; EU – Serbia; New Zealand – Malaysia; Hong Kong, China – New Zealand; India – Japan; Japan – Peru; EU – Central America; Hong Kong, China – Chile; Eurasian Economic Union; Japan – Australia; Gulf Cooperation Council – Singapore; Australia – China; China – Korea; Japan – Mongolia; Mexico – Panama; Costa Rica – Colombia; Pacific Alliance (Chile, Colombia, Peru, Mexico); EU – Bosnia and Herzegovina.

There are variations, but those affect residual aspects that do not alter the structure of the PCOs and, in any event, allow considering all of them as part of the same category.

4.2 PRUDENTIAL CARVE-OUTS IN PTAS

Contrary to what is provided under the corresponding provision in the Annex on Financial Services of the GATS, some preferential PCOs do not refer to 'any other provisions of the Agreement' but limit their coverage either to the Chapter, Annex or Protocol on financial services[22] or to various chapters disciplining trade in services.[23]

Mercado Común del Sur (MERCOSUR), EU–Chile and Hong Kong–Chile include a 'reasonableness test' in their preferential PCOs. In the absence of a more stringent requirement, the efficacy of this clause is only limited to the duty of the regulating Member to prove, in the event of a controversy, the existence of a 'genuine link' between the domestic measure and the prudential objective it aims to pursue.

The PCO in the Japan–Switzerland PTA, in context, contains a reference to internationally agreed standards, contrary to the original provision of the GATS that, as explained in Chapter 2, does not do so. Paragraph 2 of Article VI ('Domestic Regulation') of the Annex on Financial Services of the aforementioned agreement reads:

> Each Party shall make its best endeavours to ensure that the Basel Committee's "Core Principles for Effective Banking Supervision", the standards and principles of the International Association of Insurance Supervisors and the International Organisation of Securities Commissions' "Objectives and Principles of Securities Regulation" are implemented and applied in its Area.

The language is hortatory rather than dispositive and, although it is in the same Article as the PCO, it is not in and of itself a condition for lawfulness of prudential measures under the bilateral trade agreement. However, its inclusion in Article VI confers upon the paragraph at issue at least the value of 'context' in the interpretation of the provision. A deviation from standards when enacting prudential measures does not amount to a violation of Article VI, but standards may constitute a useful benchmark for the allocation of the burden of proof in the event of a controversy. In other words, there must be a presumption of lawfulness of measures adopted following the recommendations of BCBS, IAIS and IOSCO, and then, in case the regulating Member wants to move to a higher level of protection than that under the standards previously mentioned, it must show why its choice is still prudential and not protectionist.

---

[22] MERCOSUR, Japan–Singapore, EU–Chile, Japan–Malaysia, Pakistan–Malaysia, Japan–Indonesia, Brunei Darussalam–Japan, China–New Zealand, Japan–Philippines, Japan–Switzerland, Japan–Vietnam, Australia–China, Pacific Alliance.

[23] Chile–Japan, India–Japan, Japan–Peru, China–Korea, Japan–Mongolia.

Finally, the PCOs in the EU–Chile, the EU–Central America, Hong Kong–Chile, Mexico–Panama and Pacific Alliance FTAs contain an indicative list of three groups of prudential purposes according to which Members are free to regulate notwithstanding their obligations or commitments. Contrary to the wording of the prototypical provision in the GATS, Article 125 ('Prudential Carve Out') of the FTA between EU and Chile and Article 195 ('Prudential Carve Out') of the EU–Central America FTA read, in relevant part:

(a) the protection of investors, depositors, financial market participants, policy-holders, or persons to whom a fiduciary duty is owed by a financial services supplier;
(b) the maintenance of the safety, soundness, integrity or financial responsibility of financial services suppliers; and
(c) ensuring the integrity and stability of a Party's financial system.

This language is the same as that adopted in the PCO under the chapter on financial services of NAFTA. However, because both provisions provide a final clause whose content is along the lines of the last provision of the PCO in the Annex on Financial Services of the GATS, the two PCOs just mentioned are nevertheless considered to be part of the 'GATS-like' category.

The provisions falling under this category are typically drafted as 'provisions that exclude the application of other provisions' rather than exceptions. None of them includes one of the three limitations, the occurrence of which would lead this study to confer upon the PCO the status of exception (namely, a necessity test, National Treatment or chapeau language).

4.2.2.2 NAFTA-Like

Another category of PCOs replicates the text that first appeared in Paragraph 1 of Article 1410 ('Exceptions') of the North American Free Trade Agreement, which reads as follows:

Article 1410: Exceptions

1. Nothing in this Part shall be construed to prevent a Party from adopting or maintaining reasonable measures for prudential reasons, such as:

(a) the protection of investors, depositors, financial market participants, policyholders, policy claimants, or persons to whom a fiduciary duty is owed by a financial institution or cross-border financial service provider;

(b) the maintenance of the safety, soundness, integrity or financial responsibility of financial institutions or cross-border financial service providers; and

(c) ensuring the integrity and stability of a Party's financial system.

This type of PCO appears in nine FTAs:

> North American Free Trade Agreement (NAFTA); Colombia–Mexico; Panama–El Salvador (Panama–Central America); Panama–Chinese Taipei; Panama–Costa Rica (Panama–Central America); Panama–Honduras (Panama–Central America); Panama–Guatemala (Panama–Central America); Panama–Nicaragua (Panama–Central America); Peru–Mexico.

The first distinctive feature that is worthy of note after the lengthy discussion of the GATS PCO in the previous Chapters is the absence of the circular final clause that is common the category of PCOs discussed in the previous subsection. Moreover, NAFTA-like PCOs typically apply to the Chapters on financial services of their respective agreements ('*Nothing in this Part...*').

Also this category presents deviations from the original pattern. In particular, seven of the PCOs belonging to the category under analysis do not provide a 'reasonableness' requirement.[24] With regard to coverage, almost all NAFTA-like PCOs apply to the obligations in the Chapters on Financial Services of the respective agreements, except for the PCO in Colombia–Mexico, which refers to the whole Agreement, and the PCO in Peru–Mexico, which makes reference to various chapters on trade in services of the Agreement.

Given the importance of NAFTA in the realm of preferential agreements, the interpreter of the provision has access to a series of studies and documents that may provide some clarification as regards how the chapter on financial services and the positions of the various negotiating teams. Moreover, contrary to the rest of the provisions analysed in the present chapter, the NAFTA PCO was effectively invoked in a dispute. In any event, a caveat must be added: NAFTA documents and case law are only strictly relevant within NAFTA, and the conclusions drawn from the consultation of the latter should not be exported to other PTAs.

---

[24] Panama–El Salvador (Panama–Central America), Panama–Chinese Taipei, Panama–Costa Rica (Panama–Central America), Panama–Honduras (Panama–Central America), Panama–Guatemala (Panama–Central America), Panama–Nicaragua (Panama–Central America), Peru–Mexico.

4.2.2.2.1 Negotiating History and Rationale According to Cameron and Tomlin, there are three main factors that shaped the negotiations of NAFTA: i) asymmetry of powers, ii) contrasting domestic institutions and iii) differences in the management alternatives.[25] All three factors played a role in the negotiations of the chapter on financial services of the Agreements.

The first substantive proposals on financial services were put forward at the end of December 1991, mainly following pressure from US insurance companies and financial institutions. The negotiating teams regarding the negotiations of Chapter 14 were composed of officials from the US Treasury Department and the Canadian Finance Department. The negotiating team of Mexico consisted of officials from various branches of the government and from the central bank, led by a trade official.[26]

At the beginning, Mexico opposed any negotiation on financial services, whereas the United States made it clear that in the absence of substantial liberalisation in that sector, there would be no NAFTA at all. In reality, the Mexican negotiators were privately reassuring their counterparts, confirming that they were willing to proceed with unilateral liberalisation and that a trade agreement would have helped them sell the change domestically more easily.[27] There were also frictions between Canada and the United States, as the former was trying to win Washington's resistance concerning the possibility for Canadian financial institutions to establish branches in the United States. In particular, the foregoing would have required the modification of the Glass-Steagall Act.[28]

At the Dallas meeting in February 1992, positions moved towards convergence. Mexico had abandoned its fight for a permanent cap on foreign equity and accepted the principle of National Treatment. However, Canada and the United States still had not reached a solution regarding the establishment of Canadian branches.

In August 1992, the seventh and final round for the negotiations took place at the Watergate complex in Washington. By that time, tensions had

---

[25] Maxwell A. Cameron and Brian W. Tomlin, *The Making of NAFTA – How the Deal Was Done* (Ithaca and London: Cornell University Press, 2000) 264.

[26] Ibid. (p. 98).

[27] Anecdotal evidence suggests that Mexico had just reprivatised its banks at the time of the negotiations of the Agreement.

[28] Interestingly, the issue was already debated during the negotiations of the FTA between Canada and the United States. More detailed information on the negotiating positions can be found in Cameron and Tomlin, *The Making of NAFTA – How the Deal Was Done* (p. 99).

diminished. The main issue that was left on the table concerned the justiciability of controversies on financial services. Parties reached a deal according to which the provisions on dispute settlement would also apply to the domain of financial services, with panelists appointed from a roster of financial experts. This was mainly due to the US resistance to having trade experts sitting on panels dealing with financial services issues.

4.2.2.2.2 Law The NAFTA approach towards financial services differs from that of the Annex on Financial Services of the GATS. The latter is characterised by the fact that it sets out a rule-based framework for the liberalisation of cross-border trade in financial services.[29] In contrast, the NAFTA Chapter on Financial Services focuses on the way financial institutions are to be treated and has a less flexible structure.[30]

Various provisions of the Agreement deal with prudential measures and their interplay with trade rules in addition to the PCO. Paragraphs 2, 3 and 4 of Article 1406 ('Most Favored Nation Treatment') of the Agreement provide a discipline for the recognition by a Party of prudential measures of another Party (or even a non-Party). Such recognition can be accorded unilaterally, achieved through harmonisation or can be the subject of an agreement between the governments involved. The provision, then, requires that in cases where recognition occurs, the Party that unilaterally accorded recognition must provide 'adequate opportunity' to any other Party requesting similar treatment to demonstrate that it is in a comparable situation.

Article 1407 ('New Financial Services and Data Processing') sets out the requirements for regulators in case foreign suppliers of new financial services demand market access. First, the provision contains an obligation for the Parties to allow access to the market to new financial services that are similar to those already authorised domestically. When a financial service supplier needs an authorisation to operate in the market, Article 1407 requires supervisory bodies to make a decision in a reasonable time and allows them to refuse authorisation only for 'prudential reasons'.[31]

---

[29] Jeffrey Simser, 'Financial Services under NAFTA: A Starting Point', *Banking & Finance Law Review*, 10 (1994–5) (pp. 201 and ff.).
[30] Krista Nadakavukaren Schefer, *International Trade in Financial Services: The NAFTA Provisions* (The Hague/Boston: Kluwer Law International, 1999) (p. 119).
[31] It is worth noting that prudential measures are only defined in Article 1410(1) by means of a non-exhaustive list, hence supervisory bodies still enjoy substantial autonomy in the authorizing processes.

Article 1415 ('Investment Disputes in Financial Services') provides for a filter mechanism with regard to investment disputes in which the prudential defence is invoked. If the Party that invokes the provision so requires, the Tribunal shall refer the matter in writing to the Financial Services Committee for a decision and may not proceed while that is pending. The Financial Services Committee is composed of State officials of the Parties of NAFTA that are domestically responsible for financial services.[32] The Committee, in the event a claim under Article 1410 is referred to it, shall decide if the PCO is a valid defence against the claim brought before the Tribunal. The decision issued by the Committee and transmitted to the Tribunal is binding on the latter. In case the Committee does not issue its decision in 60 days, the complainant (be it the investor or the Party of the investor) can request the establishment of a specific arbitral panel, whose composition should follow the requirements set out in Article 1414.[33] Again in this case, the report issued by this arbitral tribunal shall be binding on the Tribunal before which the original dispute is pending. Where the Financial Services Committee has issued a decision in 60 days and a request for the establishment of a panel was not made in the course of the ten following days, the original Tribunal can decide on the matter.

4.2.2.2.3 Standards
The Chapter on Financial Services of NAFTA does not make reference to international standards.[34]

4.2.2.2.4 Case Law
In 2006, an Arbitral Tribunal[35] constituted under Chapter Eleven of NAFTA issued an award that, for the first and only time

---

[32] The Committee is disciplined in Article 1412 ('Financial Services Committee').
[33] As in the case of the GATS, NAFTA provides for specific rules as regards the composition of the panels that are called to decide on issues related to trade in financial services. Article 1414 ('Dispute Settlement'). The Parties to NAFTA must agree by consensus on a roster of maximum fifteen individuals. The individuals in the roster must be experts in financial services law or practice and be chosen on the basis of 'objectivity, reliability and sound judgment', in addition to meeting the conditions set out in Article 2009 (b) and (c), namely being independent and comply with the Code of Conduct established by the NAFTA Free Trade Commission.
[34] Nadakavukaren Schefer affirms that international standards like those set up by the BCBS can be of relevance in the evaluation of whether measures adopted for prudential reasons are reasonable or not. However, she points out that standards are no panacea and that they have objective limits; therefore their role as benchmark in the event of a dispute cannot be pushed too far. See Nadakavukaren Schefer, *International Trade in Financial Services* (pp. 232 and ff.).
[35] Fireman's Fund Insurance Company v Mexico, ICSID Case No. ARB(AF)/02/01, Award (17 July 2006).

4.2 PRUDENTIAL CARVE-OUTS IN PTAS

thus far, touched upon the NAFTA PCO, albeit only in an *obiter dictum*. Fireman's Fund, a wholly owned subsidiary of Allianz America, in turn a Delaware-based corporation fully owned by Allianz AG of Munich, issued a complaint against Mexico in relation to the alleged expropriation of its property. The plaintiff also claimed that Mexico had aided national companies in purchasing debentures denominated in Mexican pesos and, by so doing, had discriminated against it. The award declared the issue of whether the measures were in line with the requirements of the NAFTA PCO moot because the tribunal had not found the challenged measures to constitute expropriation under NAFTA.

The decision examines Article 1410(1) of NAFTA in paragraphs 156–68. First, the Tribunal qualifies the provision as 'exception', in line with its heading. However, it does so in a non-technical fashion, in the sense that it only clarifies that the provision may kick in to justify domestic measures that, at first sight, may be considered in violation of other provisions of the Agreement.[36] The Tribunal also dismissed the arguments of the complainant according to which, were a measure to be found unreasonable, it would give rise to a presumption of liability. Moreover, the Tribunal also did not accept the interpretation advanced by the plaintiff according to which a measure whose effects amount to a discrimination between national and foreign service suppliers would not be considered reasonable according to Article 1410(1) of NAFTA. Quoting a passage from the decision:

> The Tribunal, noting that the exception applies to all provisions of Part Five ("Investments, Services and Related Matters") of the NAFTA applicable to Financial Services, including the National Treatment article (Article 1405), concludes that Article 1410(1) permits reasonable measures of a prudential character even if their effect (as contrasted with their motive or intent) is discriminatory. The Tribunal rejects the contention that a measure discriminatory in effect is *eo ipso* unreasonable.[37]

Subsequently the Tribunal, quoting a passage from a scholarly work by Olin L. Wethington, negotiator for the United States of the Chapter on Financial Services of NAFTA, went on to affirm that the objective of the provision is twofold. On the one hand, NAFTA PCO establishes a 'regulatory prerogative' to ensure the integrity of the financial system. On the other hand, the provision prevents abuses of such prerogative, which could mainly take place in the form of arbitrary measures connected with, inter

---

[36] *Fireman's Fund Insurance*, para 159.   [37] *Fireman's Fund Insurance*, para. 162.

alia, individual firm applications or licensing requests. In a nutshell, the Tribunal agreed with the author that the NAFTA PCO permits substantial regulatory autonomy in the domain of financial services with one caveat: backhanded avoidance of National Treatment and other obligations cannot be tolerated.[38]

To what extent 'backhanded avoidance of National Treatment' differs from the concept of 'discrimination' is a complicated question to pose. One may guess that the former relates to attempts to circumvent trade obligations, but neither the text of the law nor case law shed more light on the issue. Nevertheless, the Tribunal did not test the consistency of the challenged measures with the PCO because it had not found those measures to constitute expropriation under the relevant obligations of NAFTA. The discussion was still reported in this volume as the *Fireman's Fund* case is the closest a NAFTA Arbitration Panel came to interpreting the PCO in that Agreement.

4.2.2.2.5 Analysis The description of the NAFTA PCO, put in the context of the relevant discipline on financial services of the Agreement, reveals that despite the differences in structure and wording, the provision does not substantially differ from the GATS. The function performed by the provision is, substantially, that of giving regulators a wide margin of discretion in addressing micro and macroprudential concerns. In particular, the very idea of 'integrity and stability' of the financial system is, in and of itself, wide and leaves space for domestic sovereignty with regard to the policy choices regulators consider appropriate.

Furthermore, notwithstanding the heading of the provision ('Exception'), a closer look at the provision indicates that no stringent conditions are required for the successful invocation of the prudential defence. The only real condition that must be satisfied before the PCO can operate is the requirement according to which measures adopted for prudential reasons must be 'reasonable'. This requirement has not yet been scrutinised in case law, and the only arbitral tribunal that has so far analysed the PCO did not clarify its meaning. However, NAFTA case law at least clarifies that the PCO allows discriminatory behaviour.

Can the 'reasonableness' requirement be seen as a 'proportionality test'? In the absence of authoritative interpretation of the test in case law, it is complicated to provide a conclusive answer. Trachtman explored the issue in an article published in 1996 at the dawn of the first experiences of

[38] *Fireman's Fund Insurance*, paras. 163–5.

inclusion of financial services in trade agreements.[39] He correctly points out that NAFTA introduces a 'necessity test' in the general exception provision dealing with cross-border trade in services.[40] To be justified under the exception, measures must not be unjustifiably discriminatory and should not represent a disguised barrier to trade (similar to what is required by the chapeau of the exception provisions in the GATT 1994 and the GATS). Such language is, therefore, not alien to the legal system set up by the Agreement.

Trachtman argues:

> This exception for any reasonable prudential measures might be a basis for discipline of prudential measures, or might be an avenue of defection from NAFTA financial services obligations. It would be a source of discipline if the "reasonableness" requirement is read as a proportionality requirement: the trade restriction must be proportionate to the prudential regulation benefit. For this to be the case, it is necessary for the dispute resolution process to be active, and in effect, to play a legislative-type role.[41]

Trachtman acknowledges that it was at least difficult to foresee such role for the dispute settlement system of NAFTA. It is also worth noting that the situation envisaged by Trachtman is also not likely to materialise because of structural obstacles that are difficult to overcome. First and foremost, as explained earlier, at least in the case of investment arbitration panels, upon request of the Party whose measure is challenged in the dispute, the Tribunal must refer the matter to the Financial Services Committee. Article 1412 of NAFTA, which is the provision disciplining the composition and powers of the body, is not entirely clear. It seems that there is no fixed number with regard to the members of the Committee, and the provision only requires that the 'principal representative' of one Party is an official of the Party's authority that is responsible for financial services.[42] Moreover, the Agreement does not set out the rules of procedure of the committee, the voting system or its exact composition (nor even how many members the committee shall have).

---

[39] Joel P. Trachtman, 'Trade in Financial Services under GATS, NAFTA and the EC: A Regulatory Jurisdiction Analysis', *Columbia Journal of Transnational Law* (1996), 34:1, 37–122.
[40] Article 2101(2) of the NAFTA ('General Exceptions').
[41] Trachtman, 'Trade in Financial Services under GATS, NAFTA and the EC' (p. 90).
[42] Annex 1412.1 of the NAFTA clarifies which are the competent authorities for the three Parties: for Canada, the Department of Finance; for Mexico, the Secretaría de Hacienda y Crédito Público; for the United States of America, the Department of the Treasury for banking and other financial services and the Department of Commerce for insurance services.

Second, financial services are still considered to be sensitive, and only one arbitral Tribunal to date has dealt with the NAFTA PCO, and only in an *obiter dictum*.[43] The world has experienced financial crises and bank runs, but not exactly a rush to courts to put under judicial scrutiny the regulatory development that ensued in the domain of financial services worldwide.

Third, when an agreement distinguishes between rules to be applied to all cases and *lex specialis* that applies when it comes to idiosyncratic cases, concepts and requirements from other sources should be borrowed with caution. Therefore, there can be grounds to argue that the proportionality requirements set out in Article 2101(2) of NAFTA do not equate to a 'reasonableness' test as provided by the PCO.

What is the meaning of the word 'reasonable' in the NAFTA PCO? Contrary to National Treatment, for instance, according to which the standard of treatment for the foreign service supplier is determined on a relative basis (the treatment accorded to domestic like service suppliers), the reasonableness principle sets out an 'absolute' standard of treatment to be determined on the basis of what the provision specifically requires. However, because it is a standard and not a rule, it involves the exercise of discretion.

Continental European and American scholarships differ with regard to the identification of the principle of 'reasonableness'. For European lawyers, the issue of 'reasonableness' is traditionally connected to the 'proportionality test' developed in German administrative law and familiar to most continental European legal orders.

It is possible to distinguish between 'substantive' and 'procedural' requirements connected with the proportionality test.[44] With regard to the substantive dimension, German constitutional theory has identified three sets of tests, in order of intensity: the 'suitability test', the 'necessity test' and the 'proportionality test'.[45] Under the suitability test (which can be also described as a 'means/ends test') the question is whether the measure adopted by the government is an effective means to achieve the aim pursued by the administration. It is an absolute test, in which the measure under scrutiny is evaluated autonomously, without any inquiry regarding

---

[43] See the discussion on the Fireman's Insurance Fund dispute supra.
[44] Federico Ortino, 'From 'Non-Discrimination' to 'Reasonableness': A Paradigm Shift in International Economic Law?', *Jean Monnet Working Paper* (New York: New York University, 2005), 59 (p. 33).
[45] Jan H. Jans, 'Proportionality Revisited', *Legal Issues of Economic Integration*, 27:3 (2000), 239–65.

the strength of the correlation between the means and the end[46] or a comparison with other theoretically available measures. The second test is the necessity test, according to which the scope of the scrutiny is to evaluate whether other less intrusive and trade restrictive means are available.[47] Finally, the proportionality test requires an investigation into whether the costs imposed by the measure outweigh its benefits, thus representing the most stringent test in the sequence. All three tests are referred to in the literature as classifiable in the realm of the proportionality/reasonableness principle.

Which one applies to the NAFTA PCO? The test that most comfortably fits the case at hand is the first, because the provision does not place emphasis on the issue of the 'restrictions to trade' that usually appears in exception provisions in trade agreements (and in Article 2101 NAFTA). The *Fireman's Insurance Fund* award acknowledges that a measure can be at the same time discriminatory and reasonable and that, under the 'reasonableness' requirement, only measures that are manifestly not linked with a prudential objective and lead to the backhanded avoidance of obligations or commitments can be targeted.[48] Analyses with regard to the evaluation of costs and benefits are not appropriate, nor are evaluations of less restrictive means.

Those more familiar with US law, however, may link the reading of the 'reasonableness test' introduced in the PCO of NAFTA to the homonymous test developed under US administrative law, although the two contexts are clearly different. In 1984, the US Supreme Court issued a historic decision in *Chevron U.S.A., Inc. v. Natural Resources Defense Council, Inc.*[49] in which a new standard of review for the interpretation of statutes by agencies was established: the so-called Chevron doctrine.[50]

The Chevron doctrine consists of two phases. First, the courts applying it have to ask themselves whether a statute interpreted by the agency clearly addresses the situation of fact and law brought about before them.

---

[46] Ortino, 'From 'Non-Discrimination' to 'Reasonableness': A Paradigm Shift in International Economic Law?' (p. 34).

[47] The issue is developed in greater detail in the Chapter 5, with a focus on the evolution of the jurisprudence of the WTO on the subject.

[48] See the summary of the relevant passages of the award supra.

[49] US Supreme Court, *Chevron U.S.A., Inc. v. Natural Resources Defense Council, Inc.*, 467 U.S. 837 (1984).

[50] For two authoritative works on this topic see Antonin Scalia, 'Judicial Deference to Administrative Interpretations of Law',*Duke Law Journal*, 1989:3 (1989), 511–21 and Cass R. Sunstein, 'Law and Administration after "Chevron"', *Columbia Law Review*, 90:8 (1990), 2071–120.

If the answer to this first question is negative and the statute is silent or ambiguous, the court proceeds to the final stage of the analysis, which consists of evaluating whether the interpretation advanced by the agency was 'reasonable' or 'permissible'. The Chevron doctrine can be read as a power shift from courts to agencies. Courts are asked to be deferential towards the administration and to step in only if the interpretations advanced by agencies are patently unreasonable or lead the latter to exercise powers that go beyond their competences.

In other words, the *Chevron* doctrine is about minimising the extent of judicial activism. By the *Chevron* doctrine, it is assumed that, except for extreme cases, adjudicators should refrain from intervening because instances of proportionality (or reasonableness) had been taken care of by the regulator.

After all, it does not differ substantially from what is required under the final clause of the GATS PCO. However, the 'reasonableness test' under the NAFTA, probably also because it derives from the US legal tradition and hence there are solid references to it in the literature and in case law, seems to be better structured and easier to understand.[51]

4.2.2.2.6 Conclusions on NAFTA In the absence of specific conditions that Members must meet to be entitled to benefit from the PCO, notwithstanding the heading of the provision, it is difficult to consider the provision under analysis as being an 'exception'. Rather, it seems that the provision belongs to realm of 'provisions that exclude the application of other provisions' because the only real condition on Members is that measures adopted or maintained for prudential measures ought to be 'reasonable'.

4.2.2.3   US post-2004–like

The provision, as it first appeared in the US–Singapore FTA, reads:

> **Article 10.10 (Exceptions)**
>
> 1. Notwithstanding any other provision of this Chapter or Chapters 9 (Telecommunications), 14 (Electronic Commerce), or 15 (Investment), including specifically Article 9.15 (Relationship to Other Chapters), and in addition Article 8.2.2 (Scope and Coverage) with respect to the supply of financial services in the territory of a Party by an investor of the other Party or a covered investment, a Party shall not be prevented from

---

[51] For a discussion on the Chevron doctrine and the possibility of importing it to the realm of international trade, see Steven P. Croley and John H. Jackson, 'WTO Dispute Settlement Procedure, Standard of Review and Deference to National Governments', *The American Journal of International Law*, 90:2 (1996), 193–213.

4.2 PRUDENTIAL CARVE-OUTS IN PTAS

adopting or maintaining measures for prudential reasons[10-5] including for the protection of investors, depositors, policy holders or persons to whom a fiduciary duty is owed by a financial institution or cross-border financial service supplier, or to ensure the integrity and stability of the financial system. Where such measures do not conform with the provisions of this Agreement referred to in this paragraph, they shall not be used as a means of avoiding the Party's commitments or obligations under such provisions.

[10-5] It is understood that the term "prudential reasons" includes the maintenance of the safety, soundness, integrity or financial responsibility of individual financial institutions or cross-border financial service suppliers.

This third recurring category of PCOs was conventionally named 'US post-2004-like' because it first appeared in the trade agreements signed by the United States in 2004 and because it seems to be a recurring provision in all the Chapters on Financial Services in the FTAs concluded by the United States with their commercial partners ever since. This category of PCO appears in the following eighteen Agreements:

> US–Singapore, US–Chile, US–Australia, US–Morocco, Dominican Republic–Central America–United States Free Trade Agreement (CAFTA-DR), Panama–Singapore, US–Bahrain, Nicaragua–Chinese Taipei, US–Oman, US–Peru, Australia–Chile, Canada–Peru, Canada–Colombia, Korea–US, Panama–Peru, US–Colombia, US–Panama, Canada–Panama, Korea–Australia, Canada–Korea, Canada–Honduras.

First, one of the distinguishing features of this category is that it covers provisions of the Chapter on Financial Services as well as provisions in other Chapters disciplining trade in services (from telecommunications to e-commerce). In this respect, only the Panama–Peru FTA differs by expanding the coverage of the provision from a selected number of chapters to the whole agreement. With regard to the content of the PCOs, all the FTAs falling in this category refer to the traditional two categories of prudential reasons as they were codified in Paragraph 2(a) of the Annex on Financial Services of the GATS. All the previously mentioned Agreements (US–Colombia and US–Panama being the only exceptions) provide for a vague final clause identical in wording to that provided by the PCO in the GATS. Apart from these differentiations, the agreements falling in the category under analysis show an impressive record of consistency with a limited number of outliers. Considering the fact that this is the second largest category in the study, it is a remarkable result.

None of these agreements introduces more stringent requirements for the prudential clause to operate. It is fair to conclude that these PCOs perform the functions of 'provisions that exclude the application of other provisions' without substantial conditions to be met by Parties to the agreement that may want to benefit from them.

4.2.2.4 EFTA Third-Party-Like

The first example of this category of PCOs appeared in the FTA between EFTA and Mexico and reads:

Article 36 – Prudential Carve-Out

1. Nothing in this Section shall be construed to prevent a Party from adopting or maintaining reasonable measures for prudential reasons, such as:
   (a) the protection of investors, depositors, policy-holders, policy-claimants, persons to whom a fiduciary duty is owed by a financial service supplier, or any similar financial market participants; or
   (b) the maintenance of the safety, soundness, integrity or financial responsibility of financial service suppliers; or
   (c) ensuring the integrity and stability of a Party's financial system.
2. These measures shall not be more burdensome than necessary to achieve their aim, and shall not discriminate against financial service suppliers of another Party in comparison to its own like financial service suppliers.

The fourth family of PCOs owes its name to the fact that it is commonly present in the FTAs signed by the EFTA with third parties. In addition to the FTA between the EFTA and Mexico, similar provisions appear in the following FTAs:

EFTA–Singapore, EFTA–Korea, EFTA–Colombia, EFTA–Ukraine, Ukraine–Montenegro, EFTA–Central America (Costa Rica and Panama).

A characteristic feature is the requirement that measures adopted or maintained for prudential reasons be 'reasonable' and not more burdensome than necessary to achieve their prudential goal (the so-called necessity test). The degree of variation in this category is higher compared with the others identified in this study. In short, all of the agreements comprised in this family have some peculiarities.

a. EFTA–Mexico The PCO in EFTA–Mexico differentiates between three classes of prudential measures, as in NAFTA-like PCOs. Moreover, it requires that prudential measures do not discriminate between foreign financial services suppliers and like domestic ones (National Treatment of prudential measures).

b. EFTA-Singapore The PCO in this agreement again contains a classification of the indicative prudential measures in three categories. In addition, it contains identical wording to the chapeau of Article XIV of the GATS.

c. EFTA-Korea The PCO in EFTA-Korea deviates from the example provided at the beginning of the section because it contains wording similar to the final clause of the PCO in the Annex on Financial Services of the GATS.

d. EFTA-Colombia The PCO in the FTA between EFTA and Colombia requires Members not to discriminate between foreign financial services suppliers and like domestic services suppliers in the enactment or maintenance of prudential measures. Another distinctive feature can be found in Paragraph 3 of Article 6 ('Domestic Regulation') of the treaty, which makes direct reference to internationally agreed standards and reads as follows:

> 3. Each Party shall make its best endeavours to ensure that the Basel Committee's "Core Principles for Effective Banking Supervision", the standards and principles of the International Association of Insurance Supervisors and the International Organisation of Securities Commissions' "Objectives and Principles of Securities Regulation" are implemented and applied in its territory.

e. EFTA-Ukraine, Ukraine-Montenegro and EFTA-Central America (Panama and Costa Rica) These three PCOs are treated jointly because they are identical in all aspects. They are extremely relevant for the sake of the present work because they are the only provisions in the present study where all the various features identified at the beginning of the present chapter appear. Quoting from the PCO in EFTA-Ukraine:

> Article 5 – Domestic Regulation
>
> 1. Notwithstanding any other provisions of this Chapter, a Party shall not be prevented from adopting or maintaining reasonable measures for prudential reasons, including for:
>   (a) the protection of investors, depositors, policy-holders, policy-claimants, persons to whom a fiduciary duty is owed by a financial service supplier, or any similar financial market participants; or

(b) ensuring the integrity and stability of that Party's financial system.
Where such measures do not conform with the provisions of this Chapter, they shall not be used as a means of avoiding that Party's commitments or obligations under this Chapter.
2. Measures referred to in paragraph 1 shall not be more burdensome than necessary to achieve their aim or constitute a disguised restriction on trade in services, and shall not discriminate against financial services or financial service suppliers of another Party in comparison to the Party's own like financial services or like financial service suppliers.
3. Each Party shall make its best endeavours to ensure that the Basel Committee's "Core Principles for Effective Banking Supervision", the standards and principles of the International Association of Insurance Supervisors and the International Organisation of Securities Commissions' "Objectives and Principles of Securities Regulation" are implemented and applied in its territory.

As can be seen, the provision requires that prudential measures are reasonable, necessary and non-discriminatory. Moreover, there is a final clause identical to the one in the PCO of the Annex on Financial Services of the GATS as well as a sentence similar to the chapeau of Article XIV of the GATS ('General Exceptions'). Finally, the provision makes explicit reference to the standards set up by BCBS, IAIS and IOSCO.

In sum, given the presence of stringent requirements, the provisions in this category are classified as 'exceptions'.

4.2.2.5 EU 2014

On 27 June 2014, the European Union signed Association Agreements with Georgia, the Republic of Moldova and Ukraine. All three agreements provide for identical PCOs. The PCO in the Agreement between EU and Ukraine reads as follows:

Article 126 – Prudential Carve-Out

1. Each Party may adopt or maintain measures for prudential reasons, such as:
   (a) the protection of investors, depositors, policy-holders or persons to whom a fiduciary duty is owed by a financial service supplier;
   (b) ensuring the integrity and stability of a Party's financial system.
2. These measures shall not be more burdensome than necessary to achieve their aim, and shall not discriminate against financial service suppliers of the other Party in comparison to its own like financial service suppliers.
3. Nothing in this Agreement shall be construed to require a Party to disclose information relating to the affairs and accounts of individual

4.2 PRUDENTIAL CARVE-OUTS IN PTAS

consumers or any confidential or proprietary information in the possession of public entities.

4. Without prejudice to other means of prudential regulation of cross-border trade in financial services, a Party may require the registration of cross-border financial service suppliers of the other Party and of financial instruments.

These PCOs follow the traditional classification of the indicative list of prudential objectives in two subcategories, similar to that provided in the GATS PCO. They all require prudential measures to be non-discriminatory and no more burdensome than necessary to achieve their aim.

Another aspect of these three agreements is the way in which they address the standard of treatment for branches and representative offices of juridical persons of another Party. The relevant provision in the EU–Ukraine Agreement (identical in wording to those that appear in the agreements that the EU signed with Georgia and the Republic of Moldova) reads as follows:

> Article 91 – Standard of Treatment for Branches and Representative Offices
>
> 1. The provisions of Article 88 of this Agreement do not preclude the application by a Party of particular rules concerning the establishment and operation in its territory of branches and representative offices of legal persons of the other Party not incorporated in the territory of the first Party, which are justified by legal or technical differences between such branches and representative offices as compared to branches and representative offices of companies incorporated in its territory or, as regards financial services, for prudential reasons.
> 2. The difference in treatment shall not go beyond what is strictly necessary as a result of such legal or technical differences or, as regards financial services, for prudential reasons.

Prudential reasons, in this case, can justify a higher regulatory burden for foreign companies willing to establish a branch or a representative office in the host country, provided that the measures enacted or maintained are not more burdensome than necessary to achieve their aim. The presence of a necessity test and a National Treatment obligation permits to classify the provisions under this category as 'exceptions'.

4.2.2.6 Other

Not all PCOs analysed in the current study fall under the preceding categories. In fact, there are some genuine outliers. It is important to also take account of these because there are some remarkable deviations from the typical structures of PCOs presented in the previous sections.

4.2.2.6.1 EFTA   Article 31 of the EFTA reads as follows:

> **Article 31 – Financial Market Regulation**
>
> 1. In respect of financial services, this Chapter does not prejudice the right of the Member States to adopt measures necessary for prudential grounds in order to ensure the protection of investors, depositors, policy holders, or persons to whom a fiduciary duty is owed, or to ensure the integrity and stability of the financial system. These measures shall not discriminate against natural persons, companies or firms of the other Member States in comparison to its own natural persons, companies or firms.

This provision, the coverage of which is confined to other provisions dealing with trade in financial services, belongs to the category of exceptions. It requires prudential measures to be necessary and not to discriminate between foreign services suppliers and like domestic competitors. With regard to the structure of the provision, it includes the traditional bifurcation of examples of legitimate prudential goals originally set up in the GATS PCO. This PCO is classified as an 'exception' because of the presence of a necessity test, which calls for the adoption of measures that are the least trade restrictive available to the regulating Party.

4.2.2.6.2 Australia–New Zealand (ANZCERTA)   The PCO in the ANZCERTA agreement reads as follows:

> **Article 5 – National Treatment**
>
> 1. Each Member State shall accord to persons of the other Member State and services provided by them treatment no less favourable than that accorded in like circumstances to its persons and services provided by them.
> 2. Notwithstanding paragraph 1 of this Article, the treatment a Member State accords to persons of the other Member State may be different from the treatment the Member State accords to its persons, provided that:
>   (a) the difference in treatment is no greater than that necessary for prudential, fiduciary, health and safety or consumer protection reasons; and
>   (b) such different treatment is equivalent in effect to the treatment accorded by the Member State to its ordinary residents for such reasons.

3. The Member State proposing or according different treatment under paragraph 2 of this Article shall have the burden of establishing that such treatment is consistent with that paragraph.
4. No provision of this Article shall be construed as imposing obligations or conferring rights upon either Member State with respect to Government procurement or subsidies.

This PCO is, among the provisions that have been analysed in this work, the one with the strictest requirements for the invoking Member. This is probably due to the depth of the trade agreement to which it belongs. Market integration between Australia and New Zealand is historically deep given the geographic and cultural proximity between the two countries as well as their shared cultural roots. In addition, they have proven to be deeper than other FTAs in aspects in which trade agreements are not traditionally very strong such as free movement of professionals, for instance.[52] As such it comes as no surprise that they are also more advanced with regards to the way both jurisdictions deal with prudential policies.

First, the PCO is contained in the provision on National Treatment, and this in itself is a peculiarity. Second, prudential aims are listed among the reasons (together with fiduciary, health, safety and consumer protection aims) that can allow Members to deviate from the obligation to give the same treatment to domestic and like foreign service suppliers alike. However, deviations are necessary and are put in place to restore equivalence in treatment between residents and foreigners from the preferential counterpart. This alone reveals that the structure of the provision is rather that of an 'exception'. Further, the provision is the only one among those that were examined in this work in which the burden of proof regarding the satisfaction of the conditions in order to invoke the provision is explicitly allocated to the regulating Member. This implies a radically different approach to the majority of the PCOs analysed in the present study because, in this case, the provision aims to circumscribe to the highest possible extent the regulatory autonomy of the Members to the PTA to preserve their obligations and commitments.

4.2.2.6.3 East African Community
The relevant provision in the Agreement reads:

---

[52] See Julia Nielson, 'Labor Mobility in Regional Trade Agreements', in Aaditya Mattoo and Antonia Carzaniga (eds.), *Moving People to Deliver Services* (Washington, DC: World Bank and Oxford University Press, 2003), 93–110.

Article 25 – General Exceptions

1. The free movement of capital may be restricted upon justified reasons related to:
   (a) prudential supervision;
   (b) public policy considerations;
   (c) money laundering; and
   (d) financial sanctions agreed to by the Partner States.
2. Where a Partner State adopts a restriction under paragraph 1, the Partner State shall inform the Secretariat and the other Partner States and furnish proof that the action taken was appropriate, reasonable and justified.

The East African Community (EAC) is an intergovernmental agreement among Burundi, Kenya, Rwanda, the United Republic of Tanzania and the Republic of Uganda. Strictly speaking, the EAC Agreement does not contain a PCO but only a provision according to which Members can restrict the free movement of capital for, inter alia, policy reasons belonging to the realm of prudential supervision. The regulating Member has the duty to inform the Secretariat not only of the actions taken but also of the appropriateness and reasonableness of the latter together with an obligation to provide a justification in that regard. The provision was classified as 'exception' because it imposes stringent conditions as well as the burden of proof on the regulating party.

4.2.2.6.4 Singapore–Australia

The PCO in the FTA between Singapore and Australia has some peculiar aspects. It reads as follows:

Article 3 – Prudential and Regulatory Supervision

1. Nothing in this Agreement shall be construed to prevent a Party from taking measures for prudential reasons, including measures for the protection of investors, depositors, policy holders or persons to whom a fiduciary duty is owed by a financial service supplier, or to ensure the integrity and stability of a Party's financial system. Where such measures do not conform with the provisions of this Agreement, they shall not be used as a means of avoiding the Party's commitments or obligations under this Agreement.
2. These measures shall not constitute a means of arbitrary or unjustifiable discrimination against financial service suppliers of the other Party in comparison to its own like financial service suppliers, or a disguised restriction on trade in services. Each Party shall endeavour to ensure that these measures are not more burdensome than necessary to achieve their aim.

4.2 PRUDENTIAL CARVE-OUTS IN PTAS

> 3. Nothing in this Agreement shall be construed to require a Party to disclose information relating to the affairs and accounts of individual customers or any confidential or proprietary information in the possession of public entities.

The first part of the provision is similar to the PCO in the Annex on Financial Services of the GATS. The second paragraph, then, adds a requirement similar to the chapeau of the general exceptions in the GATT or the GATS. Moreover, the provision contains a hortatory requirement (*'Each party shall endeavor*[53] *to ensure...'*) not to enact measures more burdensome than what is necessary to achieve their prudential aim. This provision was classified as an 'exception'.

4.2.2.6.5 Japan–Mexico

> Article 110 – Exceptions
>
> Notwithstanding the provisions of this Chapter, Chapter 7 and Chapter 8, a Party shall not be prevented from adopting or maintaining measures for prudential reasons with respect to financial services, including for the protection of investors, depositors, policy holders, policy claimants or persons to whom a fiduciary duty is owed by a financial institution or a cross-border financial service supplier, or to ensure the soundness, integrity and stability of a Party's financial system.

The provision restricts the coverage to the Chapters on Investment, Cross-border Trade in Services and Financial Services. For the rest, it maintains the structure of the PCO in the Annex on Financial Services of the GATS with the notable exclusion of the ambiguous final clause, an account of which has been given earlier in this text. Given the absence of relevant requirements, this PCO was classified as a 'Provision that excludes the application of other provisions'.

4.2.2.6.6 EU–CARIFORUM States Economic Partnership Agreement

Article 104 of the EU–CARIFORUM States Economic Partnership Agreement (EPA) reads:

> Article 104 – Prudential Carve-Out
>
> 1. The EC Party and the Signatory CARIFORUM States may adopt or maintain measures for prudential reasons, such as:
>   (a) the protection of investors, depositors, policy-holders or persons to whom a fiduciary duty is owed by a financial service supplier;
>   (b) ensuring the integrity and stability of their financial system.

---

[53] The original text of the provision is in American English.

This provision does not clarify its coverage or provide conditions according to which prudential measures can be adopted. As for the indicative list of legitimate prudential objectives that a party can pursue, it repeats the traditional division of two categories that first appeared in the Annex on Financial Services of the GATS. This PCO was also classified as a 'provision that excludes the application of other provisions'.

4.2.2.6.7 ASEAN–Australia–New Zealand

Article 3 of the Annex on Financial Services of the FTA between ASEAN, Australia and New Zealand reads as follows:

Article 3 – Domestic Regulation

1. Notwithstanding any other provision of this Agreement, a Party shall not be prevented from taking measures for prudential reasons, including for the protection of investors, depositors, policy holders or persons to whom a fiduciary duty is owed by a financial service supplier, or to ensure the integrity and stability of the financial system or to ensure the stability of the exchange rate[7] subject to the following:
   (a) where such measures do not conform with the provisions of this Agreement, they shall not be used as a means of avoiding the Party's commitments or obligations under this Agreement;
   (b) for measures to ensure the stability of the exchange rate such measures shall be no more than necessary and phased out when conditions no longer justify their institution or maintenance; and
   (c) for measures to ensure the stability of the exchange rate such measures shall be applied on a most-favoured-nation basis.

----

[7] The measures to ensure the stability of the exchange rate shall not be adopted or maintained for the purpose of protecting a particular sector

The provision includes measures enacted to ensure the stability of the exchange rate in the indicative list of prudential objectives in the pursuance of which Members may deviate from their obligations or commitments under the agreement. However, with regard to this latter category of prudential objectives, the conditions for the lawful invocation of the PCO are stricter because those measures have to be necessary to achieve their aim. A procedural requirement, then, provides that they must be phased out when the change of conditions does not justify their permanence into force and they should be applied on a most-favoured-nation basis. Finally, footnote 7 adds that such measures cannot be adopted as a means of protecting a market sector. With regard to the other categories of prudential objectives, the only real condition for their invocation is a requirement similar in wording to the final clause of the GATS PCO. This PCO is a provision of a 'hybrid' nature as it works as a 'scope provision' for some measures, and as an 'exception' for others.

4.2.2.6.8 EU–Korea

Article 7.38 – Prudential Carve-Out[39]

1. Each Party may adopt or maintain measures for prudential reasons[40], including:
   (a) the protection of investors, depositors, policy-holders or persons to whom a fiduciary duty is owed by a financial service supplier; and
   (b) ensuring the integrity and stability of the Party's financial system.
2. These measures shall not be more burdensome than necessary to achieve their aim, and where they do not conform to the other provisions of this Agreement, they shall not be used as a means of avoiding each Party's commitments or obligations under such provisions.
3. Nothing in this Agreement shall be construed to require a Party to disclose information relating to the affairs and accounts of individual consumers or any confidential or proprietary information in the possession of public entities.
4. Without prejudice to other means of prudential regulation of cross-border trade in financial services, a Party may require the registration of cross-border financial service suppliers of the other Party and of financial instruments.

----

[39] Any measure which is applied to financial service suppliers established in a Party's territory that are not regulated and supervised by the financial supervisory authority of that Party would be deemed to be a prudential measure for the purposes of this Agreement. For greater certainty, any such measure shall be taken in line with this Article.

[40] It is understood that the term 'prudential reasons' may include the maintenance of the safety, soundness, integrity or financial responsibility of individual financial service suppliers.

The PCO in the FTA between the EU and Korea does not clarify its coverage at the beginning. The provision contains the traditional division of the indicative list of prudential measures and adds to the wording of the recurring last clause of the PCO of the Annex on Financial Services of the GATS a necessity test. In addition, the last paragraph of the provision allows a Party to the Agreement to require the registration of cross-border financial service suppliers of the other Party as well as financial instruments. That feature is peculiar to the PCO under examination. Although it cannot be considered odd because it is common practice across jurisdictions to require registration for all financial institutions, both domestic and foreign, for them to operate, this is the only case in which it appears in the context of the PCO.

The language in the footnotes of the provision is extremely interesting. Footnote 39 essentially establishes a 'presumption of prudence' for measures applied to services or service suppliers that are not regulated and supervised by the competent authorities of the territory of the other Member. It then adds that, 'for greater certainty', such measures shall be taken in line with the requirements of the provision but opens the door to a potentially unlimited power for the regulating countries.[54] This PCO was classified as an 'exception'.

4.2.2.6.9 EFTA–Hong Kong

Article 5 – Domestic Regulation

1. Notwithstanding any other provisions of Chapter 3 of the Agreement, a Party shall not be prevented from adopting or maintaining measures for prudential reasons, including for:
   (a) the protection of investors, depositors, policy-holders, policy-claimants, persons to whom a fiduciary duty is owed by a financial service supplier, or any similar financial market participants; or
   (b) ensuring the integrity and stability of that Party's financial system.
   Where such measures do not conform with the provisions of Chapter 3 of the Agreement, they shall not be used as a means of avoiding that Party's commitments or obligations under Chapter 3 of the Agreement.
2. Each Party shall make its best endeavours to ensure that the Basel Committee's "Core Principles for Effective Banking Supervision", the standards and principles of the International Association of Insurance Supervisors and the International Organisation of Securities Commissions' "Objectives and Principles of Securities Regulation" are implemented and applied in its Area.
3. Nothing in Chapter 3 of the Agreement shall be construed to require a Party to disclose information relating to the affairs and accounts of individual customers or any confidential or proprietary information in the possession of public entities.

The first part of the provision reflects the wording of the GATS PCO, whereas the second paragraph explicitly refers to standards issued by relevant standard-setting bodies and requires Members to make their best endeavours to implement them in their domestic jurisdictions. Given its

---

[54] Mitchell et al. consider the EU–Korea FTA 'unique' in this regard. See Andrew Mitchell et al., 'Dear Prudence' (p. 794).

characteristics, this PCO was classified as a 'provision that excludes the application of other provisions'.

4.2.2.6.10 Malaysia–Australia
The PCO in the Agreement between Malaysia and Australia reads:

> Article 5 – Prudential and Regulatory Supervision
>
> 1. Notwithstanding any other provisions of this Agreement, a Party shall not be prevented from taking measures for prudential reasons, including for the protection of investors, depositors, policy holders or persons to whom a fiduciary duty is owed by a financial service supplier or financial institution, or to ensure the integrity and stability of the financial system. Where such measures do not conform with the provisions of this Agreement, they shall not be used as a means of avoiding the Party's commitments or obligations under this Agreement.
> 2. These measures shall not constitute a means of arbitrary or unjustifiable discrimination against financial service suppliers or financial institutions of the other Party in comparison to its own like financial service suppliers or financial institutions, or a disguised restriction on trade in services.
> 3. Nothing in this Agreement shall be construed to require a Party to disclose information relating to the affairs and accounts of individual customers or any confidential or proprietary information in the possession of public entities.

This PCO adds to the traditional language of the GATS PCO a requirement similar in wording to the *chapeau* of Article XIV of the GATS. The presence of such requirement is the reason why this provisions is classified as an 'exception'.

4.2.2.6.11 EU–Colombia and Peru

> Article 154 – Prudential Carve-Out
>
> 1. Notwithstanding other provisions of this Title or Title V (Current Payments and Movements of Capital), a Party may adopt or maintain for prudential reasons, measures such as:
>   (a) the protection of investors, depositors, policy-holders or persons to whom a fiduciary duty is owed by a financial service supplier;
>   (b) ensuring the integrity and stability of its financial system.
> 2. Measures referred to in paragraph 1 shall not be more burdensome than necessary to achieve their aim, and shall not discriminate against financial services or financial service suppliers of another Party in comparison to its own like financial services or like financial service suppliers.

3. Nothing in this Agreement shall be construed to require a Party to disclose information relating to the affairs and accounts of individual customers or any confidential or proprietary information in the possession of public entities.
4. Without prejudice to other means of prudential regulation of the cross-border supply of financial services, a Party may require the registration or authorisation of cross-border suppliers of financial services of another Party and of financial instruments.

The PCO in the Agreement among the EU, Colombia and Peru is also sui generis. First of all, the coverage of the provision is limited to the chapters on trade in financial services and current payments and movements of capitals of the FTA. Moreover, the second paragraph of the provision adds a necessity test as well as a National Treatment requirement. This provision is classified as 'exception' for the sake of the current analysis.

4.2.2.6.12 Switzerland–China

Article 11 – Domestic Regulation

1. Notwithstanding any other provisions of this Chapter, a Party shall not be prevented from adopting or maintaining reasonable measures for prudential reasons, including for:
   (a) the protection of investors, depositors, policy-holders, policy-claimants, persons to whom a fiduciary duty is owed by a financial service supplier, or any similar financial market participants; or
   (b) ensuring the integrity and stability of that Party's financial system.

Where such measures do not conform with the provisions of this Chapter, they shall not be used as a means of avoiding that Party's commitments or obligations under this Chapter. Such measures shall not constitute a disguised restriction on trade in services and shall not discriminate against financial services or financial service suppliers of the other Party in comparison to the Party's own like financial services or like financial service suppliers.

The PCO in the Agreement between Switzerland and China builds on the pattern established by the Annex on Financial Services of the GATS. It deviates from the original template to the extent that the coverage of the provision is limited to the provisions of the Chapter on trade in financial services and adds a National Treatment requirement. Furthermore, it obliges Members not to enact prudential measures as a means of introducing disguised restrictions to trade. For these reasons, this provision is classified as an 'exception'.

4.2.2.6.13 Japan–Thailand

Article 109 – Prudential Measures and Measures to Ensure the Stability of the Macroeconomy or the Exchange Rate

1. Notwithstanding any other provisions of this Chapter, a Party shall not be prevented from taking:
   (a) measures for prudential reasons, including for the protection of investors, depositors, policy holders or persons to whom a fiduciary duty is owed by an enterprise supplying financial services, or to ensure the integrity and stability of the financial system; or
   (b) measures to ensure the stability of the macroeconomy or the exchange rate.
   Note: The measures referred to in subparagraph (b) above include measures relating to monetary policy or measures to deter speculative capital flows.[55] Such measures shall be no more than necessary to meet the objectives of ensuring the stability of the macroeconomy or the exchange rate. Measures to ensure the stability of the macroeconomy or the exchange rate do not cover measures relating to promotion or protection of a particular sector.
2. Where such measures do not conform with the provisions of this Chapter, they shall not be used as a means of avoiding the Party's commitments or obligations under this Chapter.

The PCO in the FTA between Japan and Thailand is sui generis. First of all, it narrows the coverage of the provision to the sole Chapter on Trade in Financial Services. Second, and most notably, it adds to the traditional indicative list of prudential reasons another legitimate policy goal according to which Parties are allowed to deviate from their obligations or commitments: the stability of the macroeconomy or the exchange rate. The note to the first paragraph requires measures adopted to pursue monetary policy or avoid speculative capital flows to be no more burdensome than necessary to achieve their goal of leading to the stability of the macroeconomy or the exchange rate. Then, more generally, the final sentence of the provision requires that all the measures be not put in place solely to promote a particular market sector. The final clause of the PCO under analysis is similar to that in the GATS PCO. This PCO contains different requirements with regard to the particular types of obligations that a

---

[55] It is important to note how vague this wording is. It is almost impossible to objectively draw a line between profit seeking and speculative capital flows. Most likely, the negotiating governments wanted to keep regulatory freedom to intervene in the event of 'runs' against national currencies.

146   CARVE-OUTS IN PREFERENTIAL TRADE AGREEMENTS

Member may deviate from in pursuance of prudential objectives. Therefore, it is classified as a provision of a 'hybrid' nature.

4.2.2.6.14 ASEAN–Korea

2. Prudential Measures, Exchange Rate and Financial Stability

(a) Notwithstanding any other provisions of this Agreement, a Party shall not be prevented from taking measures for prudential reasons, including for the protection of investors, depositors, policy holders or persons to whom a fiduciary duty is owed by a financial service supplier; to ensure the integrity and stability of the financial system; or to ensure the stability of the exchange rate[1], including to prevent speculative capital flows, subject to the following:
   (i) where such measures do not conform with the provisions of this Agreement, they shall not be used as a means of avoiding the Party's commitments or obligations under this Agreement;
   (ii) for measures to ensure the stability of the exchange rate including to prevent speculative capital flows, such measures shall be no more than necessary, and phased out within one year or when conditions no longer justify their institution or maintenance; and
   (iii) for measures to ensure the stability of the exchange rate including to prevent speculative capital flows, such measures shall be applied on a Most-Favoured-Nation basis.
(b) Nothing in this Agreement shall be construed to require a Party to disclose information relating to the affairs and accounts of individual customers or any confidential or proprietary information in the possession of public entities.

----

[1] The measures to ensure the stability of the exchange rate including to prevent speculative capital flows shall not be adopted or maintained for the purpose of protecting a particular sector.

The PCO in the Agreement between ASEAN and Korea also adds the objective of ensuring the stability of the exchange rate (including those measures aiming to prevent speculative capital flows) to the list of prudential goals typically contained in other PCOs. The provision adds extra requirements for measures adopted to ensure the stability of the exchange rate: they must be necessary to achieve their aim and phased out within one year after the conditions that justified their imposition elapse. Moreover measures adopted for the stability of the exchange rate have to be adopted on a MFN basis and must not be imposed with the sole purpose of protecting a particular market sector. Like the previous provision, this provision is 'hybrid' in nature.

4.2.2.6.15 Korea–Vietnam

2. Prudential Carve-Out[1], Exchange Rate and Financial Stability

(a) Notwithstanding any other provision of this Agreement, a Party shall not be prevented from taking measures for prudential reasons[2], including for the protection of investors, depositors, policy-holders or persons to whom a fiduciary duty is owed by a financial service supplier, to ensure the integrity and stability of the financial system, or to ensure stability of the exchange rate[3] including to prevent speculative capital flows, subject to the following:
  (i) where such measures do not conform with the provisions of this Agreement, they shall not be used as a means of avoiding that Party's commitments or obligations under this Agreement;
  (ii) for measures to ensure the stability of the exchange rate including to prevent speculative capital flows, such measures shall be no more than necessary, and shall be phased out within one year or when conditions no longer justify their institution or maintenance; and
  (iii) for measures to ensure the stability of the exchange rate including to prevent speculative capital flows, such measures shall be applied on a Most-Favored-Nation basis.
(b) Nothing in this Agreement shall be construed to require a Party to disclose information relating to the affairs and accounts of individual service consumers or any confidential or proprietary information in the possession of public entities.
(c) Without prejudice to other means of prudential regulation of cross-border trade in financial services, a Party may require the registration of cross-border financial service suppliers of the other Party and of financial instruments.

----

[1] Any measure which is applied to financial service suppliers established in a Party's territory that are not regulated and supervised by the financial supervisory authority of that Party would be deemed to be a prudential measure for the purposes of this Agreement. For greater certainty, any such measure shall be taken in line with this paragraph.

[2] It is understood that the term "prudential reasons" may include the maintenance of the safety, soundness, integrity, or financial responsibility of individual financial service suppliers.

[3] The measures to ensure the stability of the exchange rate including to prevent speculative capital flows shall not be adopted or maintained for the purposes of protecting a particular sector.

Although this provision is based on the text of the GATS PCO, it contains a number of distinctive features that make it different from the rest of the provisions examined in precedence. First of all, footnote 1 establishes a presumption of prudence for measures adopted with regard to financial services suppliers established in the territory of a Party to the Agreement but are not regulated or supervised by the authorities of that Party. Second, the provision specifies that measures aiming at maintaining the integrity of a single financial service supplier fall within the notion of 'prudential reasons' for the purpose of the application of the provision. Third, the measure includes the stability of the exchange rate and the prevention of speculative capital flows among the prudential reasons justifying a deviation from the other obligations of the agreement.

As regards the limits that both Parties face for the lawful invocation of the provision, the text establishes different tests, in accordance with the objective pursued. In general, regulating Members have to abide by a test that is written in an identical fashion to the vague final clause of the GATS PCO. Concerning measures aimed at ensuring the stability of the exchange rate, three restrictions apply: (i) they should not be more trade restrictive than necessary, (ii) they should not discriminate among the parties' like services and service suppliers and (iii) they should be phased out when the conditions for their maintenance are no longer valid.

For the same reasons as the previous two examined provisions, this PCO is classified as being of a 'hybrid' nature.

4.2.3 Conclusion on the Scope and Function of PCOs in FTAs

The analysis conducted thus led to the following results.

Scope of application: Twenty-five PCOs apply in derogation to any other provision of the agreement; thirty-three to the chapter, part or annex on financial services; twenty-seven to various but not all chapters, one to the obligations on free movement on capital, one to the discipline on National Treatment and six do not specify their ambit of application. Because the provision comes into play when the measure adopted 'affects' trade in financial services, the distinction as to the declared scope of application of the provisions is of limited explanatory value. However, the data are provided for the sake of completeness of the taxonomy that this study puts forward.

Content: The overwhelming majority of preferential PCOs (seventy-one) follow the traditional catalogue of examples of prudential reasons set out by the prototype contained in the GATS. In contrast, twenty PCOs are based on a list of three categories of reasons similar to the pattern provided by Article 1410 of NAFTA. Four PCOs deviate from the two most popular options: the PCO in the EAC PTA covers measures adopted in pursuance of 'justified reasons related to prudential supervision', the ANZCERTA PTA simply refers to 'prudential measures' and the PCOs in the ASEAN–Australia–New Zealand and Korea–Vietnam PTAs add measures enacted 'to ensure the stability of the exchange rate' to the traditional list.

Reasonableness: This requirement, according to which measures adopted to attain prudential goals have to be reasonable, appears in fourteen PCOs.

Necessity test: It is not common for PCOs to provide a necessity test. In fact, only nineteen do. Four PCOs submit the availability of the PCO to the respect of a necessity test only with regard to a specific category of prudential measures. The PCO in the ASEAN–Australia–New Zealand FTA introduces a necessity test for measures adopted to ensure the stability of the exchange rate. The same provision in the ASEAN–Korea and Korea–Vietnam PTAs requires that measures enacted for the stability of the exchange rate or the prevention of speculative capital flows are no more burdensome than necessary to achieve their aim. The PCO in the Japan–Thailand PTA introduces a necessity test for measures pursuing the stability of the macroeconomy and the exchange rate.

National Treatment: Thirteen of ninety-four PCOs require prudential measures not to discriminate between domestic services and service suppliers and like foreign services and service suppliers. This requirement is the strongest tool available to treaty drafters to ensure that PCOs are not used to afford protection to domestic services and service suppliers.

Chapeau language: A limited number of FTAs (eight) have introduced such language in the PCOs, whereas eighty-six of ninety-four have not introduced a similar wording.

GATS PCO final clause: The final clause of the GATS PCO is more popular than other requirements that constitute the subject of this analysis. Seventy PCOs contain a similar wording.

Standards: Only six of ninety-four PCOs make reference to standards. However, standards are not referred to as benchmarks for legality of prudential measures. In fact, all those PCOs contain a generic and hortatory call for Parties to make their best endeavours to implement internationally agreed standards in their jurisdictions. The standards typically referred to are those issued by BCBS, IAIS and IOSCO.[56]

Legal function: Based on the criteria set out above, preferential PCOs have been classified as 'exceptions' (if they include either a 'necessity test',

---

[56] For an overview on the composition and functioning of these standard-setting bodies, see Chapter 2.

or a 'National Treatment requirement' or language similar to that of the chapeau of Article XX of the GATT 1994), 'provisions that exclude the application of other provisions' (if parties invoking the PCO do not have to comply with substantial requirements to avail of it) or 'hybrid' if they present features of both categories applying to different sets of measures. Only seventeen PCOs can be classified as 'exceptions'. Four PCOs are of a hybrid nature and seventy-three (77.65 per cent of the total) instead can be considered as 'provisions that exclude the application of other provisions (or 'scope' provisions).

On the basis of this analysis, it is now possible to raise more delicate questions. The first is whether some categories of PCOs are more common after the 2007–8 financial crisis. To answer this, trends of the different categories of PCOs year after year are analysed, looking at the date in which the relevant PTAs have been signed. The date of the signature rather than the date of entry into force of the agreements is determinative because the former refers to the time in which negotiations were concluded, whereas the latter may take place at a later point in time. The three main results of this investigation are that the GATS-like category is still the most used worldwide, also at the preferential level, and that trend is constant. The second result is that there is an increasing number of PTAs that recur to tailor-made PCOs (the residual category 'Other') than before. Finally, all the PTAs on trade in financial services signed after the 2007–8 financial crisis contain a PCO.

Two caveats must be stated here. First, we are dealing with small numbers. There are not thousands of agreements, and as such it is complicated to identify trends (see Figure 4.4). Second, the number of PTAs signed has not been homogeneous through the years, and therefore any conclusion must be drawn with caution.

The second question is whether PCOs at the bilateral level tend to be stricter or more lenient than the example set up in the GATS PCO. This issue is a particularly complex one because a number of factors should be taken into account, including the existence of a mechanism for the resolution of disputes in each of the agreements considered as well as the structure of the agreements and the depth of the commitments on cross-border trade in financial services that the Parties to the agreements have exchanged.

With that caveat in mind, it is nevertheless possible to examine the data collected to provide a realistic approximation of whether WTO Members opt for more stringent rules at the bilateral level as compared to the case of the GATS PCO.

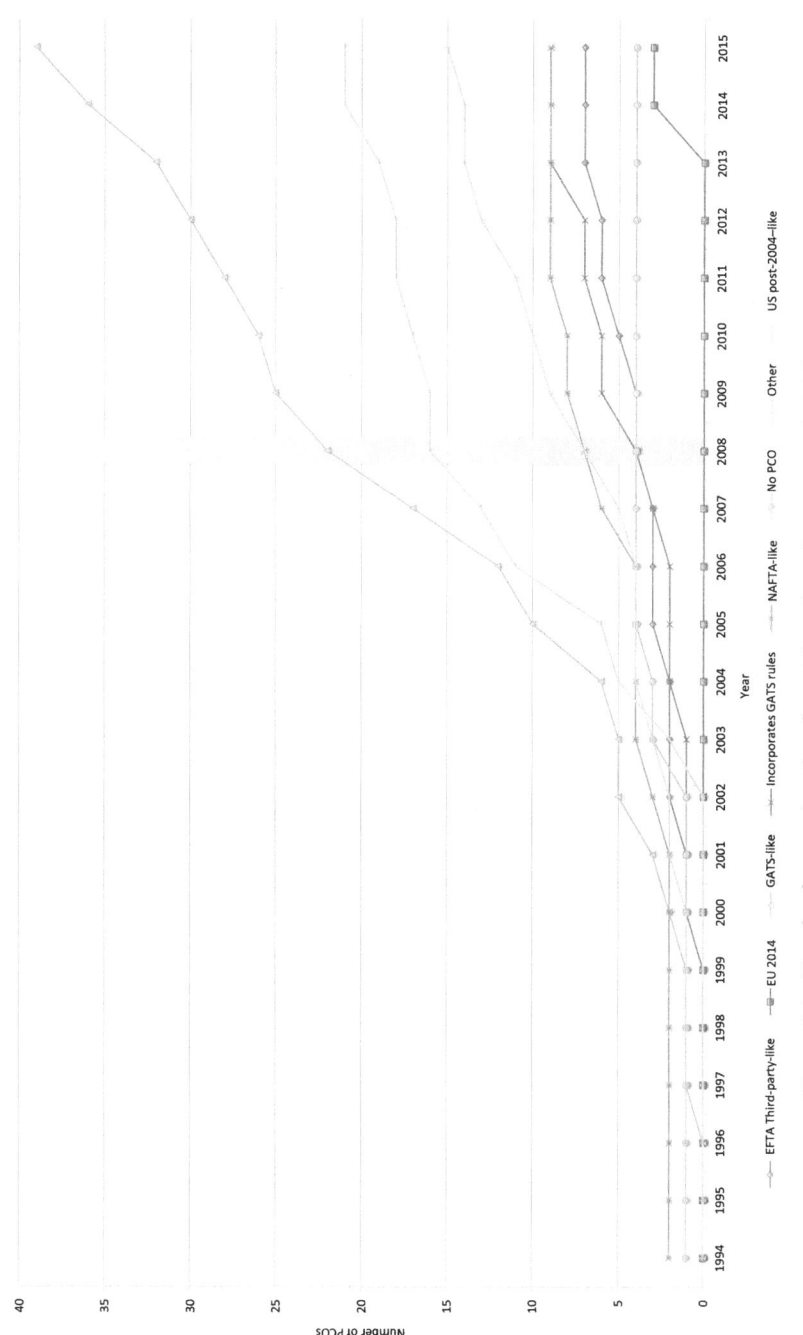

Figure 4.4 Trends of categories of preferential prudential carve-outs (PCOs) over time

A 'PCO restrictiveness index' is constructed to present the data collected in the most coherent fashion possible. Six requirements have been identified: reasonableness, the necessity test, National Treatment, the Chapeau of Article XX GATT' language, the GATS PCO final clause and reference to international standards. Each requirement was assigned a value of 1 or 0 depending on whether it features in the PCO under analysis. The decision was taken not to assign different values to different features in order not to arbitrarily set a hierarchy of restrictiveness among the various requirements. The average of these data was then calculated to assign each PCO a value in a range from 0 to 1 (on a scale from 0 to 1, each requirement is given a value of approximately 0.17, rounded to the closest decimal point):

No requirements: 0.00
One requirement: 0.17
Two requirements: 0.33
Three requirements: 0.50
Four requirements: 0.67
Five requirements: 0.83
Six requirements: 1.00

Keeping in mind that, according to this scale, the PCO of the GATS would have a restrictiveness index of 0.17, the numbers show that the majority of PCOs at the bilateral level have the same value. Summing up those PCOs with a restrictiveness index of 0 to those with an index of 0.17, Table 4.1 shows that 72.33 per cent of all bilateral PCOs have either one

Table 4.1 *Prudential carve-out (PCO) restrictiveness index*

PCO restrictiveness index	Frequency	%
0.00	11	11.7
0.17	57	60.63
0.33	16	17.02
0.50	5	5.31
0.67	2	2.12
0.83	0	0
1.00	3	3.19

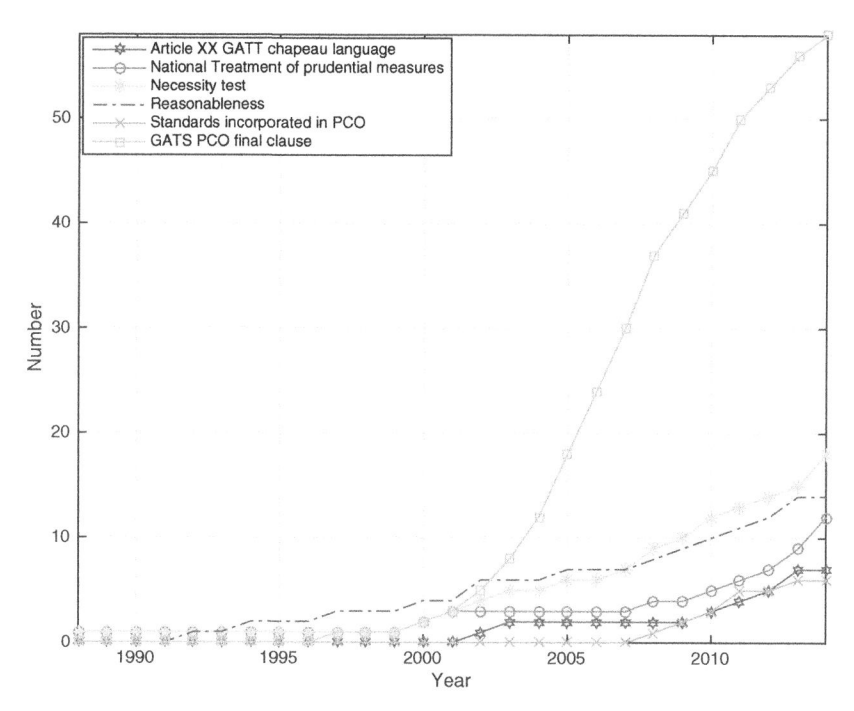

Figure 4.5 Frequency of requirements in preferential prudential carve-outs (PCOs)

or no requirement to be satisfied for the prudential defence to be lawfully invoked by a government.

Each of these requirements was then analysed to identify possible trends over time. In other words, this study verifies how often these requirements have appeared in bilateral PCOs since the late 1990s. The figures are broken down by year and cumulated to establish trends (Figure 4.5).

All trends appear to be relatively homogeneous with the remarkable exception of the final clause of the PCO in the GATS, which appears in seventy PCOs.

The main aim of this analysis was to keep track of the evolution of the formulation of PCOs in PTAs in order to understand what lessons could be learned at the multilateral level. In particular, the most delicate issue with regard to the examination of the defences for prudential measures in trade agreements is that pertaining to the legal function that they perform. The argument is crucial because the classification of a provision, in one way or another, has an impact on the allocation of the burden of proof in the event of a dispute as well as the deference that adjudicators are required to pay to domestic regulators. There is a net prevalence of PCOs (seventy of ninety-four) performing the function of 'scope provisions' or – more appropriately – 'provisions that exclude the application of other provisions'. This means that there is a general tendency in trade agreements to consider financial regulation to be the reserved domain of States and prudential concerns to be of overriding importance when confronted with trade liberalisation obligations. Only a minority of PCOs are drafted in a way that makes them work as exceptions, due to the introduction of stricter requirements that parties have to respect to make use of the prudential defence.

Three requirements are considered for the purposes of this study as being indicators of a different legal function for the PCO: the necessity test, National Treatment and the introduction of a test similar to the chapeau of Article XX of the GATT 1994 and Article XIV of the GATS. Only seventeen PCOs contain at least one of such requirements.

The way these provisions are drafted, in any event, shows that trading nations have the legal arsenal to address the issue differently if they wish to do so. The fact that the overwhelming majority of the PCOs are drafted in a peculiar way, in contrast to traditional exception-type provisions in trade agreements, is perhaps an indication that the PCO in the Annex on Financial Services of the GATS is not accidentally ambiguous, but is deliberately drafted in that manner for fear that governments would not be able to control the spreading of financial turmoil any longer or that stricter rules would lead to regulatory chill and put them in a situation of inability to intervene in the presence of turbulence in financial markets (or in anticipation thereof).

4.3 Ongoing Negotiations

After two decades since the entry into force of the Annex on Financial Services of the GATS and given the experience acquired by all WTO Members in the negotiation of PTAs (and the evolution of trade rules that took place at the preferential level, an account of which was given in the previous section), it is important to understand how prudential concerns are addressed at a time of dramatic changes for the international trade landscape.

The current situation differs previous negotiations of trade agreements. Ongoing negotiations, in fact, are taking place in the aftermath of what was

4.3 ONGOING NEGOTIATIONS

probably the most severe financial crisis in the history of modern world. In particular, the interconnectedness of financial systems worldwide made it easier for the crisis to find transmission channels and to spread its consequences to various jurisdictions. Some commentators have spoken out against trade agreements for allegedly forcing States to water down their rules on financial markets. In this respect, it is interesting to recall a passage from the conclusions of the Stiglitz Commission Report:

> [T]hreats have been exacerbated by financial market integration. Countries that have fully opened their capital accounts, have engaged in financial market liberalization, and have relied on private finance from international capital markets are among those likely to be most adversely affected. Many countries have come to rely on foreign banks, some from countries that were poorly regulated and followed inappropriate macroeconomic policies and that now find their capital badly impaired. These institutions are now repatriating capital, with adverse effects on developing countries. The difficulty is compounded by the fact that many developing countries have entered into free trade agreements (FTAs), bilateral investment treaties (BITs) and World Trade Organization commitments that enshrine the policies of market fundamentalism noted above and further limit their ability to regulate financial institutions and instruments, manage capital flows, or protect themselves from the effects of financial market protectionism.[57]

The following subsections provide an account of PCO negotiations in the following PTAs: a preferential agreement on trade in services between twenty-three like-minded Members of the WTO with the aim of advancing the liberalisation agenda of the GATS (the Trade in Services Agreement, TiSA); a 'mega-regional' agreement (the Trans-Atlantic Trade and Investment Partnership [TTIP] between the EU and the United States); and the EU–Canada Comprehensive Economic and Trade Agreement (CETA).

These negotiations are likely to affect a larger number of consumers across the world and come at a time where some lessons on trade rules can be considered to be learnt, therefore it is interesting to understand how the issue of the interplay between prudential regulation and financial services trade liberalisation is being dealt with.

---

[57] Report of the Commission of Experts of the President of the United Nations General Assembly, 'Reforms of the International Monetary and Financial System' (commonly known as the 'Stiglitz Commission's Report'), 21 September 2009, para. 51, available at www.un.org/ga/econcrisissummit/docs/FinalReport_CoE.pdf.

4.3.1 The Negotiations of the PCO in the TiSA

The negotiations for a preferential agreement on trade in services were launched in 2013. Talks are taking place among twenty-three Members of the WTO with the EU counting as one (the so-called Really Good Friends of Services [RGFS]).[58] The aim is to further liberalise cross-border trade in services among WTO Members that are willing to do so, while leaving the door open for others to join in at a later stage.

In strict legal terms, this agreement could qualify as a PTA according to the principles set out in Article V of the GATS. However, the intention of the parties is more ambitious. Some of the RGFS, in fact, want to negotiate a 'plurilateral' agreement, which is in principle compatible with the structure of the GATS with the aim of leaving the door open for latecomers to eventually join.[59]

Plurilateral agreements are covered under Annex 4 of the WTO Agreement.[60] Article II.3 of the WTO Agreement clarifies that they only create obligations for those Members that have accepted them and not for those who decided to remain outside. Article X.9 of the WTO Agreement requires Members to agree by consensus in case they want to add another agreement to the list. For a plurilateral agreement to be valid and recognised under WTO law, therefore, all WTO Members, including those that are not parties to it, have to agree. This requirement will probably not be met easily because there have already been some resistance regarding new parties seeking admission to the negotiating table.[61]

---

[58] Australia, Canada, Chile, Chinese Taipei (Taiwan), Colombia, Costa Rica, the European Union, Hong Kong, Iceland, Israel, Japan, Liechtenstein, Mauritius, Mexico, New Zealand, Norway, Pakistan, Panama, Peru, Republic of Korea, Switzerland, Turkey and the United States.

[59] On the different hypotheses taken into considerations before the launch of the negotiations, see Gary Clyde Hufbauer, J. Bradford Jensen and Sherry Stephenson, 'Framework for the International Services Agreement', *Peterson Institute for International Economics – Policy Brief* (2012), 1–45.

[60] To date, these agreements are the Agreement on Civil Aircraft (CA) and the Agreement on Government Procurement (GPA). The WTO General Council, by consensus, decided to eliminate the International Dairy Agreement (IDA; see WTO Docs. IDA/8 of 30 September 1997, and WT/L/252 of 27 December 1997) and the International Bovine Meat Agreement (IBM; see WTO Docs. IMA/8 of 30 September 1997 and WT/L/252 of 17 December 1997) from the list.

[61] See the press release issued by the European Commission reporting the intention by the former EU Commissioner for Trade earlier in 2014 in support of the Chinese application to join the negotiations. The communiqué acknowledges that '[t]he debate over China's participation has been difficult, however, due to concerns expressed by some TiSA

4.3 ONGOING NEGOTIATIONS

It would be difficult to imagine that a WTO Member excluded from the negotiations of a plurilateral agreement would not oppose the same agreement's enlistment under Annex 4 of the WTO Agreement. Moreover, there are institutional problems that deserve careful attention.[62]

Negotiations have been put on hold at the end of 2016, and it is not clear whether and when they will resume. The RGFS met in Geneva, outside the WTO, for twenty-one rounds of negotiations. Despite the fact that negotiations were not open to the public, some information have circulated with regard to the structure of the Agreement and parts of its content. A future TiSA – should it be concluded and duly ratified – would adopt a 'negative list' approach with regard to National Treatment commitments,[63] whereas it would keep the GATS structure with regard to Market Access.[64] This in itself would not represent a problem in the context of an Article V of the GATS PTA. Questions would arise with regard to the compatibility with the existing structure of the GATS, should RGFS manage to find a way into the WTO for the agreement.

With regard to specific disciplines on sectoral negotiations, little information is available at this stage.[65] However, in the summer of 2014, WikiLeaks leaked the draft text of the Chapter on Financial Services of the TiSA.[66] The Chapter adopts a hybrid approach along the lines of what was anticipated before with regard to Market Access and National Treatment

---

participants'. The document is available at http://europa.eu/rapid/press-release_IP-14-352_en.htm.

[62] For a detailed analysis of the pros and cons connected to the choice of the 'plurilateral track', see Bernard M. Hoekman and P. C. Mavroidis, 'Embracing Diversity: Plurilateral Agreements and Trade in Services', *World Trade Review*, 14:1 (2015), 101–16.

[63] That is, Members have to specifically list those subsectors and modes of supply in which they are not willing to make commitments according to which they will treat foreign services and service suppliers in a non-discriminatory way compared with national like services and service suppliers.

[64] Pierre Sauvé, 'A Plurilateral Agenda for Services? Assessing the Case for a Trade in Services Agreement (TISA)', *NCCR Trade Regulation Working Paper* (2013) (p. 11).

[65] Commentators have stressed the problems connected with this lack of transparency, and some criticisms were expressed with regard to the fact that the negotiating partners agreed not to declassify the text of the agreement until five years after the entry into force of the agreement or after the closure of the negotiations. See, in particular, Jane Kelsey, 'Memorandum on Leaked TISA Financial Text' (https://wikileaks.org/tisa-financial/Analysis-of-secret-tisa-financial-annex.pdf, 2014, MIMEO, 1–17.

[66] See https://wikileaks.org/tisa-financial.

requirements. It also adds a stand-still clause according to which parties to the TiSA agree to lock in the current levels of liberalisation.[67]

Article X.17 of the Chapter on Financial Services of the TiSA, as leaked in 2014, reads:

> **Article X.17: Prudential Measures**
>
> 1. Notwithstanding any other provision of the Agreement, a Party shall not be prevented from [**PA, EU:** taking] [**US:** adopting or maintaining] measures for prudential reasons, including for:
>   (a) the protection of investors, depositors, [**PA, US** financial market users], policy-holders or persons to whom a fiduciary duty is owed by a financial service supplier; or
>   (b) to ensure the integrity and stability of a Party's financial system.
> 2. Where such measures do not conform with the provisions of this Agreement, they shall not be used as a means of avoiding the Party's commitments or obligations under the Agreement.

The current text of the PCO in TiSA clearly draws inspiration from the GATS PCO and carries with it all the connected interpretative problems that were raised in the previous chapter.[68] Alongside the 'stability' of the financial system, it adds the objective of ensuring its 'integrity'. However, the two concepts are so intertwined that the distinction does not seem to be meaningful. As a final note on the draft text of the PCO of the TiSA, it must be recalled that the circulated document represents the current state of the art of the negotiations on the topic at the time of the leak and that it is not sure yet that – assuming the treaty will see the light of the day – this will be the definitive formulation of the provision.

4.3.2 The Negotiations of the PCO in the TTIP

Trade rules are also evolving at a bilateral level. In particular, the negotiations of an agreement between the EU and the United States, in light of the importance of the two players in the world market for financial services, cannot be overlooked in the context of the present overview.

---

[67] Trade in Services Agreement (TiSA) Financial Services Annex, WikiLeaks release: 19 June 2014 (https://wikileaks.org/tisa-financial/WikiLeaks-secret-tisa-financial-annex.pdf).

[68] Kelsey, in a memorandum published on the WikiLeaks website together with the draft text of the Chapter on Financial Services, warns against such formulation. In her words: 'The TISA negotiations were an opportunity to revise this exception and provide a meaningful protection for the right of governments to regulate for precautionary and remedial reasons. Instead, TISA extends countries' exposure to the rules and then repeats the same impossibly circular language.' Kelsey, 'Memorandum on Leaked TISA Financial Text' (p. 12).

4.3 ONGOING NEGOTIATIONS

The talks for the negotiation of a comprehensive PTA between the EU and the United States were launched in July 2013. At the time of writing, it is not clear whether the negotiations will reach a successful conclusion. With regard to financial services, in particular, the situation is even more complicated.

As explained in Chapter 2 of this volume, reforms in financial market regulations in the main domestic jurisdictions were coordinated at the international level by means of recommendations or standards. The bodies that issued those documents such as the G-20 or the BCBS cannot be considered full-fledged international organisations and, most of all, their recommendations are not legally binding, despite the fact they are actually implemented at the domestic level. Furthermore, given that such requirements are usually written in terms of 'minimum standards' or 'obligations of result', implementation at the domestic level has not usually led to the same results in the EU and the United States, where different approaches were followed.[69] Therefore many voices, particularly in the private sector, have pointed to the opportunity to address the regulatory divergence between the two shores of the Atlantic through means of regulatory cooperation or mutual recognition.[70]

Positions with regard to the inclusion of financial services in the TTIP have been different between the two Parties. On one hand, the representatives of the United States have repeatedly insisted that they would not allow trade agreements to limit the ability of the administration to regulate financial markets. On the other hand, the EU, as it always does in its negotiations with preferential trading partners, insisted on having an agreement as comprehensive as possible and on tackling barriers that limit the access to the US market for European financial institutions.[71]

Negotiations are not yet concluded, and the documents of the negotiations are not all publicly available. Because of the change in the US administration, negotiations have been put on hold, waiting for the publication of the new negotiating strategy of the current administration. Although a substantial deal on financial services seems to be unlikely, talks took place

---

[69] For an explanation of the different approaches adopted by the EU and the United States in the aftermath of the crisis, see Chapter 2.

[70] See, for instance, Klaus Deutsch, 'Transatlantic Consistency? Financial Regulation, the G20 and the TTIP', *Deutsche Bank Research – EU Monitor, Global Financial Markets* (2014), 27 (p. 20).

[71] For an overview of the initial positions, see Simon Johnson and Jeffrey J. Schott, 'Financial Services in the Transatlantic Trade and Investment Partnership', *Peterson Institute for International Economics – Policy Brief* (2013), 1–11.

between the two delegations with regard to the introduction of measures addressing the issue of regulatory cooperation between the jurisdictions.[72]

In particular, the EU pushed for the establishment of a framework for regulatory cooperation according to the following principles:

- Joint work to ensure timely and consistent implementation of internationally agreed standards for regulation and supervision.
- Mutual consultations in advance of any new financial measures that may significantly affect the provision of financial services between the EU and the US and to avoid introducing rules unduly affecting the jurisdiction of the other party.[2]
- Joint examination of the existing rules to examine whether they create unnecessary barriers to trade.
- A commitment to assessing whether the other jurisdiction's rules are equivalent in outcomes.[73]

------

[2] Unless there are overriding prudential reasons.

Although financial services are not, at the time of the submission of the present work, on the negotiating agenda, talks on the general chapter on trade in services did take place and, and at the start of 2014, a German newspaper leaked the text of the provisional chapter on trade in services.[74] It contains a PCO that reads as follows:

Article 52 Prudential Carve-Out

1. Each Party may adopt or maintain measures for prudential reasons, such as:
   (a) the protection of investors, depositors, policy-holders or persons to whom a fiduciary duty is owed by a financial service supplier;
   (b) ensuring the integrity and stability of a Party's financial system.
2. These measures shall not be more burdensome than necessary to achieve their aim.
3. Nothing in this Agreement shall be construed to require a Party to disclose information relating to the affairs and accounts of individual consumers or any confidential or proprietary information in the possession of public entities.

---

[72] Corporate Europe Observatory, a non-governmental organisation, has published the leak of the EU proposal on 'Regulatory Cooperation on Financial Services in TTIP'. The text is available at http://corporateeurope.org/sites/default/files/attachments/regulatory_coop_fs_-_ec_prop_march_2014-2_0.pdf.
[73] European Commission, EU–US Transatlantic Trade and Investment Partnership (TTIP) – Cooperation on Financial Services Regulation, available at http://trade.ec.europa.eu/doclib/docs/2014/january/tradoc_152101.pdf.
[74] The German newspaper *Die Zeit* leaked the Chapter on Trade in Services on 27 February 2014. The text is available at www.bilaterals.org/?eu-us-fta-ttip-eu-draft-proposal&lang=en.

The provision clearly follows the pattern set out in the Annex on Financial Services of the GATS. The only relevant difference in the structure of the carve-out is the introduction of a necessity test. This variation would make the proposed text of the TTIP PCO (assuming this will be the final text) look like an exception-type provision, contrary to the majority of PCOs that have been examined in the present volume.

4.3.3 The Negotiations of the PCO in the EU–Canada Comprehensive Economic and Trade Agreement

In 2014, Canada and the EU concluded the negotiations of the CETA. The Agreement entered into force provisionally on 21 September 2017 and will only enter into force completely once all EU Member States have completed their respective ratification processes.[75] It is an interesting agreement, for various reasons. For instance, Canada is considered, among commentators, as the developed country whose financial system was hit less severely by the financial turmoil than the United States and the EU experienced.[76]

The agreement presents some important innovations with regard to the discipline on trade in services and, more specifically, on financial services. The rules on services adopt a 'negative-listing approach', that is that National Treatment, Market Access and Most Favoured Nation obligations apply to all services except those specifically indicated by the Parties. Moreover, Canada and the EU have committed to full transparency with regard to non-conforming measures in the financial services sector. The latter will be listed in the parties' schedules to be easily identified.[77]

The CETA contains important elements for the current analysis also regarding the institutional dimension. The Agreement introduces a

---

[75] Information as regards the process are available at http://ec.europa.eu/trade/policy/in-focus/ceta/.

[76] Bordo et al. claim that Canada was better prepared to face the outbreak of the 2007 and 2008 financial crisis for reasons that have mainly to do with the structure of its financial system. In fact, the composition of the Canadian financial market, so their argument goes, can be described as an 'oligopoly', with large banks involved more in traditional and less risky activities than, for example, their equivalent in the United States. See Michael D. Bordo, Angela Redish and Hugh Rockoff, 'Why Didn't Canada Have a Banking Crisis in 2008 (or in 1930, or in 1907, Or...)?', NBER Working Paper Series (2011), 1–40, available at www.nber.org/papers/w17312.pdf.

[77] Lang and Conyers stress that, on the Canadian side, both federal and local non-conforming measures will be listed. Andrew Lang and Caitlin Conyers, 'Financial Services in EU Trade Agreements', *Study for the ECON Committee of the European Parliament* (2014), 1–47 (p. 16).

Financial Services Committee, whose composition and functions are set out in Article 18 of the Chapter on Financial Services. The Committee, which will decide by consensus, will be composed of representatives of domestic authorities that are in charge of financial services. The Article clarifies that, in the case of Canada, the delegate to the Committee shall be an official from Finance Canada. There is no corresponding classification for the EU, but anecdotal evidence suggests that this was because, at the time of the conclusion of the agreement, the European Commission was undergoing reorganisation with different allocation of staff and competences and with the creation of new directorate-generals. In any event, no additional information was added at the end of the legal review process. This element is relevant because it proves, once again, that the division of competences and tasks between trade departments and finance departments in this area is always a delicate matter and that the latter are typically not willing to give up their regulatory prerogatives. The Committee will meet annually and be in charge of the supervision of the implementation of the Chapter.

The CETA is relevant for the current analysis as it introduces three innovative elements compared with other agreements: (i) the PCO deviates from the main categories identified in the study; (ii) the Agreement provides for a filter mechanism in investor–state disputes concerning prudential measures, similar to what is provided for by NAFTA; and (iii) there is an Annex providing guidance on the application of the PCO.

4.3.3.1 The PCO in CETA

The PCO in the Agreement between Canada and the EU reads:

Article 13.16: Prudential Carve-Out

1. This Agreement does not prevent a Party from adopting or maintaining reasonable measures for prudential reasons, including:
   (a) the protection of investors, depositors, policy-holders, or persons to whom a financial institution, cross-border financial service supplier, or financial service supplier owes a fiduciary duty;
   (b) the maintenance of the safety, soundness, integrity, or financial responsibility of a financial institution, cross-border financial service supplier, or financial service supplier; or
   (c) ensuring the integrity and stability of a Party's financial system.
2. Without prejudice to other means of prudential regulation of cross-border trade in financial services, a Party may require the registration of cross-border financial service suppliers of the other Party and of financial instruments.

4.3 ONGOING NEGOTIATIONS

> 3. Subject to Articles 13.3 [National Treatment] and 13.4 [Most-favoured nation], a Party may, for prudential reasons, prohibit a particular financial service or activity. Such a prohibition shall not apply to all financial services or to a complete financial services sub-sector, such as banking.

The provision is peculiar for many reasons. First and foremost, its formulation turns the logical premises of the text of the GATS PCO. Rather than carving out the scope of application of the provision by clarifying that 'notwithstanding any other obligation' under the Agreement Members can still pursue prudential objectives, it is framed as a bold and clear reaffirmation of the Members' rights to regulate, which is in no way compressed by the Agreement, in and of itself.

The structure of the provision appears similar to the PCO in NAFTA at first sight. Paragraph 1 of the PCO in CETA reflects the formulation of Article 1410 of NAFTA, including the 'reasonableness' requirement that was discussed earlier. The provision then adds the possibility for a Party to require the registration of financial instruments and financial service suppliers of the other one. Finally, the PCO authorises Parties to prohibit a particular financial service or activity for prudential purposes. However, such prohibition cannot apply to all financial services or to an entire sub-sector (as an example, the provision makes reference to the 'banking' sub-sector). This is, in all aspects, an important evolution of trade law in the domain of prudential policy. In particular, it is a powerful tool to address the distortions that the boom of new financial instruments may cause, as regulators are often unprepared to the technological shocks and are usually in the position of chasing new financial instruments to exercise their regulatory powers. The possibility to intervene in the presence of new and not properly understood financial instruments is not uncontested across all jurisdictions, and as such, this innovation is substantial in nature.[78]

The provision seems to belong to the realm of 'provisions that exclude the application of other provisions' rather than to that of exceptions. No particular conditions, apart from a not better qualified 'reasonableness requirement' along the lines of the wording of the PCO in NAFTA, must be respected by Parties when they deviate from their obligations in pursuance of prudential goals.

---

[78] Sometimes not even the operators in financial markets are aware of the instruments they are working with. The story of the boom of high-frequency trading is particularly telling of how regulators struggle to catch up with financial innovation. A good account of the story is provided by Michael Lewis, *Flashboys – Cracking the Money Code* (London: Allen Lane, 2014), 274.

4.3.3.2 The Filter Mechanism in Investment Disputes on Financial Services

Article 13.21 ('Investment Disputes in Financial Services') of the Chapter on Financial Services of the CETA provides for a peculiar discipline with regard to the invocation of the prudential shelter in investment disputes. The issue is not new to the domain of trade agreements as NAFTA also provides for a similar filter mechanism.

The provision sets out a special discipline.[79] Essentially, the most important elements are the following: (a) unless the parties agree otherwise, when Article 13.16 is invoked, the tribunal shall be constituted from the list provided for under the provision that requires that financial

---

[79] Article 13.21: Investment Disputes in Financial Services:

1. Section F of Chapter Eight (Resolution of investment disputes between investors and states) applies, as modified by this Article and Annex 13-B, to: (a) investment disputes pertaining to measures to which this Chapter applies and in which an investor claims that a Party has breached Article 8.10 (Treatment of investors and of covered investments), 8.11 (Compensation for losses), 8.12 (Expropriation), 8.13 (Transfers), 8.16 (Denial of benefits), 13.3, or 13.4; or (b) investment disputes commenced pursuant to Section F of Chapter Eight (Resolution of investment disputes between investors and states) in which Article 13.16.1 has been invoked.
2. In the case of an investment dispute under subparagraph 1(a), or if the respondent invokes Article 13.16.1 within 60 days of the submission of a claim to the Tribunal under Article 8.23 (Submission of a claim to the Tribunal), a division of the Tribunal shall be composed, in accordance with Article 8.27.7 (Constitution of the Tribunal) from the list established under Article 13.20.3. If the respondent invokes Article 13.16.1 within 60 days of the submission of a claim, with respect to an investment dispute other than under subparagraph 1(a), the period of time applicable to the composition of a division of the Tribunal under Article 8.27.7 (Constitution of the Tribunal) commences on the date the respondent invokes Article 13.16.1. If the CETA Joint Committee has not made the appointments pursuant to Article 8.27.2 (Constitution of the Tribunal) within the period of time provided in Article 8.27.17 (Constitution of the Tribunal), either disputing party may request that the Secretary-General of the International Centre for Settlement of Investment Disputes ("ICSID") select the Members of the Tribunal from the list established under Article 13.20. If the list has not been established under Article 13.20 on the date the claim is submitted pursuant to Article 8.23 (Submission of a claim to the Tribunal), the Secretary-General of ICSID shall select the Members of the Tribunal from the individuals proposed by one or both of the Parties in accordance with Article 13.20.
3. The respondent may refer the matter in writing to the Financial Services Committee for a decision as to whether and, if so, to what extent the exception under Article 13.16.1 is a valid defence to the claim. This referral shall not be made later than the date the Tribunal fixes for the respondent to submit its counter-memorial. If the respondent refers the matter to the Financial Services Committee under this paragraph the periods of time or proceedings referred to in Section F of Chapter Eight (Resolution of investment disputes between investors and states) are suspended.

services disputes shall be adjudicated by experts selected from a specific list; (b) the respondent in the dispute may refer the matter in writing to the Financial Services Committee as to whether and, if so, to what extent the defence under Article 13.16 of the Agreement constitutes a valid counterargument for the claim raised by the complainant; (c) if the Committee accepts the arguments raised by the respondent, the claim shall be considered to be dismissed (totally or partially) and the rest of the dispute shall proceed before the original panel; (d) the Committee has three months to render its decision, otherwise the investor may proceed with its claim; (e) in case the respondent does not raise the defence in its first intervention in the proceedings, it shall not be prevented from doing so at a later stage; (f) finally, the Tribunal shall not draw adverse inferences from the lack of a joint determination on the matter by the Financial Services Committee or by the CETA Trade Committee.

4.3.3.3 Understanding on the Application of Articles 13.16.1 (Prudential Carve-Out) and 13.21 (Investment Disputes in Financial Services)

Annex 13 B to the CETA provides guidance in the application of the PCO as well as of Article 13.21 of the Chapter on Financial Services (as already

4. In a referral under paragraph 3, the Financial Services Committee or the CETA Joint Committee, as the case may be, may make a joint determination as to whether and to what extent Article 13.16.1 is a valid defence to the claim. The Financial Services Committee or the CETA Joint Committee, as the case may be, shall transmit a copy of the joint determination to the investor and the Tribunal, if constituted. If the joint determination concludes that Article 13.16.1 is a valid defence to all parts of the claim in their entirety, the investor is deemed to have withdrawn its claim and the proceedings are discontinued in accordance with Article 8.35 (Discontinuance). If the joint determination concludes that Article 13.16.1 is a valid defence to only parts of the claim, the joint determination is binding on the Tribunal with respect to those parts of the claim. The suspension of the periods of time or proceedings described in paragraph 3 then no longer applies and the investor may proceed with the remaining parts of the claim.
5. If the CETA Joint Committee has not made a joint determination within three months of referral of the matter by the Financial Services Committee, the suspension of the periods of time or proceedings referred to in paragraph 3 no longer applies and the investor may proceed with its claim.
6. At the request of the respondent, the Tribunal shall decide as a preliminary matter whether and to what extent Article 13.16.1 is a valid defence to the claim. Failure of the respondent to make that request is without prejudice to the right of the respondent to assert Article 13.16.1 as a defence in a later phase of the proceedings. The Tribunal shall draw no adverse inference from the fact that the Financial Services Committee or the CETA Joint Committee has not agreed on a joint determination in accordance with Annex13-B.

detailed). The Understanding is opened by preamble in which the parties acknowledge the relevance of prudential regulation and commit to act in good faith. It recalls procedural issues concerning the application of Article 13.21, which was the object of the preceding analysis. The document then sets out non-exhaustive principles.

Appropriate level of prudential regulation: Each party is free to set out its appropriate level of prudential regulation. It is clarified, importantly, that such level can be higher than that set out in international forums. This innovation is meaningful because it provides clarity with regard to the margin of manoeuvre that regulators enjoy in this domain. Moreover, it introduces concepts that are familiar to other fields of trade law. In fact, 'appropriate level' recalls the expression 'adequate level of protection' introduced in Article 2.2 of the SPS Agreement of the WTO. Contrary to the latter, however, there are not stringent procedural requirements to be met under the CETA for a party to deviate from internationally agreed standards in the setting out of its appropriate level of prudential regulation. The foregoing can be explained because the concept of 'adequate level of protection' under Article 2.2 of the SPS Agreement requires a scientific risk assessment to be conducted, whereas this is not the case in the context of the PCO under CETA. Moreover, the CETA does not list the relevant standards in the field, as opposed to the SPS Agreement.

Relevant considerations: When dealing with the PCO, adjudicators must give consideration to the available information as well as to the urgency of the situation at the time in which the measure was issued.

Deference: The Understanding acknowledges the highly specialised nature of prudential regulation and requires adjudicators to defer 'to the highest degree possible' to the laws and regulations of the Parties' jurisdictions as well as to the determinations made by domestic authorities with regard, for example, to risk assessments and other factual determinations. Given the high level of asymmetry of information in this domain, the Understanding acknowledges that domestic authorities are in a better position to evaluate the situations of potential danger for financial institutions and the financial system taken as a whole.

Indicators of lawfulness/unlawfulness: The Understanding provides indicators with regard to the possibility of benefitting from the PCO in the event of a dispute. A measure should be considered in compliance with Article 13.16 – according to the principle set out in the Understanding – if it has a prudential objective and it is not manifestly disproportionate to the attainment of its stated aim. On the contrary a Party cannot take advantage of the discipline set out in the PCO when it enacts a regulation that amounts to a disguised restriction on foreign investment or an arbitrary and unjustifiable discrimination towards foreign investors that are in a situation comparable to that of like domestic investors.

Presumption of lawfulness: A measure, provided that it does not amount to a disguised restriction and does not discriminate arbitrarily and unjustifiably among investors in comparable situations, shall be deemed to be in compliance with Article 13.16 in four cases: when the measure is in line with international standards on prudential regulation; when it is adopted in pursuance of the resolution of a financial institution that is no longer viable or likely to be no longer viable; when it pursues the recovery of a financial institution under stress or to the management of the latter; and when it is approved in response to a systemic financial crisis to preserve or restore financial stability. This is a rather broad list of cases and, in addition thereto, the last element has a remarkably broad reach.

Finally, a section titled 'Periodic Review' concludes the Understanding. The Financial Services Committee may amend the Understanding and shall review it at least once every two years. Moreover, the Financial Services Committee may develop a 'common understanding' on the application of the PCO based on the discussions within that body as well as the developments taking place in the context of international forums.

4.4 Conclusion

This Chapter examined how prudential concerns are addressed in PTAs on financial services. The study reveals a general tendency to replicate the rules already contained in the GATS Annex on Financial Services, although the degree of differentiation is increasing.

Such differentiation proves that a series of tools is available to treaty drafters and that they can certainly introduce more stringent rules when they aim to compress the margin of manoeuvre of domestic regulators. Overall, this has happened rarely thus far.

Interestingly, the study shed light on a series of elements and requisites that, if added to the existing text of the GATS PCO, could substantially reduce the degree of uncertainty of its current vague and circular wording. This is elaborated on in the final chapter of this study, where options for reform are put forward.

5

A Possible Alternative Approach

5.1 Introduction

Chapter 3 gave an account of the interpretation advanced by the Panel in *Argentina – Financial Services* and by scholars earlier regarding the scope of application and the legal function of the GATS PCO. The current mainstream approach classifies it as an exception-type provision and sees the last sentence of the PCO as being comparable to the chapeau of Article XX of the GATT 1994 and Article XIV of the GATS. Such an interpretation may be reassuring for international trade scholars because it links the interpretation of the PCO to that of well-known provisions, thus making the former less of an uncharted territory. However, there are solid textual, historical and economic reasons that cast doubts on the extent to which the mainstream understanding is the only permissible one.

The aim of this chapter is to set forth an alternative approach to the interpretation of the PCO of the GATS, which is more consonant with its negotiating history and economic rationale.[1]

5.2 Problems with the Current Mainstream Approach

The vast majority of scholars who have ventured into the interpretation of the PCO have insisted that the latter should be considered a provision performing the same legal function as that assigned by the treaties to 'general exceptions'. The Panel in *Argentina – Financial Services* took the same approach, whereas the Appellate Body seems to have left the door open to other permissible readings of the provision.[2]

The classification of the PCO as an exception is problematic for a number of reasons. First, the structure of the PCO differs substantially from

---

[1] Some of the ideas put forward in this chapter were anticipated in Carlo M. Cantore, "'Shelter from the Storm': Exploring the Scope of Application and Legal Function of the GATS Prudential Carve-Out", *Journal of World Trade*, 48:6, 1223–46.

[2] See the review of the literature and the overview of the Panel and Appellate Body Reports on *Argentina – Financial Services* in Chapter 3.

5.2 PROBLEMS WITH THE CURRENT MAINSTREAM APPROACH 169

that of the paradigmatic GATS exception – Article XIV. The latter, in fact, has the following three features:

- it opens with a chapeau, which, like that of Article XX of the GATT 1994, addresses 'the manner in which [the questioned measure] is applied'[3] – in other words, it requires that measures be applied in a non-arbitrary or unjustifiably discriminatory fashion, or that they do not constitute a disguised restriction to trade in services;
- it provides for an exhaustive list of the policy objectives covered; and
- at least for the policy objectives included in subparagraphs (a), (b) and (c), it requires that a necessity test be met, that is, that measures ought not to be more burdensome than necessary to achieve their objective.

None of those features appears in the text of the PCO. Actually, the structure of the latter is different from that of the exception-type provisions of the WTO Agreements. Those differences, together with other aspects that are examined later in this chapter, contribute to construct the PCO in a way that is different from the traditional mainstream interpretation.

Deviating from an 'exception-type' interpretation scheme has implications with regard to the allocation of the burden of proof in the event of a dispute and, ultimately, with the degree of deference that WTO panels will have to pay vis-à-vis regulators. Each of the three aforementioned elements are analysed in turn.

5.2.1 The Chapeau

The discussion carried out in Chapter 3 of this volume highlighted how most commentators have seen similarities between the chapeau of Article XIV of the GATS and the final sentence of the PCO. The implications deriving from finding similarity between the two clauses are potentially huge, since that may lead to the importation of established case law on the chapeau in the interpretation of the PCO, which might not be warranted. WTO adjudicators, in the past, have already attracted criticisms when they relied on established case law under other agreements to clarify the meaning and standards of review of different provisions.[4] Because

---

[3] Appellate Body Report, *US – Gasoline*, p. 22.
[4] The criticisms made by Mavroidis of the Appellate Body's case law on the Agreement on Technical Barriers to Trade (TBT) are illustrative in this regard. See Petros C. Mavroidis,

the Panel in *Argentina – Financial Services* did not analyse the final clause of the GATS PCO, it is necessary to unravel the consequences of a strict parallel between the latter and the chapeau of Article XIV of the GATS. To do so, both terms of the comparison are reported here.

The chapeau of Article XIV of the GATS reads as follows:

> Subject to the requirement that such measures are not applied in a manner which would constitute a means of arbitrary or unjustifiable discrimination between countries where like conditions prevail, or a disguised restriction on trade in services, nothing in this Agreement shall be construed to prevent the adoption or enforcement by any Member of measures...

The last sentence of the PCO, in turn, reads:

> Where such measures do not conform with the provisions of the Agreement, they shall not be used as a means of avoiding the Member's commitments or obligations under the Agreement.

Whilst the wording of the chapeau points to a hierarchy in legitimate policy objectives that can be pursued lawfully, the final clause of the PCO, in contrast, addresses the issue of the possible circumvention of trade obligations when the domestic measures at issue does not pursue a genuine prudential goal.

The interpreter is assisted by extensive case law on the meaning of the requirements of the chapeau as well as on the specific function it performs. The WTO Agreements are living agreements and our understanding of the balance of the Members' rights and obligations becomes clearer over time because of the work conducted by the WTO Panels and Appellate Body. It is important, therefore, to consider the evolution of the case law on the chapeau to understand what its terms mean and what its function is.

Two are the main sources of concern with regard to the importation of the ideas and the concepts expressed in the chapeau of the General Exceptions provisions of the GATT 1994 and the GATS in the PCO. The first relates to the non-negligible differences in the wording, and the second relates to the problems that may arise should WTO panels import, lock stock and barrel, the case law that was referred to in the analysis of the consistency of a measure with the final clause of the GATS PCO.

'Driftin' too Far from Shore – Why the Test for Compliance with the TBT Agreement Developed by the WTO Appellate Body Is Wrong, and What Should the AB Have Done Instead', *World Trade Review*, 12:3 (2013), 509–31.

5.2.1.1 The Chapeau in WTO Case Law

The Appellate Body in *US – Gambling* found that a set of measures adopted by the United States aimed at the prohibition of online gambling, provisionally justified under Article XIV (a) of the GATS on the grounds that they were necessary to protect public morals, were in fact inconsistent with the requirements of the chapeau. The Appellate Body did not find evidence of discrimination in favour of domestic suppliers in the application of the measures at issue but outlawed the scheme on the grounds that, potentially, some provisions could be read as allowing domestic suppliers to provide remote betting services for horse racing. Quoting the Appellate Body report in relevant parts:

> We have found instead that those measures satisfy the "necessity" requirement. We have also upheld, but only in part, the Panel's finding under the chapeau. We explained that the only inconsistency that the Panel could have found with the requirements of the chapeau stems from the fact that the United States did not demonstrate that the prohibition embodied in the measures at issue applies to both foreign and domestic suppliers of remote gambling services, notwithstanding the IHA – which, according to the Panel, "does appear, on its face, to permit" domestic service suppliers to supply remote betting services for horse racing. In other words, the United States did not establish that the IHA does not alter the scope of application of the challenged measures, particularly vis-à-vis domestic suppliers of a specific type of remote gambling services. In this respect, we wish to clarify that the Panel did not, and we do not, make a finding as to whether the IHA does, in fact, permit domestic suppliers to provide certain remote betting services that would otherwise be prohibited by the Wire Act, the Travel Act, and/or the IGBA.
>
> Therefore, we modify the Panel's conclusion in paragraph 7.2(d) of the Panel Report. We find, instead, that the United States has demonstrated that the Wire Act, the Travel Act, and the IGBA fall within the scope of paragraph (a) of Article XIV, but that it has not shown, in the light of the IHA, that the prohibitions embodied in these measures are applied to both foreign and domestic service suppliers of remote betting services for horse racing. For this reason alone, we find that the United States has not established that these measures satisfy the requirements of the chapeau. Here, too, we uphold the Panel, but only in part. [Footnotes omitted][5]

The Appellate Body interprets the chapeau of Article XIV of the GATS in light of the longer and more established case law on Article XX of the GATT 1994. It first clarified so in *US – Gambling*, where it stated that the

---

[5] Appellate Body Report, *US – Gambling*, paras. 371 and 372.

two provisions set out general exceptions to the provisions of the respective agreements in a comparable fashion. Both provisions aim to allow Members to pursue legitimate identified objectives, following the requirements set out therein.[6]

The same decision, following consolidated case law on Article XX of the GATT 1994, reads the discipline provided by Article XIV of the GATS as one that requires a 'two-tier analysis'.[7] The idea was first expressed in the landmark *US – Gasoline* report of the Appellate Body, which explained the test as follows:

> In order that the justifying protection of Article XX may be extended to it, the measure at issue must not only come under one or another of the particular exceptions – paragraphs (a) to (j) – listed under Article XX; it must also satisfy the requirements imposed by the opening clauses of Article XX. The analysis is, in other words, two-tiered: first, provisional justification by reason of characterization of the measure under XX(g); second, further appraisal of the same measure under the introductory clauses of Article XX.[8]

Ever since, the Appellate Body has given the chapeau an important function in the analysis of the compatibility of the various domestic measures that were subjected to its scrutiny to verify their compatibility with the requirements of Article XX of the GATT 1994. The idea is as follows: when a measure is found to be in violation of one or more provisions of the GATT 1994, for it to be justified under Article XX of the GATT 1994, it must first pass one of the tests provided for by letters (a) to (j) of the provision under analysis. After this first step is completed, the measure has to pass the test under the chapeau.

The chapeau, according to the interpretation advanced by the Appellate Body and constantly repeated in the following reports, focuses on the way in which the measure is applied. The Appellate Body has clarified what this condition means in *US – Gambling*[9]:

> The focus of the chapeau, by its express terms, is on the application of a measure already found by the Panel to be inconsistent with one of the obligations under the GATS but falling within one of the paragraphs of Article XIV. By requiring that the measure be applied in a manner that does not constitute "arbitrary" or "unjustifiable" discrimination, or a "disguised

---

[6] Appellate Body Report, *US – Gambling*, para. 291.
[7] Appellate Body Report, *US – Gambling*, para. 292.
[8] Appellate Body Report, *US – Gasoline*, p. 22.
[9] Appellate Body Report, *US – Gambling*, para. 339.

restriction on trade in services", the chapeau serves to ensure that Members' rights to avail themselves of exceptions are exercised reasonably, so as not to frustrate the rights accorded other Members by the substantive rules of the GATS.

The Appellate Body has also distinguished between the burden of proof under the specific exceptions of the provision and the burden of proof under the chapeau. Since *US – Gasoline*, it has clarified that the Member invoking an exception has the burden of demonstrating that a measure that was provisionally found to be consistent with one of the exceptions in the body of Article XX of the GATT 1994 does not constitute an abuse of such an exception.[10]

In other terms, the chapeau serves the necessary role of striking a balance between the possibility of a Member deviating from its obligations in pursuit of other (legitimate) interests and the competing claim of other WTO Members to have their rights preserved and not disproportionately harmed by the unilateral action of the regulating government. Concretely, this line of equilibrium is substantiated by the requirements that the measures are not applied in a manner that would constitute 'arbitrary discrimination between countries where the same conditions prevail'; 'unjustified discrimination between countries where the same conditions prevail' or 'a disguised restriction to international trade'. This is consonant with the original idea of the GATT in the 1940s that trade liberalisation does not trump social preferences as long as the latter are 'genuine' and there is no abuse of right.

It is important at this stage to review how the concepts of 'arbitrary or unjustifiable discrimination' and 'disguised restriction on trade' have evolved over the years. In *US – Gasoline*, the Appellate Body made it clear that the three requirements are necessary terms of the same equations and that one cannot make a rigid distinction between the three requirements and read them in isolation. The Appellate Body, in particular, clarified the following:

> "Arbitrary discrimination", "unjustifiable discrimination" and "disguised restriction" on international trade may, accordingly, be read side-by-side; they impart meaning to one another. It is clear to us that "disguised restriction" includes disguised discrimination in international trade. It is equally clear that concealed or unannounced restriction or discrimination in international trade does not exhaust the meaning of "disguised restriction." We consider that "disguised restriction", whatever else it covers, may properly

[10] Appellate Body Report, *US – Gasoline*, p. 22.

be read as embracing restrictions amounting to arbitrary or unjustifiable discrimination in international trade taken under the guise of a measure formally within the terms of an exception listed in Article XX. Put in a somewhat different manner, the kinds of considerations pertinent in deciding whether the application of a particular measure amounts to "arbitrary or unjustifiable discrimination", may also be taken into account in determining the presence of a "disguised restriction" on international trade. The fundamental theme is to be found in the purpose and object of avoiding abuse or illegitimate use of the exceptions to substantive rules available in Article XX.[11]

The Appellate Body, in *US – Shrimp* clarified the scope of application and the function of the chapeau in more detail. In particular, the report clarified that the policy goal of the measure under analysis cannot provide the justification under the standards of the chapeau because that particular scrutiny is reserved to the test under one of the ten specific policy objectives in the exhaustive list set out in the body of Article XX of the GATT 1994.

In that case, the Appellate Body took a long detour to clarify its understanding of the test of the chapeau. To begin with, the Appellate Body put the analysis of the chapeau against the background of the preamble of the WTO Agreement, in the context of a dispute that concerned issues related to the protection of the environment and the ecosystem. In the words of the Appellate Body, the preamble, insofar as it reflects the intentions of the negotiators of the WTO, 'must add colour, texture and shading to our interpretation of the agreements annexed to the WTO Agreement'.[12]

The Appellate Body identified the chapeau as setting forth a test according to which each of the exceptions listed in paragraphs (a) to (j) of Article XX of the GATT 1994 has to be considered to be limited and conditional.[13] In other words, the chapeau represents the last test that domestic measures in compliance with the requirements of one of the paragraphs of Article XX of the GATT 1994 must meet. To back this interpretation of the chapeau, the Appellate Body decided to seek confirmation in the negotiating history of the provision. In so doing, the adjudicators revealed that there was an initial proposal, tabled by the United States, according to which the exceptions should be made available to the Members of the GATT 1947 without any other condition to be satisfied. In the discussion that followed, other Members (including Belgium and the Netherlands) took

---

[11] Appellate Body Report, *US – Gasoline*, p. 25.
[12] Appellate Body Report, *US – Shrimp*, para. 153.
[13] Appellate Body Report, *US – Shrimp*, para. 157.

5.2 PROBLEMS WITH THE CURRENT MAINSTREAM APPROACH 175

other positions and, in the end, the United Kingdom advanced a position of compromise on which the negotiating teams agreed. The parties agreed that Article XX of the GATT 1947 should provide for an exhaustive list of *limited* and *conditional* exceptions to the obligations provided for in the Agreement.[14]

The Appellate Body went on with the clarification of its understanding of what the chapeau means for the architecture of the GATT 1994. According to the Appellate Body, the language of the introductory sentences of Article XX of the GATT 1994 is in essence, 'one expression of the principle of good faith', and, more in detail, the very aim of the chapeau should be that of avoiding situations in which Members may abuse their rights to deviate from their substantive obligations.[15] Then, in what is arguably one of the most often quoted (although not exactly the clearest) passages of WTO case law, the Appellate Body famously stated:

> The task of interpreting and applying the chapeau is, hence, essentially the delicate one of *marking out a line of equilibrium* between the right of a Member to invoke an exception under Article XX and the rights of the other Members under varying substantive provisions... The location of the line of equilibrium, as expressed in the chapeau, is not fixed and unchanging; the line moves as the kind and the shape of the measures at stake vary and as the facts making up specific cases differ. [Emphasis added][16]

The Appellate Body points out that the focus under the chapeau should consist of scrutiny of the application of the measure, the rationale of which was already assessed in the analysis under one of the ten paragraphs of Article XX of the GATT 1994. However, the Appellate Body makes it clear that the analysis under the chapeau should not be seen as exclusively dealing with procedural aspects because substantive requirements also come under scrutiny.[17]

The issue in the *US – Shrimp* dispute concerned a requirement by the US administration according to which, for shrimp to be sold in the US market, they had to be fished with a particular technique that involved the use of specific nets (*Turtle Excluder Devices*, TEDs). The measure was already found to be in compliance with the requirements of Article XX (g) of the

---

[14] See Appellate Body Report, *US – Shrimp*, para. 157 (and the footnotes) for the details of the discussion during the negotiations of the GATT 1947.
[15] Appellate Body Report, *US – Shrimp*, para. 158.
[16] Appellate Body Report, *US – Shrimp*, para. 159.
[17] Appellate Body Report, *US – Shrimp*, para. 160.

GATT 1994 ('the protection of natural exhaustible resources'), but it was outlawed because it failed to pass the test under the chapeau. The problem there was that the United States was, de facto, imposing on other WTO Members the burden of adopting exactly the same regulatory program as the one imposed on US fishing companies and they were not given the possibility to adopt others that were comparable in their effects.[18]

The main problem for the Appellate Body, therefore, consisted of the imposition of a rigid and unbending requirement that, although non-discriminatory on the face of it (because it was imposed on US companies and foreign companies alike), caused de facto disproportionate effects and imposed an excessive burden on foreign firms that were put in a position where they could not export shrimp to the United States.[19]

The Appellate Body addressed the issue with clear and unequivocal words. It is worth reporting another key passage from the report, as it will be useful in the analysis of the difference between the chapeau of Article XX of the GATT 1994 and the final clause of the PCO:

> [I]t is not acceptable, in international trade relations, for one WTO Member to use an economic embargo to *require* other Members to adopt essentially the same comprehensive regulatory program, to achieve a certain policy goal, as that in force within that Member's territory, *without* taking into consideration different conditions which may occur in the territories of those other Members. [Emphasis in the original text][20]

The Appellate Body found that the applicants were right in pointing to the rigidity of the US measure with specific regard to two issues: the measure did not allow all foreign exporters to the United States to enter negotiations with the administration; moreover, it did not allow for shrimp fished through means as efficient as TEDs to enter the US market.

Essentially, the absence of flexibility in the application of the measure led the Appellate Body to find in favour of the applicants in the case that the measures adopted by the United States were inconsistent with the requirements of the chapeau of Article XX of the GATT 1994 because they amounted to arbitrary and unjustifiable discrimination between countries where the same conditions prevailed.

Another important case in the chapeau saga is *Brazil – Retreaded Tyres*. Brazil had imposed a restriction on imports of remoulded tyres to protect the environment and to avoid the spreading of diseases connected

---

[18] Appellate Body Report, *US – Shrimp*, para. 163.
[19] Appellate Body Report, *US – Shrimp*, para. 164.
[20] Appellate Body Report, *US – Shrimp*, para. 164.

5.2 PROBLEMS WITH THE CURRENT MAINSTREAM APPROACH 177

to the particular processes adopted in the treatment of used pneumatics. However, Brazil had also introduced an exemption for imports of retreaded tyres from MERCOSUR countries following a decision by an arbitral tribunal under MERCOSUR law. The measure was challenged before WTO courts and gave the Appellate Body another occasion to put forward its understanding of the chapeau.

The Panel had justified the difference in treatment between tyres from MERCOSUR and tyres from other parts of the world on the basis of the limited trade in that particular good among MERCOSUR countries.[21] In its appellant submission, the European Union challenged the conclusions of the Panel report, calling into question the availability of a ruling from a MERCOSUR tribunal as a legitimate justification for the imposition of a discriminatory application of a measure and arguing that, following the ruling, Brazil could have lifted the import ban vis-à-vis all importers.[22]

The Appellate Body did not accept the existence of a decision by a MERCOSUR tribunal as a legitimate justification for the discrimination between MERCOSUR countries and third countries. It ruled as follows:

> In our view, the ruling issued by the MERCOSUR arbitral tribunal is not an acceptable rationale for the discrimination because it bears no relationship to the legitimate objective pursued by the Import Ban that falls within the purview of Article XX(b), and even goes against this objective, to however small a degree. Accordingly, we are of the view that the MERCOSUR exemption has resulted in the Import Ban being applied in a manner that constitutes arbitrary or unjustifiable discrimination.[23]

The case under analysis here is also important because it clarified that the terms 'arbitrary' and 'unjustifiable' of the chapeau are not tantamount to 'capricious' or 'random'. According to the Appellate Body, rational behaviour from the legislator may also lead to arbitrary or unjustifiable discrimination because it may be based on a decision that may be totally unconnected from the rationale of the measure or may even contradict it.[24]

The Appellate Body had the opportunity to analyse the chapeau of Article XX of the GATT 1994 in *EC – Seal Products*, in the spring

---

[21] Panel Report, *Brazil – Retreaded Tyres*, paras. 7.354–5.
[22] Appellate Body Report, *Brazil – Retreaded Tyres*, para. 220.
[23] Appellate Body Report, *Brazil – Retreaded Tyres*, para. 228.
[24] Appellate Body Report, *Brazil – Retreaded Tyres*, para. 232.

of 2014. The European Union had approved a regulation whereby it imposed an import ban on seal products with limited exceptions. One of these exceptions – the 'Inuit community exception' (IC exception) – allowed seal products that were the result of hunts conducted by indigenous communities of Greenland following traditional methods, providing that the ultimate purpose of the harvesting was the subsistence of the local community. The same possibility, however, was not conceded to the indigenous communities of Canada and Norway, whose governments challenged the regulatory scheme approved by the EU before a WTO panel. The Appellate Body found the regulatory scheme to comply with the requirements set forth in Article XX(a) of the GATT 1994 because it was considered to be a necessary measure for the protection of public morals.

However, the measure did not meet the test under the chapeau. The Appellate Body asked itself the question of whether the same conditions prevailed within the EU and other countries that lamented discriminatory treatment. It found out that the EU failed to sufficiently explain what made the conditions of the Inuit communities of Greenland different from that of the indigenous communities of Canada that they required different treatment.[25] The Appellate Body found that the scheme was construed in a way to make it, de facto, available only to Greenland and that this circumstance was not due to the inaction of Canadian exporters to seek authorisation.[26] The Appellate Body concluded as follows:

> In sum, we have identified several features of the EU Seal Regime that indicate that the regime is applied in a manner that constitutes a means of arbitrary or unjustifiable discrimination between countries where the same conditions prevail, in particular with respect to the IC exception. First, we found that the European Union did not show that the manner in which the EU Seal Regime treats seal products derived from IC hunts as compared to seal products derived from "commercial" hunts can be reconciled with the objective of addressing EU public moral concerns regarding seal welfare. Second, we found considerable ambiguity in the "subsistence" and "partial use" criteria of the IC exception. Given the ambiguity of these criteria and the broad discretion that the recognized bodies consequently enjoy in applying them, seal products derived from what should in fact be properly characterized as "commercial" hunts could potentially enter the EU market under the IC exception. We did not consider that the European Union has sufficiently explained how such instances can be prevented in the

---

[25] Appellate Body Report, *EC – Seal Products*, para. 5.317.
[26] Appellate Body Report, *EC – Seal Products*, paras. 5.333–4.

5.2 PROBLEMS WITH THE CURRENT MAINSTREAM APPROACH

application of the IC exception. Finally, we were not persuaded that the European Union has made "comparable efforts" to facilitate the access of the Canadian Inuit to the IC exception as it did with respect to the Greenlandic Inuit. We also noted that setting up a "recognized body" that fulfills all the requirements of Article 6 of the Implementing Regulation may entail significant burdens in some instances.

For these reasons, we find that the European Union has not demonstrated that the EU Seal Regime, in particular with respect to the IC exception, is designed and applied in a manner that meets the requirements of the chapeau of Article XX of the GATT 1994. It follows that the European Union has not justified the EU Seal Regime under Article XX(a) of the GATT 1994.[27]

The case law reveals how the original understanding of the chapeau has evolved. It was initially conceived as an obligation upon WTO Members to apply their justified WTO-inconsistent measures in a way that is not abusive of their limited and conditional right to do so. Over the years, WTO panels and Appellate Body have indulged in pervasive analyses regarding the design and structure of the measures under scrutiny, thus setting a high threshold that domestic measures have to meet to satisfy the test.

5.2.1.2 The Problems with the Parallelism between the Final Clause of the PCO and the Chapeau of Article XX of the GATT 1994

The introduction of a separate test of consistency of the domestic measures under the chapeau is a judicial construction that does not plainly stem from the text of the provision and its negotiating history. It is not surprising, therefore, that its meaning and functions are being called into question by recent literature.[28] However, because this work is not primarily concerned with the interpretation of the chapeau of the exception provisions of the GATT 1994 and the GATS, it is necessary to turn the attention to analysing the main problems concerning the parallelism with the final clause of the PCO that has been advocated by some international trade scholars.

---

[27] Appellate Body Report, *EC – Seal Products*, paras. 5.338–9.
[28] See, in this regard, Petros C. Mavroidis, *Sealed with a Doubt – EU, Seals and the WTO*, MIMEO (2015). See also Lorand Bartels, 'The Chapeau of the General Exceptions in the WTO GATT and GATS Agreements: A Reconstruction', *American Journal of International Law*, 109:1 (2015), 95–125.

5.2.1.2.1 The Wording The chapeau deals with the application of a measure that was previously found to be in compliance with one of the paragraphs of the body of the provision (either Article XX of the GATT 1994 or Article XIV of the GATS). It requires that the measure under scrutiny, in its application, does not lead to arbitrary or unjustifiable discrimination between countries where the same conditions prevail or to a disguised restriction to trade. None of these three terms appears in the last clause of the PCO, not even in a different fashion or through the use of synonyms.

One may think, at first sight, that the terms 'applied' (in the chapeau) and 'used' (in the PCO) are to be considered as similar. They should both deal, in principle, with the application of the measures and not just with the ways in which they are designed and drafted. This distinction is a subtle one, however, and the case law has been problematic in this regard.[29]

5.2.1.2.2 The Case Law The most important issue here is that of avoiding the risk of importing 'lock stock and barrel', the case law on General Exceptions into the interpretation of the PCO. There are warning signs of this in the cases that have been analysed in the previous pages, and they are made explicit in the following sections.

The case law on 'general exceptions' has made it clear that these perform a strategic function in the legal system of the WTO, namely that of 'marking out a line of equilibrium' between the right of a Member to deviate from its trade obligations to pursue other legitimate policy objectives and the rights of other Members of the international trade community not to see their rights frustrated by arbitrary measures that, although at first glance are cosmetically designed to sound legitimate are, in reality, instruments that conceal protectionist behaviour. To do so, the drafters of the exceptions used specific concepts ('arbitrary or unjustifiable discrimination between countries where the same conditions prevail' and 'disguised restriction to trade'). The Appellate Body has gone one step further in this regard by stating that the terms used in the chapeau are to be read side by side as imparting meaning to each other so as to compose, in the end, a single test.

The Appellate Body has developed its jurisprudence on the issue, drifting from the shore of the principle of good faith – in its *abus de droit* connotation – and scrutinising in detail the policy choices made by the regulators. In one case, the Appellate Body seems to have even put into

---

[29] Especially, the Appellate Body Report in *EC – Seal Products* is problematic in this regard.

5.2 PROBLEMS WITH THE CURRENT MAINSTREAM APPROACH 181

question, following the arguments of the complainant, the effectiveness of the defensive strategy of the respondent in the case before a regional court, the implementation of the decision of which led the defending government to adopt a regulatory scheme that was afterwards struck down for lack of compliance with the chapeau. It must be recalled, moreover, that such a 'line of equilibrium' mostly depends on the conditions set up in the relevant subparagraph of the exception – Article XX of the GATT 1994 – that, in origin, could justify the derogation from the obligations under the relevant trade agreement.

The jurisprudence of the Appellate Body, moreover reveals a tendency to scrutinise the details of the instruments deployed by the regulators to address legitimate policy goals, sometimes questioning the real aim behind the adoption of particular pieces of legislation. Put in another way, governments were allowed considerable autonomy with regard to the connection between the measures enacted and their capability of being encompassed by one of the paragraphs of Article XX of the GATT 1994 or Article XIV of the GATS. However, the choice of the means for the achievement of the legitimate non-trade policy objectives pursued by the regulating Member has been strictly scrutinized.[30] This second tier of analysis has been noticeably conducted under the chapeau and has led to a more pervasive analysis of the policy strategies adopted domestically. The Appellate Body, moreover, has made it clear on several occasions that the burden of proving that the measures adopted meet the requirements of the chapeau rests on the respondent in the dispute.

This conclusion, however, derives mainly from the context against the background of which the chapeau should be read. The texts of the various letters in Article XX of the GATT 1994 and Article XIV of the GATS, which provide for limited and conditional exceptions, inform the meaning of the chapeau. Importing the case law on the chapeau in the analysis of the PCO may tilt the balance that was carefully struck in the negotiations of the Annex on Financial Services of the GATS in favour of the interests of the Members challenging the measures rather than the regulating governments.

To make the picture clearer, it must be recalled that, for instance, the Appellate Body outlawed some measures adopted by the US

---

[30] The thorough analysis provided by Sykes is illustrative in this regard. See Alan O. Sykes, 'Economic 'Necessity' in International Law', *American Journal of International Law*, 109:2 (2015), 296–323.

administration that restricted the imports of shrimp only to those fished using particular devices. The Appellate Body found that the measure, although in principle compliant with Article XX (g) of the GATT 1994,[31] could not pass the test under the chapeau because it imposed a 'single, rigid and unbending requirement' on importers to adopt the same scheme applicable to US companies with 'little or no flexibility'.[32] In the compliance proceedings of the same dispute, furthermore, the Appellate Body clarified that there was a need for the regulator to allow importers to prove that the actions undertaken by them were 'comparable in effectiveness' to what was required under US law.[33]

The practice of adopting 'single, rigid and unbending requirement(s)' is common to many regulations for services providers across the world. It is a peculiar ingredient, in particular, in the main recipes adopted by large regulatory arenas (namely the EU and the United States) in the domain of financial services in the reform packages adopted and implemented in the aftermath of the 2007-8 financial crisis.[34]

A pervasive scrutiny of domestic policy choices with regard to financial services, along the lines of that provided for by the chapeau of the general exceptions (at least in the way in which the Appellate Body has understood they do), may not be considered a welcome development by many of the actors of the international trade system. In particular, it may alter a balance that has lasted until now and that has allowed for greater flexibility and given governments the opportunity to address loopholes and shortcomings in their legislation on financial services markets.

5.2.1.2.3 Conclusion on the Differences with the Chapeau
From the preceding discussion, substantial differences are apparent in wording between the chapeau of Article XX of the GATT 1994 and Article XIV of the GATS and the final clause of the PCO. This difference is not insignificant and represents the outcome of a different drafting process and a different function performed by the provisions.

---

[31] This is not the appropriate place to raise the argument on the basis of which it is, at least, debatable whether the Appellate Body was correct in finding that turtles can be considered 'natural exhaustible resources', a category that was introduced in the text of Article XX with regard to fossils and minerals, as emerges from the negotiating history. For a thorough analysis on the issue, see Mavroidis, *Trade in Goods* (pp. 345–51).
[32] Appellate Body Report, *US – Shrimp*, para. 177.
[33] Appellate Body Report, *US – Shrimp (Article 21.5 – Malaysia)*, paras. 144 and ff.
[34] See the discussion in Chapter 2.

5.2 PROBLEMS WITH THE CURRENT MAINSTREAM APPROACH 183

The PCO was drafted to exclude prudential regulation from the coverage of trade obligations. Its final clause represents a reaffirmation of the requirement to perform treaty obligations in good faith and does not go beyond it. The chapeau of general exceptions, because of its stricter wording and the interpretations rendered by the Appellate Body, has instead acquired a quasi-autonomous and different standing in the domain of international trade law. It serves the function of marking out a line of equilibrium between the rights of the regulating Member and those of other Members who seek access to the former's market. In other words, it represents the ultimate test that domestic measures have to pass to benefit from the exception and not to be found in violation of one or more provisions of the GATT 1994 or the GATS.

It is at least debatable whether the final clause of the PCO can be understood along these lines. The absence of case law does not help us in this regard, hence leaving much room for speculation. It can certainly be read as reaffirming the principle according to which Parties to a treaty shall not abuse their rights (*abus de droit*), which is a general principle of international law and is common to most legal orders, both domestic or international. It does not, however, call for an evaluation as to whether regulating Members have afforded their trading partners the opportunity to prove that they are in a comparable situation or that their prudential measures are equivalent in effectiveness and does not warn against discrimination.

Pushing the parallel between the PCO and Article XX of the GATT 1994 or Article XIV of the GATS too far would severely impede the possibility of a correct understanding of the state of the art of liberalisation of trade in financial services and the regulatory space left for national governments with regard to prudential measures and, in particular, crisis prevention and crisis management tools.

There are reasons to believe that the last sentence of the PCO should not be interpreted as being similar to the chapeau of Article XIV of the GATS. In fact, it can be read as reaffirming the general principle of international law according to which parties to a treaty should not abuse of the rights deriving from the latter (*abus de droit*). It does not require parties to refrain from implementing measures in a discriminatory or arbitrary fashion. Moreover, contrary to the policy objectives in Article XIV of the GATS, the prudential reasons covered by the PCO are non-exhaustive, and no necessity test is required for a successful invocation of the provision.

Admittedly, the last sentence of the PCO could perhaps be read in parallel with the requirement that measures do not constitute a disguised restriction to trade. The concept of 'disguised restriction' provided by the chapeau of Article XX of the GATT (and identical to that included in Article XIV of the GATS) has been interpreted in WTO case law in a way which is reminiscent of the French doctrine of *abus de droit*. The two concepts are similar in the sense that they point to situations in which a Member, while affirming that it pursues a lawful objective, aims in reality at an illegal one. However, the parallel between the final sentence of the PCO and the chapeau of Article XIV cannot be pushed any further. First of all, the requirement provided by the chapeau of Article XIV of the GATS must be read together with the other requirements included therein, which do not apply to the PCO. Second, the final sentence of the PCO, rather than just reaffirming a general principle of law that would have applied regardless,[35] points to the fact that each provision has a definite scope. It cannot be read as if it requires a chapeau-like test to be respected. Third, given the differences in wording and context, it must be expected that in the case of the PCO the line of equilibrium between the conflicting interests of the regulating Members and those who seek access to the markets of the latter shall definitely lean much more on the side of the importing trading nation.

As stated at the beginning of this chapter, the chapeau of Article XX of the GATT 1994 provides a hierarchy of policy objectives. In this regard, case law has consistently repeated that the first indication of this function performed by the chapeau can be found in the title of the provision ('General Exceptions'). Moreover, the same case law has linked the shifting of the burden of proof to the linguistic choice of the drafters. The unique wording and title of the PCO suggest that we are in presence of something different. Rather than establishing a hierarchy of values, the aim of the PCO is that of excluding the application of trade obligations or commitments to areas of regulation that pertain to the domain of the pursuance of prudential policy objectives. Given the differences in wording and structure, the PCO deserves an autonomous evaluation, separated from the jurisprudential evolution of the general exceptions provision of the GATT 1994 and the GATS.

5.2.2 *A Non-Exhaustive List of Prudential Objectives*

Another source of distinction between the PCO and the general exceptions of the GATT 1994 and the GATS lies in the structures of the provisions. Exceptions-type provisions are typically drafted with a fixed and

---

[35] See Article 26 of the Vienna Convention on the Law of Treaties (*Pacta sunt servanda*).

5.2 PROBLEMS WITH THE CURRENT MAINSTREAM APPROACH 185

exhaustive list of policy objectives in pursuance of which Members may deviate from their international trade obligations. The PCO, on the contrary, only provides an indicative list of what can be considered 'prudential' in the domain of financial regulation.

The rationales behind the two provisions ought to be different; otherwise, it would have made little sense not to re-create what was used in other contexts within the realm of the same organisation. In this case, Article XX of the GATT 1994 (and its twin Article XIV of the GATS) on the one side and the PCO on the other pursue different aims.

Exceptions are typically in place to avoid situations that, in decision theory, are defined as 'Type II errors' – false negatives. Those are situations in which a Member is not found to have violated one or more WTO obligations even if it has done so. In simpler terms, this issue can be broken down as follows: when a violation of a trade obligation occurs, the WTO system is designed in a way in which the balance of rights and obligations has to be, in principle, restored, bringing back into compliance domestic regulations that are found to be in violation of one or more provisions of one or more agreements. The system itself makes some instruments available for those Members who have indeed committed a violation of trade obligations but have done so in pursuance of one of the policy objectives provided for by the relevant exception provision. This is arguably why the drafters of the GATT 1994 and the GATS have individuated an exhaustive list of policy objectives that can be pursued.

It is true that concepts such as 'public morals' or 'human health' may vary over time. It is also true, however, that the policy objectives cannot be stretched to encompass issues that differ substantially from the original catalogue of exceptions. In this regard, the PCO again substantially differs from the typical exception-type provisions in other WTO Agreements. The former only provides for a non-exhaustive list of reasons according to which Members are entitled to adopt prudential measures. This expands much more the scope of manoeuvre for Members that need to deviate from trade obligations and commitments. This is yet another warning sign against the comparison between exception-type provisions and the PCO.

5.2.3 Absence of Requirements for Prudential Justifications to Kick In

Finally, there is another level of difference between exception-type provisions and the PCO. The latter does not require that any condition be satisfied for prudential measures to be put in place, with the exclusion of the restatement of the obligation to perform international obligations in good faith, on which this work has already elaborated in detail above.

This amounts to another difference that cannot be ignored when one compares the structure of the PCO and that of Article XIV of the GATS, for instance. Letters (a) to (e) of the latter all provide for requirements that Members have to fulfil to legitimately deviate from their trade obligations and commitments. Letters (a), (b) and (c) require Members to adopt measures that are 'necessary' to achieve the stated aim, that is that the measures enacted by the Members have to be the least trade restrictive. Letters (d) and (e), instead, provide for less stringent requirements, but nonetheless they do not allow Members to deviate from their obligations easily. Members will still have to prove that they were entitled to depart from trade obligations according to specific conditions.

Returning to the PCO, it is self-evident that none of the previous requirements are present in the text of the provision. This may lead to a question pertaining to the hierarchy of values protected under WTO law. Members may find it more difficult to deviate from their obligations when they want to step in and modify their regulation to protect, for instance, human health, than when they want to modify their legislation with the aim to protect consumers of financial services.

How can it be that measures for the protection of financial stability or any other prudential concern do not have to meet stringent tests, whereas measures adopted in pursuance of public health objectives must be necessary to achieve their aims? Trade agreements are not the result of rigorous mathematical equations, and they do not necessarily follow a rigorous logic. Sometimes, given that they are the outcome of negotiations between governments, it may be that such governments are willing to make concessions on some issues because they wish to protect their domestic industry, especially in some strategic sectors or subsectors. Further, it should be borne in mind that the Annex on Financial Services of the GATS was negotiated at a time when information was circulating on floppy disks and not all the current options for cross-border trade in financial services were available or, perhaps, even conceivable. The Annex, hence, was mainly used to open the door to firms to access foreign markets and establish branches and subsidiaries in the territories of other trading partners. Consequently, it is not surprising that the participants in the Uruguay Round did not push for substantial liberalisation in the domain of financial services, unlike what had happened decades ago in the domain of goods. In addition, the Southeast Asian financial crisis was still fresh in the mind of negotiators, with the countries concerned being vocal concerning the

5.2 PROBLEMS WITH THE CURRENT MAINSTREAM APPROACH 187

necessity of protecting the prerogatives of financial regulators. Therefore, governments kept a higher degree of sovereignty on financial markets that in other fields, and no ex post evaluation should undo this balance and substitute it with the more refined and balanced hierarchy of values that can be found in other provisions of WTO law.

The WTO is one set of international agreements during the negotiations of which sovereign States agreed to make concessions and conceded parts of their sovereignty for the purpose of tackling barriers to trade. Admittedly, they have considered that, in the absence of stringent limitations for the invocation of certain public policy objectives, those trade agreements would have been dried up. The choice of policy objectives was made according to the preferences of the negotiators as well as the feasibility of a compromise. Against this background, for instance, it can be argued that there are more objective criteria to determine what causes harm to human health than what can and cannot be defined as prudential regulation. As the discussion in Chapter 2 revealed there is lack of unanimity in economic literature and among policy makers with regard to an exact classification of measures that can genuinely be considered as being put in place for the protection of micro- or macroprudential objectives.

The case of the PCO, therefore, seems to differ substantially from that of exception-type provisions. Rather than simply providing for a defensive instrument – that is, an exception capable of justifying measures that would otherwise be considered inconsistent with the provisions of an agreement – the PCO can be read as marking the line between what is covered and what is not under the Annex on Financial Services of the GATS. Therefore, the PCO can be interpreted as pointing out, although probably not in the clearest possible fashion, that measures adopted in pursuance of prudential objectives are not covered by the discipline of the GATS, even if the Member has listed specific commitments and the new regulations may have a detrimental impact on them. The PCO restates the right for WTO Members to step in and amend their legislation on financial markets according to prudential concerns. In so doing, it performs a function that can be seen as different from that assigned to exceptions in international trade agreements. Against this background, the interpreter has to take extra care in assigning a function to it that it does not have; otherwise the balance of rights and obligations of WTO Members may risk severe harm.

In sum, the other permissible interpretation of the PCO that this volume attempts to advance is the following. Trade liberalisation in the field of financial services, as in any other sector, was engineered in light of the normal conditions of doing business. In this respect, regulators are expected to behave in a particular way and to comply with the obligations and commitments they agreed to at the multilateral level. Regulators are also expected to work in good times to consolidate the stability of the financial system and to intervene when a crisis hits their domestic market. To do so, the GATS Annex on Financial Services provides all WTO Member with the PCO. In this sense, the way in which the PCO is drafted makes it clear that there is nothing exceptional or unforeseeable in the behaviour of a government that pursues micro- or macroprudential policy objectives. Moreover, especially in times of crisis, one cannot reasonably expect national governments to adopt a 'business-as-usual' attitude and avoid addressing the situations by using all the powers they have to avoid the proliferation of the negative consequences of financial turbulences.

5.2.4 The Availability of General Exceptions for WTO Plus Commitments

There is another potential source of problems connected with the qualification of the PCO as an exception. The Appellate Body had the chance to clarify its position with regard to the availability of Article XX of the GATT 1994 for WTO-plus obligations listed in the protocols of accession of Members that have joined the organisation at a later stage, years after the conclusion of the Uruguay Round.

By WTO-plus obligations, the international trade epistemic community commonly refers to provisions of protocols of accession (or PTAs), which are usually under the mandate of one of the WTO agreements, when it is decided to go beyond what commonly applies to all other WTO Members.[36] The discussion on the availability of general exceptions for

---

[36] Horn et al. define WTO-plus obligations, with regard to PTAs, as follows: 'The... [WTO-plus] category corresponds to those provisions of PTAs which come under the current mandate of the WTO, where the parties undertake bilateral commitments going beyond those they have accepted at the multilateral level. An example would be a reduction in tariffs.' See Henrik Horn, Petros C. Mavroidis and André Sapir, 'EU and US Preferential Trade Agreements: Deepening or Widening of WTO Commitments?', in Kyle W. Bagwell and Petros C. Mavroidis (eds.), *Preferential Trade Agreements: A Law and Economics Analysis* (Cambridge: Cambridge University Press, 2014), 150–72 (p. 151). The 2011 World Trade Report on Preferential Trade Agreements issued by the WTO Secretariat endorses this definition. See World Trade Organization, *World Trade Report 2011 – the WTO and Preferential Trade Agreements: From Co-Existence to Coherence* (p. 131).

5.2 PROBLEMS WITH THE CURRENT MAINSTREAM APPROACH 189

the violation of WTO-plus obligations fist came out in the context of the WTO in the *China – Publications and Audiovisual Products* case.[37] In that first case, the Appellate Body was confronted with paragraph 5.1 of the Chinese Protocol of Accession, which reaffirms the principle whereby Beijing must ensure all enterprises in China shall have the right to trade in all goods throughout the customs territory of China without prejudice for the regulators to adopt or maintain legislation that is compatible with WTO law. On that occasion, the Appellate Body found that that obligation did not limit China's right to avail itself of the general exceptions set forth in Article XX of the GATT 1994 when the conditions set forth therein are satisfied.

In 2012, the Appellate Body Report in the *China – Raw Materials* took a different approach, stating that, in the absence of an express reference to the conditions set forth in Article XX of the GATT 1994, the latter cannot be invoked as a justification for the violation of the obligations undersigned by China not to impose export restrictions on a particular list of goods that are instrumental for the production of technological equipment or other more complex products.[38]

In the summer of 2014, the Appellate Body had the chance to solve this apparently incoherent case law with its report in the *China – Rare Earths* dispute. At the Panel stage, the majority of the panelists took the view that, in the absence of a direct *renvoi* to Article XX of the GATT 1994 in the provisions listing WTO plus obligations in a protocol of accession, no justification is available for the breach of any of the additional obligations undertaken by China upon entry into the WTO. One dissenting panelist warned against the systemic implications of such an approach, insisting on the importance that exception-type provisions have in the context of trade agreements. According to the view of the dissenting panelist, an exception should be made available to new WTO Members even if it is not expressly referred to in their protocols of accession.[39]

The Appellate Body upheld the view of the majority of the panelists.[40] Express reference to Article XX of the GATT 1994 may not imply, ipso facto, the availability of the exception as a defence for domestic measures

---

[37] Appellate Body Report, *China – Publications and Audiovisual Products*, para. 230.
[38] Appellate Body Report, *China – Raw Materials*, para. 308.
[39] Panel Report, *China – Rare Earths*, paras. 7.118–38.
[40] Appellate Body Report, *China – Rare Earths*, paras. 5.71–74.

that may contradict WTO-plus obligations. Panels and the Appellate Body will have to carefully scrutinise the nature of the WTO-plus obligation against the background of the Working Party Report and the Accession Protocol and taking into account the overall architecture of the WTO system.

The last decision in the series makes it clear that it is highly unlikely that a WTO Member that has acceded after the conclusion of the Uruguay Round may avail itself of the general exceptions provisions to justify a departure from WTO-plus obligations unless the Protocol contains language to this effect.

The discussion conducted in this subparagraph, instead, may have an impact on the interpretation of the PCO. Should WTO panels adopt the approach proposed by the Panel in *Argentina – Financial Services*, according to which the PCO must be classified as an exception, this may lead them to adopt, *mutatis mutandis*, the same approach with regard to its applicability to WTO plus commitments in the protocols of accession of new WTO Members, compared with what has happened with Article XX of the GATT 1994.[41]

A transposition of this approach to the domain of the PCO may have a remarkable systemic impact. A classification of the PCO as an exception would probably limit (or cast doubts on) its availability for new WTO Members that have listed GATS-plus commitments. The situation is even more dramatic because specific commitments in the context of the GATS have particular relevance, given that disciplines on National Treatment and Market Access provisions only kick in upon the condition that Members have made specific commitments in their schedules. In a context like that of the GATS, where Membership is already asymmetric, the concept of WTO-plus obligations and commitments may expand and compress the ambit of application of the PCO. Such a solution is suboptimal and may unduly constrain the right to regulate of WTO Members that have joined the club after 1995. Given the degree of interconnectedness of financial systems, it is probably not even in the interest of the original WTO Members to limit the regulatory autonomy on prudential legislation for latecomers, as this may lead to the spreading of market failures from the country of origin to other markets as well. This is yet another

---

[41] It is clear that AB reports have effects only on the parties to the dispute. It is also true that the AB is not bound by its previous case law and can issue decisions in contrast with its established jurisprudence in presence of 'cogent reasons', as per Article 3.2 of the DSU.

warning sign against the classification of the PCO as an exception-type provision.

5.3 The PCO as a Tool to Address Contingencies

The PCO is broad in scope, to the extent that it is essentially able to cover any deviation from the obligations determined by the Annex on Financial Services and the commitments made by Members in their schedule under the relevant sectors and subsectors. One may wonder, at this stage, whether the presence of a provision structured with this formulation renders useless or of negligible value the rest of the discipline provided for by the Agreement itself.

From the preceding discussion, it emerges that the terms for the invocation of the PCO by a regulating Member should be almost entirely left to the considerations that the latter may make, in accordance with the political agenda pursued. In other terms, the PCO may lead a Member to intervene in the regulatory landscape and to modify it (but also to maintain regulations in place irrespective of their compatibility with internationally agreed trade obligations) according to self-judged prudential concerns. Reference to other self-judging provisions in the WTO legal system may help understand the uniqueness of the PCO and its particular role.

In a recent piece, Sykes analyses the concept of 'economic necessity' in the WTO system.[42] Among the provisions he takes into account in his work, he makes interesting points on Article XXI of the GATT 1994 and on the discipline on Safeguards under WTO law.

Sykes acknowledges that Article XXI of the GATT 1994 was never an archetypical benchmark for lawfulness of domestic measures in the context of a GATT–WTO dispute. He finds that the explanation for this is twofold. On one hand, the provision allows Members to adopt measures that they 'consider' to be necessary to achieve the stated objectives. Such wording should suggest deference to adjudicators in the scrutiny of the rationale behind measures adopted in pursuance of the objectives indicated in Article XXI of the GATT 1994. On the other hand, however, the author maintains that the provision under analysis is limited to specific concerns that, however broad, seem to leave the possibility to address industrial policy or economic problems outside of its ambit. From all of the above, Sykes draws the lesson that narrowly tailored exceptions can function well, even in cases where they are left to the discretion and the

[42] Sykes, 'Economic 'Necessity' in International Law'.

self-judgment of the regulator. Moreover, he goes even further clarifying that, noteworthy in his opinion, 'Article XXI does *not* encompass exigencies such as financial distress of a member government or domestic economic crises unrelated to war and international emergencies' [emphasis added].[43]

Clearly, Article XXI of the GATT 1994, considering its reliance on circumstances that are observable and objective, cannot serve as a useful comparator for the PCO, which seems to go even further in carving out policy space for governments when addressing policy concerns that may change over time and could not even be foreseen at the time in which the Annex on Financial Services was negotiated.

Sykes also examines Article XIX of the GATT 1994 (Emergency Action on Imports of Particular Products). The latter specifically addresses issues of economic contingencies, namely a dramatic increase in imports of a particular product that harms domestic producers of like or directly competitive goods, provided that the latter is the outcome of an unforeseen development and the effect of the trade obligations of the importing Member.

On one hand, the rationale behind a measure drafted in this way may not seem to serve the interests of the efficiency of the world's market. A broad and vague escape clause may contribute to diminishing the credibility of the concessions made during the negotiations, given the possibility for Members to withdraw them according to situations that are not specified with a great amount of detail. On the other hand, however, such a legal construction may contribute to enhancing the flexibility of the system. In other words, because not all the developments in the market can be foreseen at the time of the signing of the agreement, Members may feel safer at the time of agreeing on concessions because they will keep the autonomy to address dramatic market failures.[44] Safeguards do not provide flexibility for the sake of flexibility ex ante. Rather, they incite commitments ex post, in the sense that they ease adjustment.

To benefit from Article XIX of the GATT 1994 (to be read together with the clarifications provided by the Agreement on Safeguards), four requirements must be met[45]: a dramatic increase in quantity of imports of a

---

[43] Sykes, 'Economic 'Necessity' in International Law', p. 303.
[44] It must be borne in mind that, as a result of the negotiations of the Uruguay Round, an Agreement on Safeguards clarifies the scope of application of Article XIX of the GATT 1994 and the conditions that Member have to respect in order to adopt safeguard measures.
[45] See, among others, Petros C. Mavroidis and Mark Wu, *The Law of the World Trade Organization: Documents, Cases & Analysis* (2nd edn.; St. Paul, MN: WEST, 2013) 1072

5.3 THE PCO AS A TOOL TO ADDRESS CONTINGENCIES   193

particular good must occur that should not be the outcome of the ordinary course of trade or a mere effect of greater trade liberalisation, but should rather be the result of an 'unforeseen development'; the situation must have caused (or at least threaten to cause) injury to the domestic producers of like or similar goods; and a causal link between the increase in imports and the injury suffered by the domestic industry must be proved. Moreover, safeguard schemes must be progressively phased out after a maximum of four years and the Member that imposes them shall enter into negotiations with the exporting Member to provide the latter with compensation.

Escape clauses have been extensively debated in the literature, and political economists have also tried to formalise models for the optimal design of escape clauses in international trade agreements. Rosendorff and Milner argue that escape clauses represent an efficient equilibrium under conditions of domestic uncertainty. Uncertainty about the developments in the world economy and the potential situations of distress that the domestic industry may face is likely to lead to the creation of mechanisms for institutional flexibility.[46] However, some costs on their use must be imposed, otherwise these escape clauses will end up not performing their function efficiently. This argument is key to the explanation because a 'low-cost' solution for a Member wishing to deviate from its commitments may lead the latter to make frequent use of the escape clauses. The third element of the explanation advanced by Rosendorff and Milner is that the introduction of an escape clause allowing Members to intervene in a situation of distress makes trade agreements easier to be concluded.[47]

How is this discussion relevant for the current work? Essentially, the PCO is a provision that gives Members the freedom to address contingencies, even if their actions would dry up their trade commitments. However, it cannot be usefully compared with the discipline on safeguards because it is not detailed enough, among other things. It is true that the PCO may be used as a tool to address contingencies, but it is also something more than that and deserves a more coherent interpretation and explanation.

(pp. 503 and ff.) for an overview of the relevant provisions along with the main clarifications provided for by the case law. For a detailed analysis of the law and the economic rationale for the Agreement on Safeguards, see Alan O. Sykes, *The WTO Agreement on Safeguards – A Commentary* (Oxford: Oxford University Press, 2006) 357.

[46] See, among others, B. Peter Rosendorff and Helen V. Milner, 'The Optimal Design of International Trade Institutions: Uncertainty and Escape', *International Organization*, 55:4 (2001), 829–57.

[47] Ibid.

5.4 Conclusions on Why Classifying the PCO as an Exception Is Not the Only Permissible Option

In addition to what has been reported so far, systemic concerns must also be assessed. If we were to assume that the PCO is an exception (or a tool to address contingencies), *quod non*, the question arises as to why it was included in the Annex on Financial Services as an annotation to Article VI of the GATS ('Domestic Regulation') and not as an annotation to Article XIV of the GATS. The answer to this question lies in the structure of the GATS as well as in the negotiating history of the provision.

The GATS is the outcome of a delicate compromise. Given the initial positions of the parties involved, the conclusion of a general agreement was considered a big achievement. Contrary to the GATT, which is still going strong after seventy years in force, the GATS is a complex and convoluted agreement seeking to strike a balance between 'progressive liberalisation' and the 'right to regulate'.[48]

Progressive liberalisation and the right of Members to regulate are not in a hierarchical relation to each other. Article VI of the GATS ('Domestic Regulation') is supplementary to the obligations on non-discrimination and market access of the same Agreement.[49] In its current form it provides for some obligations regarding the domestic regulatory process and lays the foundations for future disciplines on licensing, qualification and technical standards.

5.5 What the Mainstream Approach Overlooks: Negotiating History and Economic Rationale

The fact that the language of the provision is not self-interpreting should require the recourse to all available interpretative tools. In this respect, whilst the Panel in *Argentina – Financial Services* has privileged a rigid textual interpretation in accordance with the established practice of WTO adjudicating bodies, it did not find it useful to enquire into the matter further through available supplementary means of interpretation, as per

---

[48] Quoting from the preamble of the GATS: '*Members... Wishing* to establish a multilateral framework of principles and rules for trade in services with a view to the expansion of such trade under conditions of transparency and progressive liberalization'.
[49] In the *US – Gambling* case, the AB refrained from pronouncing on the relationship between Articles VI and XVI GATS. Instead, the AB considered that 'it is neither necessary nor appropriate for us to draw, in the abstract, the line between quantitative and qualitative measures'. See WTO Appellate Body Report, *US – Gambling*, supra n. 10, para. 250.

Article 32 of VCLT. As regards the GATS PCO, a number of documents are available to the interpreter wishing to reconstruct the negotiating history of the provision and what the drafters had in mind when they agreed upon its text. Such analysis is admittedly useful because it may contribute to shed some light on the problem that is being discussed here.

5.5.1 The Negotiating History of the PCO

Until late 1989, negotiators mostly discussed which sectors to include in the multilateral agenda for negotiations. In September 1989, at the twenty-third meeting of the Group of Negotiations on Services (GNS),[50] a discussion took place concerning general issues relating to trade in financial services. Admittedly, that meeting was the first occasion when negotiators debated trade in financial services. Negotiators there made clear their views on the necessity of leaving some leeway for governments interested in adopting domestic prudential measures.

There was overall consent about the necessity of respecting national sensitivities connected to prudential regulation, and many delegations took the floor to insist on this point, with the United States and the EU at the forefront.[51] The former insisted on respect for national specificities and the need not to confuse effective market access and National Treatment with the necessity to relax fundamental prudential measures.[52] The EU, for its part, argued that progressive liberalisation of financial services markets should not lead to deregulation at the domestic level, especially in the field of prudential measures.[53] Australia advanced the view that some sort of review mechanism of national prudential schemes was needed.[54] The common view was that national prudential schemes should not be relaxed in the name of opening up markets to trade.

This preliminary discussion was the start of the negotiations on trade in financial services. In 1990, a 'Working Group on Financial Services Including Insurance' was established. The mandate of the working group was to discuss the opportunity to negotiate an Annex on Financial Services to the GATS and its possible contents. Reyna[55] and

---

[50] Uruguay Round Doc. MTN.GNS/25, 'Group of Negotiations on Services – Note on the Meeting of 18–22 September 1989', paras. 15–63.
[51] Other countries also took the same stance, namely Sweden, Brazil, Pakistan, Canada and Singapore.
[52] Uruguay Round Doc. MTN.GNS/25, paras. 16 and 31.
[53] Ibid., para. 33.   [54] Ibid., para. 34.
[55] Jimmie V. Reyna, Services, ed. Terence P. Stewart, The GATT Uruguay Round: A Negotiating History (1986–1992) (Deventer: Kluwer, 1993) 329.

Marchetti[56] report that negotiators felt that the GATS as it was imagined at this stage did not sufficiently address the intricacies of financial services. Therefore, a detailed annex specifically dealing with such services was needed. The group held only four formal meetings, where talks concerning regulatory space for prudential measures were clearly preponderant.

5.5.1.1 Five Options for a PCO – Different Starting Positions

The first meeting of the Working Group on Financial Services was held 11–13 June 1990.[57] The Chairman, when introducing the agenda item concerning a prudential 'exception', asked the members to focus on *'how and where to draw the line between those measures that were consistent with the agreement and those that might go beyond it'*.[58] To facilitate the discussion between Members, the Chairperson himself had a non-paper circulated before the meeting containing five possible options to introduce a 'carve-out' on prudential measures:

> The first option provided for a prudential carve-out limited to a qualified national treatment provision. The second option was broader, permitting all 'reasonable' prudential and fiduciary measures. Option three was a variation of option two, enumerating examples of permissible measures. Option four provided for an unqualified right to take such measures. Option five aimed at defining as precisely as possible the prudential actions that would be permitted, so as to reduce legal uncertainties.[59]

As such, from the very beginning of the negotiations on financial services, the idea to introduce a provision according to which parties could maintain a margin for manoeuvre when adopting domestic prudential regulations – notwithstanding any other GATS obligation or commitment – gathered momentum (most likely because every domestic regime had similar measures in place). It can be said that, for some delegations at least, the introduction of a carve-out was the *conditio sine qua non* to give negotiations the green light. Uruguay Round participants, however, had different views with regard to both the scope of application as well as the legal function to be assigned to the provision.

---

[56] Marchetti, 'The GATS Prudential Carve-Out'.
[57] Uruguay Round Doc. MTN.GNS/FIN/1, 'Working Group on Financial Services Including Insurance – Note on the Meeting of 11–13 June 1990'.
[58] Ibid., para. 78.   [59] Ibid.

Table 5.1 *Positions of the delegations with regard to the chairperson's proposal for a prudential carve-out*

Trading nation	Preferred option
Australia	Combination of Options 1 (prudential carve-out limited to a qualified National Treatment provision) and 2 (all 'reasonable' prudential and fiduciary measures)
Canada, Japan, India, United States	Option 2 (all 'reasonable' prudential and fiduciary measures)
Sweden (also on behalf of other Nordic countries)	Combination of options 3 (variation of option 2, enumerating examples of permissible measures) and 4 (unqualified right to take such measures)
Switzerland and South Africa	Option 5 (definition as precise as possible of the prudential actions that would be permitted to reduce legal uncertainties)
EU, Thailand, Brazil, Egypt, Singapore, Malaysia, Hungary and Poland	None of the proposed options; suggested different approaches; some of these States insisted that prudential measures should not come under the purview of WTO Panels

The subsequent discussion reveals how, notwithstanding the fact that the majority of members were clearly in favour of a relatively broad carve-out, only a limited number of Members already had a clear idea about the kind of provision that would have represented the best solution. The majority of the delegations were in favour of option 2 (a broad carve-out, permitting all reasonable prudential and fiduciary measures). That said, on a closer look at the record, some nuances can be discerned even among those delegations with the same approach. It is therefore important to list the initial positions of the delegations that expressed their preference at an early stage.

The representative from Canada stated that there was no particular need to limit the coverage of the carve-out to National Treatment.[60] Rather, it was preferable in the view of the Canadian delegation to keep the scope of application of the provision broader. In this regard, Canada

[60] Ibid., para. 79.

sought a clearer definition of 'what was prudential and what was not' to avoid misunderstandings. Canada explicitly stood in favour of the justiciability of prudential measures before WTO panels, so that WTO Members would not be tempted to abuse of the carve-out.

Japan proposed an obligation to notify domestic prudential regulatory schemes to the Secretariat to enhance transparency.[61] India argued for the need to put specific provisions into the agreement for developing countries.[62] The Indian delegate said that option 2 was preferable, suggesting specification of the examples (an indicative list) of prudential measures that Members could lawfully adopt.

The EU was in favour of regulatory diversity at the national level.[63] It did not express an opinion in favour of any of the proposals for a carve-out that had been tabled by the Chairman but stressed the importance of acknowledging different sensitivities at the national level on financial regulation. Similarly, Thailand[64] did not favour any of the proposals for a carve-out that were on the table at that meeting.

Australia[65] argued that options 1 and 2 were more attractive. However, with specific regard to option 2 – according to which all 'reasonable' prudential and fiduciary measures should be permitted – it warned about the need to reach a broad consensus on the definition of 'reasonable' and the type of measures that this term could include (because the term was not self-interpreting). As we saw earlier, the term 'reasonable' was not included in the GATS PCO. However, it was included in the corresponding provision of the Chapter on Financial Services of NAFTA, which was being negotiated approximately during the same period.

Sweden, intervening on behalf of the other Nordic countries, shared the Australian view on the 'reasonableness' test. As for the preferred option of the group it represented, the Swedish delegation was in favor of a combination of options 2 and 3:

> [I]n the sense of an illustrative list of legitimate objectives for prudential and fiduciary regulations including monetary policy objectives, protection of fair and orderly markets, protection of depositors, investors, insurance policy holders and consumers, and prevention of inappropriate practices.[66]

The United States took a strong position in favour of option 2: a positive conclusion of the negotiations on a prudential carve-out was 'vital' for the

---

[61] Ibid., para. 80. [62] Ibid., para. 81. [63] Ibid., para. 82.
[64] Ibid., para. 83. [65] Ibid., para. 84. [66] Ibid., para. 85.

5.5 WHAT THE MAINSTREAM APPROACH OVERLOOKS 199

United States.[67] In the view of the US delegate, trading nations needed to keep as much freedom as possible when addressing prudential concerns, as long as they did not use the carve-out as a means to circumvent their multilateral obligations.

In contrast, Switzerland and South Africa[68] argued that option 5 was the best possible solution.[69] In particular, Switzerland warned that an unspecified 'reasonableness test' would put pressure on panels, whereas a more specific provision would have been more useful for the sake of legal certainty.

Brazil, Egypt and Singapore thought that it was difficult at that stage to negotiate an agreement on a prudential carve-out and refused to choose one of the tabled options.[70] Malaysia argued for the need to allow trading nations the maximum possible flexibility when regulating financial services on the basis of prudential concerns.[71] The Polish delegate stated that because his country was preparing to reconstruct its economy and its financial market, the issue deserved further consideration and that the time was not right to choose one of the proposed options.[72]

Regarding the possibility of submitting prudential measures to the scrutiny of WTO panels, Canada declared itself in favour of such an option, whereas the strongest opposition to this possibility came from Thailand, Malaysia and Hungary.[73] However, the tone of the discussion suggests that most Members did not really consider the possibility of completely excluding the justiciability of prudential measures for fear of opportunistic and protectionist behaviour.

Little at that stage was said with regard to the specific legal function that would be assigned to the PCO. Among the options proposed, only option 1 (National Treatment does not apply to prudential measures) or option 5 (exhaustive list of prudential measures excluded from the coverage of the agreement) were clearly designed in the form of exceptions to the application of other obligations or commitments. All of the other options, which were also the most popular among the Members, were designed to preserve the regulatory autonomy of the Members intervening in the regulation of their financial markets.

---

[67] Ibid., para. 86.   [68] Ibid., paras. 87–8.
[69] 'Option five aimed at defining as precisely as possible the prudential actions that would be permitted, so as to reduce legal uncertainties'.
[70] Uruguay Round Doc. MTN.GNS/FIN/1.   [71] Ibid., para. 92.
[72] Ibid., para. 93.   [73] Ibid., para. 79, para. 83 and para. 94, respectively.

Table 5.2 *Three formal proposals on prudential measures*

European Union	United States	SEACEN countries
No PCO proposed – measures to ensure that the supervision of financial institutions could override free movement of capitals	A provision that allowed trading nations to adopt all reasonable measures to address micro- and macroprudential concerns	Broad PCO; non-justiciability of prudential measures

5.5.2 *The EU, the United States and SEACEN Countries Tabled Three Formal Papers*

After these discussions, the EU, the United States and a group of South East Asian countries respectively submitted three formal papers to the Secretariat, addressing the necessity to allow WTO Member to have substantial margin for manouevre when addressing prudential concerns. The Western world was not united at that stage and showed different sensitivities with regard to the issue. The Southeast Asian countries, for their part, were extremely concerned with the idea of opening up their financial services markets. As stated earlier, Asia was recovering from a financial crisis, and financial regulators from that region were reluctant to give up on their powers at a time when their financial sectors were rebuilding and were proving to be essential for the development of these fragile economies.

The EU submitted a proposal for a draft of the Annex on financial services.[74] The document did not provide for a carve-out comparable to that approved at the end of the negotiations. Rather, the proposal by the EU aimed to remove unnecessary obstacles to the free movement of capital account transactions. However, *en passant*, the proposal submitted by the EU contained a reference to measures with the aim of ensuring wide powers for central banks and similar authorities to operate the prudential supervision of financial institutions.[75]

---

[74] Uruguay Round Doc. MTN.GNS/FIN/W/1, 'Working Group on Financial Services Including Insurance – Communication from the European Communities – Proposal by the European Community Draft Financial Services Annex to the Agreement on Trade in Services', 10 July 1990.

[75] Interestingly, because the last sentence of Article 14.2 does not include the measures provided in its letter d) among those which can have the effect of impeding capital movements, we can infer *a contrario* that – according to the EU proposal – measures for the prudential

5.5 WHAT THE MAINSTREAM APPROACH OVERLOOKS 201

Article 14 of the EU proposal, under the heading 'Payments and transfers for capital account transactions', read:

> 14.1. Each party shall permit payments and transfers for capital account transactions other than those referred in Article XIII.1 of the Agreement, to be made to or by a financial services provider of another party, freely and without delay into and out of the territory of the first party in a freely convertible currency at the spot exchange rate on the date of the transfer with respect to spot transactions, to the extent that such payments and transfers relate to the provision of cross-border services which are not prohibited by such party.
>
> 14.2. Notwithstanding the provisions of paragraph 1, any party may adopt or maintain:
>
> a) restrictions on payments and transfers for capital account transactions that are applied pursuant to Article 15 of this Annex;
> b) measures required to prevent infringement of their laws and regulations, inter alia, in the field of taxation;
> c) procedures for the declaration of capital movements for purposes of administrative or statistical information or in order to verify the authenticity of the transactions;
> d) *measures to ensure the prudential supervision of financial institutions.*
>
> The measures and procedures referred to in letters b) and c) above shall not have the effect of impeding capital movements. [Emphasis added]

The United States,[76] in contrast, stressed its main concerns in relation to a multilateral framework for the negotiations on trade in financial services. In relation to prudential measures, it noted:

> [A]ny agreement covering financial services should respect the traditional duties, rights, and responsibilities of finance ministers, central bank governors, and other regulators and officials in the financial services sector. More specifically, any such agreement must contain a provision which permits a Party to take reasonable actions necessary for prudential reasons, for the protection of investors and depositors, or for the protection of persons to whom a fiduciary duty is owed by a financial service provider.

In the view of the US delegation, therefore, members of the new agreement on financial services should have the possibility to adopt 'reasonable' microprudential measures, in addition to the macroprudential

---

supervision of banks and other financial institutions could also have the effect to limit (or even to impede) capital movements.

[76] Uruguay Round Doc. MTN.GNS/FIN/W/2, 'Working Group on Financial Services Including Insurance – Communication from the United States – Submission by the Unites States on Financial Services', 12 July 1990.

instruments relating to the traditional duties of central banks and governments.

The South East Asian Central Banking and Monetary Authorities Countries (SEACEN)[77] submitted a third paper. This group maintained a very strong position in favour of a broad carve-out. In the view of the Members of the group, in terms of importance prudential measures overrode all other possible provisions of the future agreement.

> The process of financial liberalization must take cognizance of the overriding importance of prudential consideration, monetary policies and national development objectives. In developing countries like SEACEN members, financial services play a pivotal role in economic development. Hence, liberalization must ensure that developments in the financial sector do not adversely affect the effectiveness of national institutions and the overall general well-being of the economy as well as allow flexibility to nations in the design and implementation of banking and credit policies which are normal functions of a central bank or monetary authority.[78]

The document underlined the importance of both micro- and macroprudential concerns in the regulation of financial services. In the SEACEN countries' view, measures taken for prudential reasons should not be subjected to any dispute settlement procedure.[79]

The SEACEN group (established informally in 1966 and provided with legal status as of 1982) already had some experience in the field of mutual assistance in developing central bank policies, facilitating exchanges among its members and respecting high prudential standards. The members of SEACEN were very active in GATS negotiations and keen on substantially liberalising their markets; their main concern was financial stability given their experience in this area.[80] Being part of a group helped

---

[77] Representing Indonesia, Korea, Nepal, Malaysia, Myanmar, Philippines, Singapore, Sri Lanka and Thailand.

[78] Uruguay Round Doc. MTN.GNS/FIN/W/3, 'Working Group on Financial Services Including Insurance – Communication from the Delegation of Malaysia', 12 September 1990.

[79] The paper submitted by SEACEN countries basically formalised the positions already expressed by Thailand in the first meeting of the negotiating group (see Uruguay Round Doc. MTN.GNS/FIN/1, para. 83).

[80] Quoting from the minutes of Uruguay Round Doc. MTN.GNS/FIN/3, 'Working Group on Financial Services Including Insurance – Note on the Meeting of 13–15 September 1990', para. 4: 'The requests of SEACEN countries, submitted in MTN.GNS/FIN/W/3, were not aimed at protecting domestic financial markets but the stability of the financial system. Liberalization should also take account of the particular characteristics of the relatively immature financial systems in developing countries and the central role of the system in fulfilling the socio-economic development objectives of countries. Hence, the position put

relatively small States have their voices heard because of their increased bargaining power.[81]

5.5.3 The Brussels Ministerial Conference (December 1990)

A draft text of the GATS was prepared for the Brussels Ministerial Conference of December 1990, which was supposed to mark the end of the Uruguay Round. Due to disagreement primarily on agricultural issues (more precisely, about the transformation of the European Common Agricultural Policy), the meeting failed to reach its ultimate goal.

There was also substantial disagreement among the parties with regard to the exact scope of an Annex on financial services. As such there were ultimately no provisions in the draft dealing with financial services.[82]

During the 1990 Brussels Ministerial Conference two proposals for a financial services Annex circulated. The first was submitted by Canada, Japan, Sweden and Switzerland.[83] It contained a provision specifically dealing with prudential measures and was intended to be an addendum to Article XIV (*General Exceptions*) of the draft agreement. The proposed text for the prudential exception advanced by the four countries read as follows:

> **Ad Article XIV: Exceptions**
>
> 1. The 'measures' referred to in the first sub-paragraph of Article XIV:1 of the Agreement include, in addition to sub-paragraphs 1(a) and 1 (b):
>
> 'reasonable measures taken for prudential reasons, to assure the protection of investors, depositors, policy holders or persons to whom a fiduciary duty is owed by a financial service provider, or to ensure the integrity and stability of a party's financial system'.

---

forward indicated a willingness to liberalize, which had been the member countries' policy anyway, but in a graduated manner.'

[81] For an analysis of the role of coalitions in trade negotiations, see: Mateo Diego-Fernández, 'Trade Negotiations Make Strange Bedfellows', *World Trade Review*, 7:2 (2008), 423–53, John S Odell, 'Three Islands of Knowledge About Negotiation in International Organizations', *Journal of European Public Policy*, 17:5 (2010), 619–32, Amrita Narlikar, *International Trade and Developing Countries: Bargaining Coalitions in GATT and WTO* (Routledge, 2003).

[82] See Reyna, *Services*: 'The text provided for a financial services annex, since the parties agreed that the GNS needed such an annex. However, there was no agreement on the scope and content for a financial services annex, due to the uncertainty over application of MFN, so the financial service annex consisted of a blank paper' (p. 55).

[83] Uruguay Round Doc. MTN.TNC/W/50, 'Trade Negotiations Committee – Communication from Canada, Japan, Sweden and Switzerland', 3 December 1990.

The second proposal was tabled by Malaysia on behalf of SEACEN countries.[84] The PCO included in the proposal tabled by the SEACEN countries was thought of as an addendum to Article VI of the GATS ('Domestic Regulation') and read as follows:

Article VI: Domestic Regulation

1. Notwithstanding any other provisions in the Agreement, a Party shall not be prevented from taking measures for prudential reasons, including for the protection of investors, depositors, policy holders or persons to whom a fiduciary duty is owed by a financial service provider, or to ensure the integrity and stability of the financial system.

The wording of the two texts was similar, although relevant differences should be pointed out. The text proposed by Canada, Japan, Sweden and Switzerland included a requirement that prudential measures had to be 'reasonable' to be justified under Article XIV. The list of prudential objectives included in the text, notably, was exhaustive. In contrast, the wording proposed by Malaysia was strikingly similar to the first sentence of the provision currently in force. Both the proposed texts did not include the current final sentence of the PCO. Concerning the proposal tabled by Canada, Japan, Sweden and Switzerland, this is explained by the fact that the exception should have played in combination with the good-faith obligation enshrined in the chapeau of Article XIV of the GATS. As regards the proposal advanced by SEACEN countries, the absence of a sentence similar to that included in the current PCO can instead be explained because deviations from WTO obligations in pursuance of prudential objectives, according to the proponents, should have not been justiciable.

With specific regard to the PCO, the parties were still far from agreeing on the formulation and the legal characterisation of a provision addressing micro- and macroprudential concerns. Whilst there was overall agreement regarding the introduction of a provision specifically addressing prudential policies and the regulatory leeway for national governments, there was still disagreement as to its justiciability and with regard to the most efficient way to strike the balance between regulatory autonomy and the need to avoid protectionist abuses.

In contrast to the view of the SEACEN countries, Canada, the EU, Japan and the United States were in favour of the application of the dispute settlement provisions to measures taken for prudential reasons.

---

[84] Uruguay Round Doc. MTN.TNC/W/52 Trade Negotiations Committee – Communication from Malaysia, 'Draft SEACEN Financial Services Annex', 4 December 1990.

5.5 WHAT THE MAINSTREAM APPROACH OVERLOOKS 205

At a GNS meeting held between 10–25 July 1991,[85] the discussions on the PCO continued. The United States put forward its views on the texts proposed by Sweden (on behalf also of Canada, Japan and Switzerland) and by Malaysia (on behalf of SEACEN countries), respectively. In particular, the delegate of the United States expressed its concerns in relation to distinct elements of the two proposals. In Washington's view, the first proposal was probably too restrictive in linking prudential regulations with the exceptions listed in Article XIV of the GATS, whereas the second proposal was too broad in that it excluded prudential measures from the scope of application of the rules on dispute settlement. The opinions expressed by the delegate of the United States are particularly relevant for the final agreement on the formulation of the provision, and hence deserve to be reported:

> The basic question was whether or not to give central banks a blank check; if this were the case there would be no reason to have a financial services annex because any binding commitment could be undermined by actions a country deemed prudential. The issue was not whether there should be a strong or a weak prudential carve-out, but whether a country should be free to take any prudential measures necessary so long as the measures were not arbitrary, unjustifiable, or discriminatory between domestic and foreign financial serviceproviders... [L]inking the prudential carve out with Article VI of the framework on domestic regulation did not result in a weak carve-out but in a balance between keeping markets open to foreigners on fair terms and ensuring adequate leeway to take necessary prudential action.[86]

The United States thus openly backed the proposal to draft the PCO as a specific formulation of WTO Members' right to regulate rather than an exception. Moreover, it put the accent on the need to avoid arbitrary discrimination vis-à-vis foreign financial services suppliers.

The delegate of Japan sided with the United States and stressed that the regulatory leeway allowed by the agreement in relation to prudential measures should not be used to restrict foreign trade.[87]

The delegate from Singapore[88] reiterated that prudential measures should not be included in the provision addressing general exceptions because prudential concerns arise in peculiar circumstances, adding that two more issues should be taken into account in the discussion on the PCO. A requirement to notify measures adopted in pursuance of

---

[85] Uruguay Round Doc. MTN.GNS/44, Group Negotiations on Services, Note on the meeting of 10–25 July 1991.
[86] Ibid., para. 19.   [87] Ibid.   [88] Ibid., para. 20.

prudential objectives should be included in the Annex on Financial Services. However, Singapore warned against the use of words such as 'arbitrary' or 'unjustifiable' because they would add confusion in the context of a delicate assessment.

The Mexican delegate[89] stressed that Members were called to strike a balance between the need to ensure that regulators and supervisors had enough powers 'to ensure the solvency and security of the financial system and the safety of the depositor' and the necessity to avoid that any future agreement on financial services would substantially give them carte blanche. Interestingly, in response to Mexico, the delegate of Singapore affirmed that 'it was necessary to correct the misimpression that if supervisors were given unlimited powers they would be given "carte blanche"; supervisors already had this, so one would not be giving away anything'.[90]

Members met again on 17–27 September 1991.[91] On that occasion, Malaysia streamlined the position of SEACEN countries with regard to the negotiations for a PCO. Quoting from the minutes of the meeting:

> Regarding a provision on prudential measures, SEACEN remained firm that it could not be part of an exception provision for the reasons expounded at earlier meetings. However, SEACEN recognized concerns about the possibility of abuse of the provision and were willing to discuss any proposals to prevent such abuses.[92]

This meeting is important because the strongest supporters of a broad PCO (SEACEN Countries) mentioned the possibility of making some concessions to draft a proposal that could be agreed on by all negotiating Members.

On 14 September 1991, the GNS co-chairman[93] had an informal note on financial services and possible elements of an Annex on Financial

---

[89] Ibid., para. 21.   [90] Ibid.
[91] Uruguay Round Doc. MTN.GNS/45, Group Negotiations on Services, Note on the meeting of 17–27 July 1991.
[92] Ibid., para. 14.
[93] At a meeting held on 25 April 1991, Colombia Ambassador Jaramillo – the GNS chairman – indicated that he would be further assisted in his tasks by Australian Ambassador David Hawes. The role of Ambassador Hawes was initially that of leading the negotiations on sectoral annexes, although he eventually replaced Ambassador Jaramillo as the sole GNS chairman. The necessity of having an additional figure with the task of coordinating the sectoral negotiations was important in light of the need to speed up the process with a view to concluding the Uruguay Round. For a discussion concerning the appointment of Ambassador Hawes as GNS co-chairman, see Yi-Chong Xu and Patrick Moray Weller, *The Governance of World Trade: International Civil Servants and the GATT/WTO* (Cheltenham: Edward Elgar, 2004), p. 158.

5.5 WHAT THE MAINSTREAM APPROACH OVERLOOKS 207

Services circulated with the negotiating delegations.[94] The text of the proposal is, unfortunately, not publicly available. On the following date, Sweden, on behalf of Canada, Japan and Switzerland, submitted an amended version of its proposal for an Annex on Financial Services.[95] The newly proposed text qualified the PCO as an exception and added reference to the necessity to avoid 'arbitrary' or 'unjustifiable' restrictions to foreign trade. There are no detailed records of the ensuing discussions, as the note on the meetings simply reports that '(d)elegations offered comments and raised questions regarding these texts'.[96]

The discussions continued on an informal basis, probably with the direct involvement of personnel from capitals and not just among negotiating delegations. In a meeting held on 20 December 1991, the Chairman of the Trade Negotiations Committee, Arthur Dunkel, issued a draft text for all the negotiating areas (the so-called Dunkel Draft).[97] The PCO provided by the Dunkel Draft had the same wording and structure of the provision now in force.

As can be seen, towards the end of the talks, parties agreed to take prudential measures out of the realm of exceptions (under which it could have been harder to justify the adoption of prudential regulatory schemes by the respondent in the event of a dispute). However, they also agreed that prudential measures could nonetheless be scrutinised and potentially outlawed by WTO panels. In light of the discussions reported thus far, it is fair to argue that Members achieved a compromise that could be defined as 'domestic regulation in exchange of justiciability'. The PCO, at least in the view of the Members that drafted the provision, was not an exception

---

[94] This information is reported in Uruguay Round Doc. MTN.GNS/46, Group Negotiations on Services, Note on the meetings of 21 October–1 November 1991 and 29 November 1991, para. 7.

[95] Uruguay Round Doc. MTN.TNC/W/50/Add.2, 'Trade Negotiations Committee – Communication from Canada, Japan, Sweden and Switzerland – Addendum n. 2', 15 October 1991: 'In addition to Article XIV of the Framework, the following shall apply: 1. Nothing in this Agreement shall be construed to prevent the adoption or enforcement by any Party of reasonable measures taken for prudential reasons, including for the protection of investors, depositors, policy-holders or persons to whom a fiduciary duty is owned by a financial service provider, or to ensure the integrity and stability of a Party's financial system. Such measures shall not be applied in a manner which would constitute a means of arbitrary or unjustifiable (a) restriction on the provision of financial services by financial service providers of another Party or (b) discrimination between domestic and foreign financial service providers or between countries.'

[96] Uruguay Round Doc. MTN.GNS/46, para. 7.

[97] Uruguay Round Doc. MTN.TNC/W/FA, 'Draft Final Act Embodying the Results of the Uruguay Round of Multilateral Trade Negotiations', 20 December 1991.

but, more finely, a specific formulation of the right for WTO Members to adopt domestic regulations in the domain of financial services when pursuing prudential objectives. A non-exhaustive sample of possible prudential objectives that were not affected by the Members' GATS obligations or commitments was incorporated in the provision.

The wording in the Dunkel Draft represented the agreed compromise on the PCO by the negotiators. Records from the negotiations reveal that, despite different sensitivities and different stages of development, Uruguay Round participants were fully aware of the intrinsic fragility of financial markets and even those pushing more strongly in favour of more market openness for financial services were not willing to give away their regulatory autonomy on prudential disciplines. On the contrary, financial services proved to be, on the whole, extremely problematic.

Trading nations did not manage to reach a conclusive agreement on the relevant rules of the game by the end of the Uruguay Round. They had an agreement on the Annex on Financial Services and the Understanding on Commitments on Financial Services, but it was an interim agreement because there was substantive disagreement on issues relating to Market Access, with the United States particularly unhappy about the initial commitments made by Japan and other Asian countries.[98] For this reason, negotiations continued until the approval, in December 1997, of the Fifth Protocol to the GATS, also known as the Financial Services Agreement.

5.5.4 Interim Conclusion on Negotiating History

The negotiators reached an agreement on a broad PCO, structured with an indicative list of policy objectives that could be considered prudential and hence not covered by the discipline of the Annex on financial services. The core of the talks moved to the issue of whether to hold measures adopted in pursuance of prudential objectives still justiciable under the dispute settlement system of the WTO. Canada, the EU, Japan and the United States were in favour of the application of the dispute settlement provisions to measures taken for prudential concerns. The SEACEN countries opposed this possibility. In the end, Members decided that prudential measures can be scrutinised by WTO panels only to the extent that they amount to backhanded avoidance of trade obligations and commitments and with

---

[98] Jarreau, 'Interpreting the General Agreement on Trade in Services and the WTO Instruments Relevant to the International Trade of Financial Services: The Lawyer's Perspective' (p. 28).

the caveat that, according to Paragraph 4 of the Annex on financial services, such disputes should be adjudicated at the panel stage by experts in the domain of financial services.

The available documentation from the Uruguay Round shows that some participants proposed to draft the provision on prudential measures following the structure and wording of typical exception-type provisions. However consensus could not be reached on this, mostly due to the opposition of the SEACEN countries. Furthermore, it should not be forgotten that negotiations on the specific disciplines on financial services were among the most complicated ones in the history of the GATT or WTO. The compromise on financial services risked to founder many times, mainly because not all the Parties were keen on making substantial concessions. The PCO, with its broad scope of application and the wide margin for manouver left to national governments, served as cornerstone for a difficult compromise. It is fair to conclude that there would not be any Annex on Financial Services of the GATS without a PCO drafted in these terms. Negotiations, in fact, could only proceed on the basis that a provision excluding prudential measures from the coverage of the Annex on Financial Services of the GATS was included in it.

The negotiating history is further backed by the economic rationale behind the drafting of the provision at the time of the Uruguay Round talks as well as the evolution of the economic thinking since the late 1990s.

5.5.5 The Negotiating History Meets the PCO's Economic Rationale

The financial sector is at the heart of modern economies, especially in industrialised countries, and the integrity and soundness of financial institutions and the financial system considered as a whole are a crucial factor for the stability of the entire economy of a country. As such, the arguments in favour of sound regulation of financial markets are solid. Deregulation occurred in some domestic jurisdictions (especially in the 1980s and 1990s) but happened with the vocal opposition of different sectors of the public and came at a cost. Moreover, the unprecedented financial crisis of 2007 and 2008 signalled the start of a new wave of financial regulation, both coordinated in international forums as well as driven by the political priorities of governments in domestic jurisdictions. We live, in fact, in re-regulation times. As shown in Chapter 2, financial regulation is justified by market failures, generally: market power, information asymmetries and negative externalities.

Against the background of those market failures, it is important to stress that the financial industry is one of the most innovative with new instruments being traded in the markets in the absence of pre-existing rules. One of the hardest tasks for financial regulators it that of keeping up with financial innovation, especially when unforeseen problems arise. This alone might be a solid basis for Members to keep freedom to regulate when negotiating an international agreement on trade in financial services. Sometimes actors in financial markets are not even exactly aware of the instruments they are using.

These market failures and their potential negative effects are so prevalent in the financial sector that national authorities are often in a condition of 'ignorance'. Borrowing from Stirling, such a condition can be defined as 'a state under which there exist neither grounds for the assignment of probabilities, nor even a basis for the definition of a comprehensive set of outcomes'.[99]

In other scientific fields, the acknowledgement of ignorance has led to the establishment of the so-called precautionary principle.[100] The rationale behind such a principle is to allow regulators, who are ignorant as to the probability of the occurrence of imminent harm, to adopt the necessary interventions to avoid negative outcomes until scientific evidence emerges. In other words, the precautionary principle allows regulators to maintain a modest but nonetheless proactive approach towards unknown developments and to avoid the potential negative outcomes, which could derive from a permissive legislation adopted on the bases of scarce scientific information. Given the importance of the protected interests, the WTO legal order in its SPS Agreement introduced the concept of 'adequate level of protection' (ALOP) and allows Members to set their own, both on a definitive level under Article 5.1 of the SPS Agreement as well as on a temporary basis under Article 5.7 of the SPS Agreement. Members must be consistent with the chosen ALOP, and their policies have to be based on scientific evidence. The case is even more dramatic when it comes to financial services. History reveals that it has proven difficult for governments and institutions entrusted with the duty of supervising

---

[99] Andrew Stirling, 'On 'Precautionary' and 'Science Based' Approaches to Risk Assessment and Environmental Appraisal', in Andrew Stirling (ed.), *On Science and Precaution in the Management of Technological Risk*, Volume II (European Science and Technology Observatory, 2001), 36–93 (p. 56).

[100] Mavroidis, *Trade in Goods* (p. 731) assesses the status of the precautionary principle under customary international law.

financial institutions to predict crises and to react promptly to avoid the spread of dramatic consequences.

This is why, especially in the aftermath of the recent crisis, both international forums and national authorities stressed the need to revise the financial regulatory architecture and to provide supervisory authorities with the necessary tools to intervene in a timely manner and limit the negative consequences of financial distress. A collapse in the financial sector is likely to trigger domino effects, potentially in all other sectors of the economy.

Moreover, the crisis and its aftermath have also shown that some governments may have the incentive to deregulate or not to regulate financial markets according to sound prudential principles because that would be costly and lead to economic losses. Therefore, they may have the incentive to free ride the prudential burdens imposed on larger jurisdictions and offer cheap and safe harbours to riskier and more lucrative speculative activities.

Members facing the challenge of a more sound financial regulation should not be prevented from taking bold steps for the protection of the stability of financial systems because of strict and debatable interpretations of WTO provisions.[101]

Therefore, against this background, it is not surprising that Uruguay Round participants decided keep sovereignty over financial regulation and to exclude prudential legislation from the coverage of WTO law. Such elasticity probably serves the interests of the WTO system as a whole, given that a strict interpretation of the PCO may lead to situations of regulatory chill under which Members may be afraid to modify their financial regulation to avoid being found in violation of WTO law.

5.6 An Alternative Approach

Having reconciled the negotiating history of the PCO with the economic rationale behind prudential regulation, it is now important to explain the contours of the other permissible approach that this volume argues for in the interpretation of the provision. Such an approach admittedly allows to give meaning to all the terms of the provision and to fit it more appropriately in its context.

---

[101] See Coffee, 'Extraterritorial Financial Regulation: Why E. T. Can't Come Home' (pp. 1297 and ff.) for a detailed analysis of the issue.

5.6.1 The Heading 'Domestic Regulation' – Nomina Sunt Consequentia Rerum

An often-quoted passage from Justinian's Institutiones is 'nomina sunt consequentia rerum'. The expression, meaning 'names correspond to the things they are attached to', is a reasonable starting point for the present discussion. The heading of the provision under analysis ('Domestic Regulation') should have warned those who attempt to interpret the PCO of the GATS about the peculiar nature of the provision, as opposed to the traditional exception-type provisions provided for by the various WTO Agreements. Indeed, the emphasis on the need not to consider the provision as an exception akin to Article XIV of the GATS was brought up by several Members in the context of the negotiation of the Annex on Financial Services.

The Annex on Financial Services of the GATS is complementary to the main framework agreement for trade in services (the GATS) and follows its structure. The idea behind the Annex is to clarify the function and scope of application of the various provisions of the GATS when disciplining Members' obligations and commitments in the domain of trade in financial services, a delicate and still heavily regulated sector at the domestic level. It provides for a *lex specialis* on some aspects of the GATS to better protect (at least this was the idea of the drafters) the Members' interests in the field.

In a contribution that can be considered seminal in terms of providing a better understanding of the instrument, Jarreau wrote:

> The Annex on Financial Services, like the Annex on Article II Exemptions, is an integral part of the GATS. The financial services annex is, however, applicable only to trade in financial services. It is a financial services supplement to the framework agreement designed to provide greater specificity with regard to trade in financial services. The Annex on Financial Services is divided into five numbered sections, each relating to a specific article or articles of the framework agreement... *The second section of the annex corresponds to Article VI of the framework agreement, Domestic Regulation.* It authorizes each WTO Member to establish 'prudential' regulatory measures to protect purchasers and beneficiaries of financial services, as well as its domestic financial system. [Emphasis added][102]

Later in the same piece the author clarifies that:

---

[102] Jarreau, 'Interpreting the General Agreement on Trade in Services and the WTO Instruments Relevant to the International Trade of Financial Services: The Lawyer's Perspective' (p. 36).

5.6 AN ALTERNATIVE APPROACH

Section 2 of the Annex on Financial Services is referred to as the 'prudential carve-out'. Notwithstanding any other provision of the GATS, Section 2 of the Annex permits Members to enact measures for 'prudential reasons'. Measures that may be deemed prudential are not defined but may include measures taken for "the protection of investors, depositors, policy holders or persons to whom a fiduciary duty is owed by a financial service supplier or to ensure the integrity and stability of the financial system". This section of the Annex affords Members considerable autonomy to enact financial regulatory measures. The freedom afforded by Section 2 may be subject to protectionist abuse as prudential measures are not considered limitations on market access or national treatment and, therefore, need not be inscribed in a Member's Schedule.[103]

Headings do not have the same power as the substantive wording of provisions.[104] They are not sources of legal obligations but certainly reflect the content of the provisions they are linked to. It may certainly be seen as an ex post evaluation, and there is indeed an element of hindsight, but in taking a closer look at the structure of the Annex on Financial Services and puts it in parallel with that of the GATS, one will find that there is a definite tendency to make the provisions of the former correspond to those of the latter and that respect is paid to the order of appearance of the various Articles. Paragraph 1 of the Annex on Financial Services (Scope and Definition) corresponds to Article I of the GATS (Scope and Definition), Paragraph 3 of the Annex on Financial Services (Recognition) corresponds to Article VII of the GATS (Recognition), Paragraph 4 of the Annex on Financial Services (Dispute Settlement) corresponds to Article XXIII of the GATS (Dispute Settlement and Enforcement) and Paragraph 5 of the Annex on Financial Services (Definitions) corresponds to Article XXVIII of the GATS (Definitions). Following this pattern, then, the PCO – should it be drafted as an addendum to Article XIV of the GATS (General Exceptions) – would have followed (and not preceded) Paragraph 3 on recognition, and moreover, it would have more probably had another heading.

Instead the order of appearance of the various provisions suggests that the PCO performs the function of an addendum to Article VI of the GATS, setting up a special discipline for domestic regulation adopted in pursuance of prudential aims in the domain of financial services. It pertains to the regulatory autonomy that Members enjoy when pursuing legitimate policy objectives in that field.

---

[103] Ibid. (p. 67). [104] A famous Latin maxim reads: *rubrica non est lex*.

It should be noted, however, that the Panel in *Argentina – Financial Services* disagrees with the foregoing. The Panel, in fact, denies any correspondence between the provisions in the Annex on Financial Services and those of the GATS. To prove its point, the Panel refers to Paragraph 4 of the Annex on Financial Services (Dispute Settlement) and argues that there is no exactly corresponding provision in the GATS, the most similar item therein being Article XXIII, with the heading 'Dispute Settlement and Enforcement'.[105]

The PCO applies 'notwithstanding any other provisions' of the Agreement, thus it covers obligations as well as specific commitments. It applies, therefore, to the general discipline set forth in Article VI of the GATS as well. An explanation for this lies in the text of the latter. The first paragraph of the provision reads:

> In sectors where specific commitments are undertaken, each Member shall ensure that all measures of general application affecting trade in services are administered in a reasonable, objective and impartial manner.

Paragraph 5(a) of the same provision adds:

> In sectors in which a Member has undertaken specific commitments, pending the entry into force of disciplines developed in these sectors pursuant to paragraph 4, the Member shall not apply licensing and qualification requirements and technical standards that nullify or impair such specific commitments in a manner which:
>
> (i) does not comply with the criteria outlined in subparagraphs 4(a), (b) or (c); and
> (ii) could not reasonably have been expected of that Member at the time the specific commitments in those sectors were made.

One explanation for the introduction of such a broad PCO could be found in between the lines of Article VI of the GATS. Members negotiated a text that could allow them to amend their existing legislation or to enact new laws even in contrast with the limitations enlisted in their schedules of specific commitments, on the basis that they had done so in pursuance of legitimate prudential policy goals.

The GATS is a negative integration agreement and does not aim for the harmonisation of domestic policies. Right from its preamble, it reaffirms Members' right to regulate according to domestic policy objectives, acknowledging, on one hand that any policy choice may affect trade but, on the other, that trade liberalisation is not 'the only game in town', as

---

[105] Panel Report, *Argentina – Financial Services*, para. 7.845.

5.6 AN ALTERNATIVE APPROACH

governments have more complex agendas and interests to protect. The PCO arguably expands the perimeter of regulatory autonomy, giving Members wider scope of manoeuver in the domain of prudential regulation, a concept that is, by its nature, evolutionary and broad.

Members of the WTO enjoy considerable regulatory autonomy and have kept sovereignty over the possibility of making modifications to their prudential regulation arsenal in ordinary and extraordinary times. Moreover, paraphrasing Jarreau, the considerable autonomy granted to Members allows them to take such measures in ordinary and extraordinary times. In other words, because nothing in the PCO indicates otherwise, 'measures for prudential reasons' may include day-to-day regulation, as well as preventive and crisis management instruments.

The Annex on Financial Services of the GATS has a specific structure. It provides for *lex specialis* to that of the GATS in the context of trade in banking services, insurance services and other types of financial services, according to the definitions and commitments contained in Members' schedules. Against this background, the PCO can be admittedly read as a *lex specialis* to the discipline of Article VI of the GATS ('Domestic Regulation'), clarifying the rights and limits that Members keep with specific regard to a broad area of financial regulation that is constantly evolving and is commonly known as prudential regulation.

If not an exception, how should the PCO then be classified? It is hereby argued that the wording, the context and the object and purpose of the provision as well as its negotiating history permit an alternative reading. If a comparison should be made with other provisions of the WTO-covered agreements, those need not be Article XX of the GATT 1994 or Article XIV of the GATS, as elaborated in the following subsection.

5.6.2 The PCO as a 'Provision That Excludes the Application of Other Provisions' against the Background of WTO Law and Case Law

The PCO can be identified as a 'provision that excludes the application of other provisions', to borrow an expression used by Grando in a seminal work.[106] On the basis of a thorough analysis of the case law of WTO Panels and the Appellate Body, Grando classifies provisions containing rules exempting WTO Members from compliance with generally applicable obligations in two main categories: (i) provisions that establish

---

[106] Michelle Grando, *Evidence, Proof and Fact-Finding in WTO Dispute Settlement*, pp. 154 and ff.

an exception to a rule and (ii) provisions that exclude the application of other provisions.[107]

That distinction is not merely formal, as it entails substantial consequences regarding the allocation of the burden of proof in the context of a dispute. In fact, in the case of exceptions, it is for the complainant to prove that the respondent has violated a general obligation and then for the respondent to prove that it was entitled to do so, having fulfilled the conditions for the lawful invocation of an exception. Conversely, as regards provisions that the exclude the application of other provisions, the complainant must prove that the defendant was not entitled to benefit from those, and, if such burden is discharged, the complainant can try to persuade the Panel that the respondent has violated a general rule.

There are a number of examples of provisions that exclude the application of other provisions in WTO case law. Article IV of the GATT 1994 ('Special Provision Relating to Cinematograph Films'), for example, serves the same function with regard to film quotas that Members can adopt to protect their domestic cultural industry. It reads:

Article IV – Special Provisions Relating to Cinematograph Films

If any contracting party establishes or maintains internal quantitative regulations relating to exposed cinematograph films, such regulations shall take the form of screen quotas which shall conform to the following requirements:

(a) Screen quotas may require the exhibition of cinematograph films of national origin during a specified minimum proportion of the total screen time actually utilized, over a specified period of not less than one year, in the commercial exhibition of all films of whatever origin, and shall be computed on the basis of screen time per theatre per year or the equivalent thereof;

(b) With the exception of screen time reserved for films of national origin under a screen quota, screen time including that released by administrative action from screen time reserved for films of national origin, shall not be allocated formally or in effect among sources of supply;

(c) Notwithstanding the provisions of subparagraph (b) of this Article, any contracting party may maintain screen quotas conforming to the requirements of subparagraph (a) of this Article which reserve a minimum proportion of screen time for films of a specified origin other than that of the contracting party imposing such screen quotas; Provided that no such minimum proportion of screen time shall be increased above the level in effect on April 10, 1947;

---

[107] Ibid.

(d) Screen quotas shall be subject to negotiation for their limitation, liberalization or elimination.

The provision is designed differently from the PCO. However, the rationale behind the former is more similar to that behind the PCO than is the case regarding exception-type provisions. The way in which Article IV of the GATT 1994 is drafted leads the interpreter to consider it more in terms of a *lex specialis* dealing with a particular type of goods. As Ehring interestingly argued:

> Article IV grants WTO members a limited right to restrict the showing of films of foreign origin. The effect of Article IV is similar to that of a qualified exception to the obligations contained in Article III (national treatment) and Article I:1 (most-favoured-nation treatment). Legally, however, Article IV is formulated not as an exception of the same type as Article XX or XXI, but as a lex specialis dealing specifically with films. It imposes obligations on members that establish or maintain internal quantitative regulations. Article IV establishes a special legal regime for internal quantitative regulations relating to cinematograph films, which partly differs from general rules such as Articles I:1 and III. In contrast, Article III:10 is an exception in the technical sense, and it exempts measures that fall under, and comply with, Article IV from the disciplines of Article III, which may otherwise apply. Article IV is thus not an exception in the technical sense, which a respondent would have to invoke, in a WTO dispute in response to a complainant's claim of a violation of other provisions of the GATT. Rather, the complainant would have to invoke Article IV as being violated and bear the burden of proof in that regard.[108]

Article IV of the GATT 1994 is not the only provision in WTO to serve this function. Other agreements also contain specific disciplines addressing particular situations and dealing with special rules applicable only to a subset of domestic regulations adopted by governments of trading nations.

Another analogy could be drawn with the precautionary principle under paragraph 7 of Article 5 of the WTO Agreement on the Application of Sanitary and Phytosanitary Measures (SPS) ('Assessment of Risk and Determination of the Appropriate Level of Sanitary or Phytosanitary Protection'), which reads:

> In cases where relevant scientific evidence is insufficient, a Member may provisionally adopt sanitary or phytosanitary measures on the basis of available pertinent information, including that from the relevant

---

[108] Lothar Ehring, 'Article IV of the GATT: An Obsolete Provision or Still a Basis for Cultural Policy', in Inge Govaere, Reinhard Quick and Marco Bronckers (eds.), *Trade and Competition Law in the EU and Beyond* (Cheltenham: Edward Elgar, 2011), 96–118 (p. 114).

international organizations as well as from sanitary or phytosanitary measures applied by other Members. In such circumstances, Members shall seek to obtain the additional information necessary for a more objective assessment of risk and review the sanitary or phytosanitary measure accordingly within a reasonable period of time.

Again, this provision differs substantially in content and structure from the PCO. However, the rationale behind it is relatively similar and allows Members to regulate in situations of uncertainty or ambiguity. It does so, however, on the condition that Members satisfy a number of conditions, namely: (1) the available relevant scientific information must be insufficient, (2) provisional measures should adopted on the basis of available pertinent information, (3) obtaining additional information will be necessary for a more objective assessment and (4) the measures adopted must be reviewed after the elapse of a reasonable period of time. None of these conditions appear in the PCO.

Although no extensive case law exists on the issue and some WTO Members understand the application of this principle as limited by the requirements of proportionality, necessity and consistency with past practice,[109] the Panel in *European Communities – Approval and Marketing of Biotech Products* clarified that Article 5.7 of the SPS Agreement must be classified as a 'qualified right', and therefore the burden of proof in the event of a dispute should follow the general '*actori incumbit probatio*' rule.[110] In other words, according to that panel, it is up to the complainant that brings the case against the regulating Member to make the case that the domestic piece of legislation goes beyond the boundaries crafted under Article 5.7 of the SPS Agreement. The latter confers on Members the right to set the level of protection they deem appropriate in a situation of insufficient scientific evidence. The Appellate Body has had the chance to clarify its understanding of the meaning of the expression 'qualified right':

> Where a Member exercises its right to adopt an SPS measure that results in a higher level of protection, that right is qualified in that the SPS measure must comply with the other requirements of the SPS Agreement, including the requirement to perform a risk assessment.[111]

Admittedly, the divide between rules and exceptions is functional in the sense that it helps clarify the allocation of burden of proof depending on

[109] See the communication by the EU: WTO Doc. G/SPS/GEN/168 of 14 March 2000.
[110] Panel Report, *EC – Approval and Marketing of Biotech Products*, para. 7.2976.
[111] Appellate Body Report, *Canada – Continued Suspension*, para 532.

the frequency distribution of transactions that the framers had in mind when drafting the specific formulation of given provisions.[112] Usually, drafters reveal their intention concerning the classification of provisions as exceptions either through the title of provision (Article XX of the GATT 1994) or by using specific words to that effect.

Case law has not always followed a coherent path in this regard. In *China – Raw Materials*, for instance, the Appellate Body dealt with the characterisation of Article XI.2 of the GATT 1994 and its interplay with Article XI.1. Despite that at first glance Article XI.2 of the GATT 1994 looks like a 'scope provision' and that the negotiating record clearly shows it was meant to perform that role, the Appellate Body held that it should be up to the defendant in case of a dispute to demonstrate that it met the conditions to lawfully impose export prohibitions or restrictions on a particular set of goods, thus characterising it as an exception.[113]

This assessment of other WTO Agreements leads to the conclusion that there are a number examples in WTO law of 'provisions that exclude the application of other provisions', although the divide between 'exceptions' and this latter category has not followed a linear path in the evolution of case law and the distinction is admittedly artificial. This volume argues that the PCO should be treated as a 'provision that ecludes the application of other provisions'. The foregoing is arguably more in line with the negotiating record of the provision as opposed to the current mainstream understanding of the GATS PCO.

5.7 Conclusion

The ordinary meaning of the PCO and the context in which it is placed suggest that Members have substantial regulatory freedom in the domain of prudential measures. The PCO is only limited by an obligation of good

---

[112] *Contra*, some authors argue that a rigid taxonomic distinction between rules and exceptions is not warranted. See, for instance, Tomer Broude, 'Genetically Modified Rules: The Awkward Rule-Exception-Right Distinction in EC-Biotech', *World Trade Review* 6:2 (2007), 215–231.

[113] See Appellate Body Report, *China – Raw Materials*, paras. 308–44. Mavroidis criticises the case law on Article XI:2 based on the negotiating history of the provision. At the time of the negotiations, several Members (including the United States) had a number of programs in place like those mentioned in Article XI.2 of the GATT 1994 and wanted to shield off similar programs from any legal challenge. See Petros C. Mavroidis, *The Regulation of International Trade: GATT* (Vol. 1) (Cambridge, MA: MIT Press, 2016), pp. 99–110.

faith unlike other provisions such as, for instance, Article 5.7 of the SPS Agreement, which are governed by the application of specific criteria that must be satisfied.

The decision by the Panel in *Argentina – Financial Services* to classify the provision as an exception, without paying the necessary attention to the wording and the context of the provision, can admittedly be criticised because a similar reasoning might unduly constrain the regulatory prerogatives of WTO Members. The fact that the Appellate Body left the window open as to how to classify the provision calls for additional thinking as to its design and function.

The classification of the provision as an exception or as a provision excluding the application of other provisions is important in light of the power for WTO panels to scrutinise whether domestic measures supposedly adopted by Members in pursuance of prudential objectives are in reality a means to surreptitiously avoid trade obligations or commitments. Because trade agreements are incomplete contracts by definition, and the PCO is a quintessential example of this given its non-exhaustive list of legitimate policy objectives and its circular wording, the interpreter has to take into account the possibility that panels may err.

Erroneous outcomes can be divided into two categories: *Type I errors – false positives* (where the court finds that the defendant has violated the rule, even though it has not) and *Type II errors – false negatives* (where the court finds that the defendant has not violated the rule even though it has). What is a more desirable outcome when an exception is invoked? And what is the case when it comes to the PCO? The answers to these questions are essential to understanding the function assigned to the PCO in the WTO legal order.

Typically, exceptions perform the task of limiting *Type II – false negative* situations, and this is why they usually have a limited scope of application. This means that they are usually designed narrowly because the gate should not be open too wide to permit Members to easily deviate from their trade obligations. Consequently a closed list of legitimate objectives together with stringent requirements to be met and a final control over the bona fide application of the measures make a Type I – false positive error a more desirable outcome in the event of a dispute.

Therefore, where an exception is invoked in a dispute, it is up to the defendant to demonstrate that its regulation, which in principle breaches one or more obligations of the agreement, satisfies the conditions set up in an exception and consequently is still lawful. A system that wants to avoid Type II errors allocates the persuasive burden in a dispute to the defendant in line with the general principle of law according to which '*quicumque exceptio invocat ejusdem probari debet*'.

In other cases, that is, when Type II errors are considered to be more desirable outcomes, the system is more deferential towards regulating Members. It accords them autonomy when regulating particularly sensitive issues; hence false negatives are considered the preferred outcome. In such cases, the burden of proof follows the general principle according to which it is up to the claimant to demonstrate that the defendant has violated the rules.

The rationale and the negotiating history of the PCO seem to suggest that the system wants to avoid Type I – false positive situations. Therefore, in the event of a dispute concerning prudential issues, the complainant would have to persuade the panel not only that the defendant has violated one or more GATS provisions or commitments but also that it has done so for reasons other than prudential purposes. Alternatively, even if it accepts that the purpose of a particular measure actually has a prudential goal, the complainant would have to show that the measure in question has been used as 'a means of avoiding a member's obligations or commitments' (something that is particularly difficult because this would require proving that the other member had acted in bad faith).[114]

The rationale for the PCO differs substantially from that which is typical of exception-type provisions in WTO agreements. The only limit that applies to Members' regulatory autonomy can be found in the final clause which, as explained earlier, only reaffirms an obligation of good faith. Because good faith is presumed, it would again be up to the complainant to demonstrate that the respondent used measures to avoid its obligations or commitments.

The PCO is a fundamental provision in the WTO framework of rules governing trade in financial services. However its wording is

---

[114] Joachim Åhman, *Trade, Health and the Burden of Proof in WTO Law* (Global Trade Law Series; Alphen aan den Rijn: Wolters Kluwer, 2012) (p. 25): 'If the persuasive burden is allocated to the claimant, the risk of Type II errors will generally be higher than the risk of Type I errors, and vice versa. This can be explained in the following way. Let us say that we have a larger number of two-party disputes, where one party claims that the other party has violated a certain rule. In the majority of the cases, the court will probably find that one party's claim seem the more probable. However, in a number of cases (the uncertain cases), the court will find that the claims of both parties seem equally probable. If the court decides that the claimants should always carry the burden, the defendants will win all the uncertain cases'. On the same issue, see also Caroline Foster, *Science and the Precautionary Principle in International Courts and Tribunals* (Cambridge: Cambridge University Press, 2011) 375 (p. 214).

self-cancelling and ambiguous, and it is left to speculation whether this situation came about by design or if it is an accident of the negotiations, given that it was the first time that the international community tried to regulate international trade in financial services in the context of a multilateral forum.

Only one WTO dispute so far has dealt with the PCO and the Panel, which on that occasion, classified it as an 'exception'. In that case, the measures for which the PCO was invoked could not avail of the provision because the Panel concluded that the link between the prudential objective pursued and the means deployed was too remote.

As has already been clarified, however, the Panel in *Argentina – Financial Services* did not examine in detail the meaning and function of the final clause of provision, and the Appellate Body deliberately refused to label it as an exception. Therefore, there is room for alternative readings.

This volume seeks to advance a possible alternative approach to the interpretation of the PCO that contradicts some of the assumptions of the mainstream contributions in the literature. This work confirms that the scope of the PCO is substantially broad and confers on Members the right to react to financial crises or to work to prevent them. It has explained why there are good reasons to believe that the PCO is not an exception in the technical sense and that, if a parallel must be drawn between the PCO and other WTO provisions, it ought to be drawn between provisions other than Article XX of the GATT 1994 or Article XIV of the GATS.

The PCO can be seen as performing as similar function to Article 5.7 of the SPS Agreement (an 'autonomous right', in the words of the Appellate Body) or to Article IV of the GATT 1994 (*lex specialis*). Moreover, the PCO goes even further, and it is clearly designed as a unique provision in the multilateral legal framework governing international trade. It has a uniquely broad scope of application due to the lack of confidence that Uruguay Round negotiators had with regard to the benefits of liberalisation of trade in financial services in terms of financial stability.

The main implications of this alternative approach relate to the allocation of burden of proof. Indeed, this is the area in which the practical consequences of the analysis conducted here seem most clear: in case of a dispute, this work suggests that the burden of proof should not fall on the defendant. The GATS and its special discipline on financial services are clear in the reaffirmation of the right of WTO Members to regulate the markets for services.

How would that have worked in the *Argentina – Financial Services* dispute? Following the arguments developed in this chapter, this volume argues that the solution provided by the Panel is suboptimal. Had the Panel followed the alternative approach that is suggested in the present volume – assuming it would still find that the measures were GATS-inconsistent, despite the reversal operated by the Appellate Body, it would have probably achieved the same objective but in a different fashion.

Recall that the Panel concluded that the measures for which the PCO was invoked did not meet the test under the first part of the provision because, in the Panel's view, they were not rationally connected to the stated aim. The Panel exercised a pervasive scrutiny as to the design and structure of the measures at issue, thus admittedly going beyond the letter of the first part of the provision, which merely calls to verify that measures were adopted 'for' prudential reasons, and not 'mainly' or 'exclusively' for prudential reasons. And despite the fact that the measures at issue distinguished among countries on the basis of non-objective criteria, it can nevertheless be argued that the imposition of restrictions vis-à-vis at least those countries for which no effective mechanisms for the exchange of information for tax purposes with Argentina was in place did contribute to the achievement of prudential objectives.

The question as to whether Argentina had tried to hide purely (or mostly) protectionist measures under the cover of the right to regulate in accordance with prudential objectives should have mattered for the sake of the test established under the second part of the provision. In that respect, the Panel should have allocated the burden on Panama to demonstrate that Argentina was abusing its right. On the basis of the arbitrariness of the criteria for the determination as to whether countries were cooperative, those measures would have probably failed to pass the test under the second clause.[115]

This volume argues that the PCO preserves the regulatory autonomy of Members in the delicate domain of prudential regulation and supervision in the financial services sector. The foregoing can be better understood if placed against the background of the preamble of the GATS which reads as follows:

> Recognizing the right of Members to regulate, and to introduce new regulations, on the supply of services within their territories in order to meet

---

[115] A separate question, in this regard, is whether the MFN analysis conducted by the Panel was correct (the Appellate Body reversed it, as explained in Chapter 3 of this volume). We do not know whether the Panel, by following a different approach in its likeness analysis, would have still found the services and service suppliers from cooperative and non-cooperative services as being like.

national policy objectives and, given asymmetries existing with respect to the degree of development of services regulations in different countries, the particular need of developing countries to exercise this right...

It is argued that the complainant should carry the burden of proving, in addition to the claimed inconsistency with regards to the general rule (namely GATS obligations or commitments), that the adopted measures amount to an attempt to avoid trade obligations and commitments without a concrete prudential objective being pursued. If we were to take the position of the majority of commentators, then the burden of proof would be allocated similarly to other exception-type provisions (as set out by the Appellate Body in *US – Gambling*).[116]

Recent developments in the aftermath of the 2007–8 financial crisis reminded the world of the unpredictable nature of financial markets and of how bad regulation (or no regulation) may severely hit the global economy. An understanding of the PCO whereby its main function is considered to be to restate the right of domestic governments to step into financial markets and modify the regulations according to the needs of financial stability is, probably, more loyal to the Uruguay Round participants' intentions.

After all, the Panel itself acknowledged that the determination as to whether a measure has been taken for prudential reasons is 'no easy task'.[117] In this respect, additional deference vis-à-vis national regulators should be warranted.

---

[116] Appellate Body Report, *US – Gambling*, para. 140.
[117] Panel Report, *Argentina – Financial Services*, para. 7.884.

6

Suggestions for Reform

The discussion conducted so far reveals that Type I errors are particularly costly if they happen in the context of trade disputes on financial services. Against that background, the classification of the GATS PCO as an exception does not provide sufficient guarantees that national governments' prerogatives are well protected.

Irrespective of the interpretative approach adopted, however, the provision as it stands does not ensure legal certainty. Proofs thereof are the divergent readings of the provision put forward by Panama and Argentina in *Argentina – Financial Services*. On that occasion, the Panel correctly dismissed Panama's claim that the heading 'Domestic Regulation' implied a narrow scope of application for the GATS PCO, covering only measures falling within the boundaries of Article VI of the GATS[1]; yet a number of issues are still unclear, including the meaning of the final clause of the GATS PCO.

WTO Members have signalled, over the years, that they were not at ease with the way in which the PCO is drafted. This volume has given account of the proposals for reform tabled at the WTO and of instances in which Members decided to reiterate their right to regulate in accordance to prudential concerns in their schedules.

A check up of the GATS PCO is particularly desirable in the current context of reforms that all major financial systems are undergoing, leading many commentators to highlight the tendency of financial services to swing towards host-country regulation as opposed to the previous tendency in the opposite direction over the previous twenty years.[2]

Recently, the need to rethink trade rules on prudential regulation emerged in the context of the FTA between Singapore and Australia. Mitchell et al. report that the two countries signed an amendment on 13 October 2016 introducing a 'filter mechanism' in Investor–State disputes

---

[1] Panel Report, *Argentina – Financial Services*, para. 6.272.
[2] See Claessens and Marchetti, 'Global Banking Regroups'.

concerning measures that the responding government deems to be prudential. In such cases, the question as to whether the measure concerned is actually prudential must be submitted to the financial services authorities of both parties to the treaty for them to jointly conduct an evaluation with regard to the validity of the PCO defence raised by the respondent.[3]

To the largest possible extent, this chapter borrows from solutions already existing at the bilateral level or in other WTO Agreements, with the objective of minimising transaction costs and increasing the likelihood of implementation. The proposals put forward in this chapter can be subdivided in procedural and substantive innovations.

6.1 Procedural Innovations

6.1.1 Filter Mechanism – Ensuring Institutional Balance

At the outset, there are legitimate doubts as to whether the review of prudential measures by a WTO Panel is appropriate. Although Paragraph 4 of the Annex on Financial Services requires that panels for disputes concerning prudential measures shall have the necessary expertise, that might not be sufficiently reassuring for the regulatory prerogatives of WTO Members in such a delicate domain.

The issue is not new to WTO litigation. For example, questions concerning institutional balance emerged in the *India – Quantitative Restrictions* dispute, which originated in a series of import restrictions adopted by India. India argued that the import restrictions applied to one-third of the tariff lines in its schedules of concessions were duly justified because they were necessary to address a balance-of-payment problem, pursuant to Article XVIII:B of the GATT 1994. In particular, India had regularly notified and consulted with the Committee on Balance-of-Payments restrictions before adopting the measures[4] and was of the opinion that the Panel had no competence to review those. In India's view, the Committee on Balance-of-Payments was the appropriate body within the WTO institutional setting to deal with the matter.[5] The Appellate Body, upholding the Panel's findings, established that dispute settlement panels are competent to review the legality of balance-of-payments restrictions, as neither the

---

[3] Mitchell et al., 'Dear Prudence: Allowances under International Trade and Investment Law for Prudential Regulation in the Financial Services Sector', p. 795.
[4] Appellate Body Report, *India – Quantitative Restrictions*, para. 2.
[5] Appellate Body Report, *India – Quantitative Restrictions*, para. 28.

GATT 1994 nor the DSU did provide for special exemptions for that kind of measures.[6]

The issue concerning prudential measures is even more delicate than that addressed in the *India – Quantitative Restrictions* dispute. The extent of the regulatory autonomy of national governments concerning the adoption of prudential measures boils down to the more fundamental questions of the balance of rights and obligations of WTO Members and, ultimately, to sovereignty.

As the discussion in Chapter 4 revealed, various FTAs opted to leave the decision as to the validity of the prudential defence to committees composed of representatives of the finance departments of the parties to the agreement. Examples in this respect can be found in NAFTA, CETA and, more recently, in the FTA between Australia and Singapore, as discussed in the introduction to this chapter. How could this work in the context of the WTO? First and foremost, it would require amendments to the GATS Annex on Financial Services and, perhaps, to the DSU. Second, the 'filter mechanism' could be designed in two ways:

- deferral of the matter to the WTO Committee on Trade in Financial Services, which will be called to decide whether the measures for which the PCO is invoked are prudential or not; or
- deferral of the matter to an ad hoc committee chaired by an independent expert nominated by both parties jointly (or by the WTO Director General in case of disagreement, similarly to the composition of Panels) and composed of delegates from the finance departments of the Members involved in the dispute.

The committee in charge of the decision on the validity of the PCO defence should be given a fixed term to decide on the matter, and meanwhile, the dispute should be put on hold. The decision of the committee should then be binding on the WTO Panel before which the dispute is pending.

6.1.2 Transparency

Transparency obligations are common to WTO Agreements. The GATS is no exception to this and dedicates one of its first provisions to the discipline of transparency: Article III. In addition to asking Members to publish in a timely manner their domestic legislation that may have an

---

[6] Appellate Body Report, *India – Quantitative Restrictions*, paras. 85–91.

impact on trade in services, paragraph 3 of the provision also requires Members to notify the Council for Trade in Services of the WTO about the enactment of new regulations or amendments to existing disciplines that affect trade in services under the sectors and modes that constitute part of the specific commitments of the given Member. Practice since the late 1990s has not been satisfactory in this area. According to Wolfe, Members seldom notify their legislation to the Council and practice is in general scarce on this issue. Moreover, transparency does not seem to be a main source of concern for most Members, and this claim seems to be valid for developed and developing Members alike.[7] Paragraph 4 requires Members to establish enquiry points to provide adequate information to other Members that may seek it. Finally, Article III gives WTO Members the possibility to notify any other Member's measures that it considers as affecting trade in services.

There is no case law dealing with transparency requirements at the WTO level. In all likelihood, the lack of an effective sanction that could be imposed on Members who do not respect the transparency requirements makes the latter, if not useless, at least redundant.[8]

The Annex on Financial Services of the GATS does not add to the discipline on transparency provided for by the main agreement. Practice in the domain of financial services (and prudential regulation) reveals a wide margin for improvement in this regard. Empirical evidence suggests that incentives (or disincentives) affect the operation of transparency requirements in the context of WTO Agreements.[9] First of all, the more the subject matter of the transparency requirement is identified in detail, the more WTO Members are expected to fulfil the task and notify the changes in relevant regulation. Second, Members tend to avoid the notification of their regulatory schemes when they fear that it will lead to new negotiations or even to dispute settlement. 'Self-incrimination', as a result, is a powerful disincentive. Given the uneasiness of many WTO Members with regard to the coverage and application of the PCO, it is probably not to be expected that Members will autonomously notify measures that could be considered to be in violation of GATS rules.

[7] Robert Wolfe, 'Letting the Sun Shine in at the WTO: How Transparency Brings the Trading System to Life', *WTO Staff Working Paper* (2013), 43.
[8] Terry Collins-Williams and Robert Wolfe, 'Transparency as a Trade Policy Tool: The WTO's Cloudy Windows', *World Trade Review*, 9:4 (2010), 551–81.
[9] Ibid. (pp. 573–5).

One suggestion for reform in this domain may be that of providing Members with a list of measures that are clearly considered as being prudential (also referring to the existing practice at the level of international standard-setting forums), with the requirement that they are notified to the Council for Trade in Services. This will not impose an excessive burden on Members but will have the merit of increasing transparency. Ultimately, this would also encourage the circulation of best practices between WTO Members.

6.1.3 Periodical Review

Prudential measures are often adopted in situations of uncertainty with regard to the conditions of the market for financial services, as clarified throughout this volume. Because they have the capacity to override commitments and obligations at the multilateral level, they may result in a permanent or semi-permanent derogations to the rules of the game on international trade that Members had agreed to abide by.

Prudential measures may be of two kinds. They may either address permanent and structural issues (such as capital requirements), or they may serve as a tool to address the market failures deriving from contingencies. Moreover, prudential measures are sometimes adopted in situations of uncertainty with regard to both the developments in the markets as well as the effectiveness of the instruments adopted. As a result, it is possible (at least in theory) that such measures unduly restrict international trade in financial services or impose an unnecessary burden on financial services providers. As such, the PCO does not impose any procedural requirement on WTO Members with regard to the phasing out of prudential measures when the contingency that called for their adoption is over.

Without constraining the right of Members to regulate financial markets and to intervene when they deem it appropriate, examples from other WTO agreements may be taken into account for the restructuring of the PCO in a way that could make the provision more in line with the goals of transparency and efficiency of the trading system. The first example may be taken from the discipline on precautionary measures set forth in the SPS Agreement. Article 5.7 of the SPS Agreement requires WTO Members to review the measure adopted in circumstances of lack of sufficient scientific evidence with regard to the harmfulness of a particular product within a (unspecified) reasonable period of time. The Agreement on Safeguards also requires measures adopted to smooth the effects of contingencies in which a surge in the imports causes a major harm to the domestic industry producing a particular good to be phased out. Article 7.1 of the Agreement on Safeguards requires Members to impose safeguard measures only for the period that is necessary to address the situation causing the injury. This period cannot exceed four years unless it is extended under the conditions provided for by Article 7.2 of the Agreement on Safeguards.

The peculiar nature of financial regulation makes the case for the periodical review of prudential measures even more compelling. Romano, for instance, argues that amidst international regulatory standards that have proven not to be high enough to avoid the disruption of a financial crisis and in light of the condition of 'ignorance' in which regulators are often placed, the rules of the game for the financial market should be periodically reviewed to better calibrate the regulatory response to the policy objectives pursued.[10]

A robust rationale lies behind the periodical review of prudential rules. Gerson convincingly argues that temporary legislation entails a different distribution of error costs compared with permanent legislation. Temporary legislation, in fact, allows national governments and legislative bodies to address the shortcomings in the initial formulation of a legislative act.[11] Moreover, temporary legislation ensures that new information is integrated into the legislative process in a timely fashion, reduces the risks of short-term biases and helps to address situations of asymmetric information.[12] In the case of the PCO, a periodical review of the measures derogating from the obligations under the GATS and its Annex on Financial Services may serve the goal of legal certainty, pushing Members to enhance transparency and to strike a more efficient balance between trade commitments and prudential concerns. In any event, even in the absence of a reform of the rules in the Annex on Financial Services, Members may autonomously decide to periodically review their prudential regulations.

The introduction of temporary legislative acts, however, raises the concern as to what happens in situations where, because of a failure to find a compromise among the various political sensitivities at the national level, a legislative measures pursuing a prudential objective is allowed to expire,

---

[10] See Roberta Romano, 'Regulating in the Dark and a Postscript Assessment of the Iron Law of Financial Regulation', *Hostra Law Review* (2014), 43:1, 25–69.
[11] Jacob Gersen, 'Temporary Legislation', *University of Chicago, John M. Olin Law & Economics Working Paper No. 126* (2006), pp. 11 and 12.
[12] Ibid., p. 15.

thus creating a gap in the legislation. Such shortcoming might be mitigated with the introduction of transitional mechanisms whereby old prudential measures remain in force *ad interim* until new legislation is agreed upon.

6.1.4 Possibility for WTO Members to Comment and Submit Observations Concerning Other Members' Legislative Reforms

A change in financial market legislation from a risk-averse government may entail losses or the reduction of opportunities for foreign firms. As a result, other WTO Members might have concerns regarding the way in which new measures are constraining the benefits accruing to them under the GATS.

In this respect, Article 5.8 of the SPS Agreement provides a useful tool that, *mutatis mutandis*, could be imported in the context of the GATS PCO. The provision reads as follows:

> When a Member has reason to believe that a specific sanitary or phytosanitary measure introduced or maintained by another Member is constraining, or has the potential to constrain, its exports and the measure is not based on the relevant international standards, guidelines or recommendations, or such standards, guidelines or recommendations do not exist, an explanation of the reasons for such sanitary or phytosanitary measure may be requested and shall be provided by the Member maintaining the measure.

A similar mechanism is envisaged in Article 2.5 of the Agreement on Technical Barriers to Trade (TBT) Agreement. Considering that Members do not have the incentives to challenge measures adopted in pursuance of prudential objectives before WTO panels, as made clear earlier in this work, a tool designed along the lines of Article 5.8 of the SPS Agreement or Article 2.5 of the TBT Agreement can enhance cooperative and transparent behaviours by governments. This could serve the cause of legal security and help to bridge the gap between trade commitments and the current tendency to repatriate financial regulation.

6.2 Substantive Innovations

6.2.1 Standards

As explained in Chapter 2, one of the main drivers for reform in financial services markets is the work conducted under the auspices on standard-setting bodies, the nature of which (public or private; formal or informal; binding or not binding) is not always clearly defined.

Contrary to practice in other WTO agreements (particularly the TBT and SPS), the GATS does not provide a sufficiently developed framework in this regard. This section suggests that internationally agreed standards could potentially represent a benchmark in the attempt to separate prudential measures from purely protectionist measures. The following subsections clarify the current status of internationally agreed standards under the GATS and what could be done to provide more clarity and integrate the multilateral discipline on trade in financial services with the guidelines and requirements set up in international forums dealing with financial regulation.

6.2.1.1 The Role of Standards in the GATS and in the Annex on Financial Services

The Annex on financial services of the GATS does not make an explicit *renvoi* to internationally agreed standards, and WTO panels not yet addressed the issue. It is interesting, therefore, to start the analysis by looking again at the negotiating history of the Annex on financial services to understand whether the negotiators debated the issue during the Uruguay Round. At the time of the negotiations, relevant standard-setting bodies in the field of financial services already existed, although their membership was limited and their role was arguably less prominent.

In the first meeting of the Working Group on Financial Services, negotiators debated the possibility of inviting experts from other institutions to participate in discussions. The Chairman proposed inviting experts from the OECD Secretariat and the BCBS because their expertise could have been of help in setting the agenda for negotiations.[13] However, this proposal was rejected due to the opposition of some countries. In particular, the representative from India raised an explicit objection to the invitation of experts from the two organisations. He referred to the decision taken by the Trade Negotiation Committee that only relevant international organisations could be invited and argued that OECD and BCBS were 'neither truly international in character, nor relevant to the work of the sectoral group'.[14]

---

[13] Uruguay Round Doc. MTN.GNS/FIN/1, 'Working Group on Financial Services Including Insurance – Note on the Meeting of 11–13 June 1990', para. 7.

[14] Ibid., para. 9.

6.2 SUBSTANTIVE INNOVATIONS

The GATS refers to international standards in Article VI ('Domestic Regulation') and Article VII ('Recognition'). Article VI of the GATS concerns obligations related to domestic regulation. It applies only in cases in which WTO members have already undertaken specific commitments to ensure that 'all measures of general application affecting trade in services are administered in a reasonable, objective and impartial manner'. The issue of the application of standards emerges in the analysis of Article VI:5 of the GATS, which contains an obligation not to apply licensing and qualification requirements and technical standards in a manner which 'does not comply with the criteria outlined in subparagraphs 4(a), (b) or (c)' and 'could not reasonably have been expected'. According to subparagraph 5(b), to assess the compliance of a Member's measures with the requirement set forth by Article VI:4 of the GATS, account shall be taken of whether such measures were adopted following standards of international organisations.

In addition, footnote 3 to Article VI:5 of the GATS provides additional explanation of what bodies should be considered as 'relevant international organizations': 'The term "relevant international organizations" refers to international bodies whose membership is open to at least all Members of the WTO.'

The text of Article VI:5 of the GATS (together with footnote 3), therefore, seems to require that two conditions must be met for internationally agreed standards to be relevant in this context: i) the standards need to have been actually applied by the Member whose measures need to be scrutinised under Article VI of the GATS and ii) only standards issued by international bodies whose membership is open to – at a minimum – all WTO Members can be usefully be considered as a benchmark to assess the conformity of a Member's measures to Article VI:5 of the GATS.

Article VII of the GATS (Recognition) is the other provision of the agreement where it is possible to find the word 'standards'. Paragraph 5 of the provision reads as follows:

> Wherever appropriate, recognition should be based on multilaterally agreed criteria. In appropriate cases, Members shall work in cooperation with relevant intergovernmental and non-governmental organizations towards the establishment and adoption of common international standards and criteria for recognition and common international standards for the practice of relevant services trades and professions.

In this case, it is difficult to consider this passage as an obligation. Indeed, it seems to suggest a route to WTO members wishing to engage in unilateral recognition schemes or in mutual recognition agreements (MRAs) – when they deem it appropriate – to work in cooperation with relevant international bodies (either intergovernmental or non-governmental) and to adopt common international standards.[15] The 'sibling provision' in the Annex on Financial Service – Paragraph 3 (Recognition) – does not make reference to international standards.

In any event, it is important to recall that to date no mutual recognition agreements concerning prudential measures have been notified to the WTO Secretariat.[16]

States are still reluctant to agree on (binding) international law disciplines on financial markets. Financial services remain a sensitive issue in terms of States' sovereignty, and there is a lack of will to delegate the regulation on the topic to international organisations. Governments are aware of the necessity of internationally agreed common practice because financial markets are highly globalised and interdependent but prefer to set the rules of the game informally, among themselves, outside the scope of international agreements. Moreover, the risks associated with bad regulation of financial services are high. Therefore, the gains for cooperation are not straightforward, and this is a possible explanation of why governments may prefer to share their views informally and to give to flexible agencies the task of issuing general orientations of non-legally binding nature.

Do standard-setting bodies of a hybrid nature such as, for instance, the BCBS fulfil the conditions set out in the GATS rules? From a formal point of view, the FSB and the BCBS, for instance, do not meet the 'opening-up' requirement of Article VI of the GATS as they are 'spin-offs' of the G-20 and consequently are not by definition open to the accession of all WTO Members.

Article VII of the GATS instead only encourages WTO members to base their recognition policies (both unilateral and bilateral) on relevant international standards. There is no reason to presume, in theory, that the BCBS might not be considered an international body issuing relevant international standards. Nonetheless this cannot be enough to legitimise recourse to standards for two sets of reasons. First of all, Article VII of the

---

[15] Two WTO Agreements, namely the TBT and the SPS have a more detailed discipline with regard to the interplay between trade rules and standards. In comparison with the latter the discipline of the GATS is rather minimalistic.

[16] Marchetti and Mavroidis provide an overview of all the MRAs notified to the WTO Secretariat until 2009 in Juan A. Marchetti and Petros C. Mavroidis, 'I Now Recognize You (and Only You) as Equal: An Anatomy of (Mutual) Recognition Agreements in the GATS'. Nothing new has emerged in recent years.

GATS only suggests that WTO members cooperate with relevant international standard-setting bodies when granting unilateral or mutual recognition of measures dealing with trade in services. Nothing in the wording of the provision suggests that it could be interpreted as an obligation of any kind. Second, the 'sibling' provision in the GATS Annex on Financial Services deals specifically with the mutual recognition of prudential measures without making any reference to standards. Therefore, the *renvoi* to relevant international standards of Article VII GATS should not be overestimated because it may even be overridden by the *lex specialis* contained in Paragraph 3 of the GATS Annex on Financial services. Moreover, the latter specifically excludes the application of Article VII:4(b) of the GATS, which requires Members that adopt or modify recognition measures to promptly inform the Council for Trade in Services about the negotiations of an MRA in order to give interested parties the opportunity to indicate their interest in the participation to such negotiations. Consequently it seems that the already shallow discipline for the accession of third parties to MRAs is even weaker with regard to financial services, leaving more leeway to the regulating jurisdictions.

Nonetheless, a formalistic approach might be somehow misleading. In the analysis of the potential interplay between the PCO and standards on prudential and sound financial regulation, some realpolitik arguments deserve to be taken into account. First of all, most standards are generally implemented in a timely manner (and interestingly not only by members to the relevant standard-setting bodies).[17]

Therefore, irrespective of their formal status as non–legally binding norms, they are undoubtedly part of the relevant rules that financial institutions have to respect because the overwhelming majority of national regulators (whether BCBS members or not) apply Basel standards, turning them into hard law crystallised in national legislative acts.

Notwithstanding the fact that standards seem not to have access to the GATS system through the main door, there are cases in which they are effectively taken into consideration. Reference to the effective application and implementation of standards via domestic legislative acts appears in various official records of WTO accession procedures after the conclusion of the Uruguay Round.[18] Furthermore, many WTO Members refer

---

[17] Daniel K. Tarullo, *Banking on Basel – the Future of International Financial Regulation* (Washington, DC: Peterson Institute of International Economics, 2008), pp. 195 and ff. reports that more than a hundred jurisdictions follow the standards set up in Basel.

[18] Michael S. Barr and Geoffrey P. Miller, 'Global Administrative Law: The View from Basel', *The European Journal of International Law*, 17:1 (2006), 15–46 (p. 42, fn. 114) and Régis

to standards in the policy statement reports they submit to the Secretariat for the Trade Policy Review Mechanism (TPRM). For instance, although not formally recognised, BCBS standards already play an important role in the GATS as they are evoked in the accession procedures and in TPRM.

Because standards are almost universally applied and they already appear in many ways in the GATS context, their value should not be underestimated.

6.2.1.2 Standards and the PCO

This work does not go as far as suggesting the adoption of internationally agreed standards as a benchmark of lawfulness for domestic measures in the domain of financial services. However, compliance with a standard may constitute a powerful argument for the responding Member in the event of a dispute to prove that the measure adopted actually pursues a legitimate objective and was not enacted with the aim of avoiding trade obligations. Members wishing to impose a level of protection that is higher than what is provided for by the standards may still be allowed to do so, but they will have to provide more evidence with regard to the clarification of the objective pursued and the insufficiency of the existing standards to that extent. A suggestion for reform may include the introduction of an Annex making explicit reference to standard-setting bodies and to the standards issued by the latter.

6.2.2 Guidelines

Chapter 3 provided an extensive overview of the evolution of carve-outs for prudential measures in FTAs. One recent development that can serve as a useful example to make the PCO in the Annex on Financial Services of the GATS more efficient and better designed is constituted by the Understanding on the application of the PCO in the CETA (the FTA between the EU and Canada), an account of which was given in Section 4.4.3.

The document contains the most advanced ideas with regard to the protection of prudential objectives in the context of agreements with the stated aim of lowering material and immaterial barriers to foreign trade in financial services. Arguably, the CETA strikes a good balance between

---

Bismuth, 'Financial Sector Regulation and Financial Services Liberalization at the Crossroads: The Relevance of International Financial Standards in WTO Law', *Journal of World Trade*, 44:2 (2010), 489–514 (pp. 510 and ff.) give detailed account of the reference to Basel standards contained in accession documents of – inter alia – Kazakhstan and Jordan.

the need for governments to keep sovereign control over financial regulation and issues of legal certainty, which, as we have seen, are sometimes sacrificed in the context of trade agreements in this particular domain.

Chapter 4 provided a detailed overview of the aforementioned Understanding, and as such it is not necessary to restate the details of the document. However, it is important, for the sake of the completeness of the argument put forward, to point out the main features of the Understanding that can be usefully replicated at the multilateral level, should there be consensus among all the Members of the WTO.

Among the other novel proposals introduced by the document, some deserve particular attention. For instance, adjudicators must give consideration to the information available as well as to the urgency of the situation; the document expressly acknowledges that regulators are in a better position to evaluate the risks that ensue from market failures in the domain of financial services, and as such adjudicators have to be deferential to them 'to the highest possible extent'; the document clearly lists the cases in which a measure is presumed to have been adopted in pursuance of legitimate prudential objectives and as a result a presumption of lawfulness of the measure must be recognised. All the preceding elements would contribute to a more reasoned decision with regard to the lawful invocation of the GATS PCO in a dispute.

6.3 Conclusion

As is submitted in this final chapter, a number of viable options are available to WTO Members should there be the political will to reform the PCO to make it more efficient. This is certainly unrealistic as things stand, in light of the difficult times that the WTO is experiencing and the context of the permanent deadlock of multilateral negotiations. However, this volume humbly tried to put forward a few options for reform, which may become useful in the coming years should the context change.

REFERENCES

Adlung, Rudolf, Morrison, Peter, Roy, Martin and Zhang, Wiewei (2013), 'FOG in GATS Commitments – Why WTO Members Should Care', *World Trade Review*, 12(1), 1–27

Admati, Anat and Hellwig, Martin (2013), *The Bankers' New Clothes: What's Wrong with Banking and What to Do about It* (Princeton, NJ: Princeton University Press)

Åhman, Joachim (2012), *Trade, Health and the Burden of Proof in WTO Law* (Global Trade Law Series) (Alphen aan den Rijn: Wolters Kluwer)

Akerlof, George A. (1970), 'The Market for 'Lemons': Quality, Uncertainty and the Market Mechanism', *The Quarterly Journal of Economics*, 84(3), 488–500

Alexander, Kern (2008), 'The GATS and Financial Services: Liberalisation and Regulation in Global Financial Markets', in Kern Alexander and Mads Andenas (eds.), *The World Trade Organization and Trade in Services* (Leiden and Boston: Martinus Nijhoff), 561–99

Ascher, Bernard (1989), 'Multilateral Negotiations on Trade in Services: Concepts, Goals, Issues', *The Georgia Journal of International and Comparative Law*, 19(2), 392–403

Avgouleas, Emilios and Goodhart, Charles (2015), 'Critical Reflections on Bank Bail-Ins', *Journal of Financial Regulation*, 1(1), 3–29

Bagwell, Kyle and Staiger, Robert W. (2002), *The Economics of the World Trading System* (Cambridge, MA: MIT Press)

Balassa, Bela (1961), *The Theory of Economic Integration* (Homewood, IL: Richard D. Irwin)

Baldwin, Robert E. (1970), *Nontariff Distortions in International Trade* (Washington, DC: Brookings Institution)

Barr, Michael S. and Miller, Geoffrey P. (2006), 'Global Administrative Law: The View from Basel', *The European Journal of International Law*, 17(1), 15–46

Bartels, Lorand (2015), 'The Chapeau of the General Exceptions in the WTO GATT and GATS Agreements: A Reconstruction', *American Journal of International Law*, 109(1), 95–125

Bhagwati, Jagdish (1984), 'Splintering and Disembodiment of Services and Developing Nations', *The World Economy*, 7(1), 133–44

(1990), 'Departures from Multilateralism: Regionalism and Aggressive Unilateralism', *The Economic Journal*, 100(403), 1304–17

Bismuth, Régis (2010), 'Financial Sector Regulation and Financial Services Liberalization at the Crossroads: The Relevance of International Financial Standards in WTO Law', *Journal of World Trade*, 44(2), 489–514

Blanchard, Olivier, Dell'Ariccia, Giovanni and Mauro, Paolo (2013), 'Rethinking Macro Policy II: Getting Granular', *IMF Staff Discussion Note*, 1–25

Blinder, Alan S. (2013), *After the Music Stopped – The Financial Crisis, the Response and the Work Ahead* (New York: Penguin), 476

Bordo, Michael D., Redish, Angela and Rockoff, Hugh (2011), 'Why Didn't Canada Have a Banking Crisis in 2008 (or in 1930, or in 1907, or ...)?', *NBER Working Paper Series*, 1–40

Broude, Tomer (2007), 'Genetically Modified Rules: The Awkward Rule-Exception-Right Distinction in EC-Biotech', *World Trade Review* 6(2), 215–31

Brummer, Chris (2012), *Soft Law and the Global Financial System – Rule Making in the 21st Century* (Cambridge: Cambridge University Press), 296

Cameron, Maxwell A. and Tomlin, Brian W. (2000), *The Making of NAFTA – How the Deal Was Done* (Ithaca and London: Cornell University Press), 264

Cantore, Carlo M. (2014), '"Shelter from the Storm": Exploring the Scope of Application and Legal Function of the GATS Prudential Carve-Out', *Journal of World Trade*, 48(6), 1223–46

Claessens, Stijn and Marchetti, Juan A. (2013), 'Global Banking Regroups', *Finance & Development*, 50(4), 14–17

Coffee, John C. (2014), 'Extraterritorial Financial Regulation: Why E. T. Can't Come Home', *Cornell Law Review*, 99(6), 1259–302

Collins-Williams, Terry and Wolfe, Robert (2010), 'Transparency as a Trade Policy Tool: The WTO's Cloudy Windows', *World Trade Review*, 9(4), 551–81

Conconi, Paola and Perroni, Carlo (2012), 'Conditional versus Unconditional Trade Concessions for Developing Countries', *Canadian Journal of Economics*, 45(2), 613–31

Cottier, Thomas and Krajewski, Markus (2010), 'What Role for Non-Discrimination and Prudential Standards in International Financial Law', *Journal of International Economic Law*, 13(3), 817–35

Croley, Steven P. and Jackson, John H. (1996), 'WTO Dispute Settlement Procedure, Standard of Review and Deference to National Governments', *The American Journal of International Law*, 90(2), 193–213

De Meester, Bart (2008), 'Testing European Prudential Conditions for Banking Mergers in the Light of the Most Favoured Nation in the GATS', *Journal of International Economic Law*, 11(3), 609–47

(2014), *Liberalization of Trade in Banking Services – An International and European Perspective* (Cambridge: Cambridge University Press), 388

Delimatsis, Panagiotis and Sauvé, Pierre (2010), 'Financial Services Trade after the Crisis: Policy and Legal Conjectures', *Journal of International Economic Law*, 13(3), 837–57

De Nicolò, Gianni, Favara, Giovanni and Ratnovski, Lev (2012), 'Externalities and Macroprudential Policy', *IMF Staff Discussion Note*, SDN/12/05, 23

Denk, Olivier and Gomes, Gabriel (2017), 'Financial Re-regulation since the Global Crisis? – An Index-based Assessment', *OECD Economics Department Working Papers, No. 1396*, OECD Publishing, Paris, 1–51

Deutsch, Klaus (2014), 'Transatlantic Consistency? Financial Regulation, the G20 and the TTIP', *Deutsche Bank Research – EU Monitor, Global Financial Markets*, 27

Dewatripont, Mathias and Tirole, Jean (2012), 'Macroeconomic Shocks and Banking Regulation', *Journal of Money, Credit and Banking*, 44 (Supplement S2), 237–254

Diamond, Douglas W. and Dybvig, Philip H. (1983), 'Bank Runs, Deposit Insurance and Liability', *The Journal of Political Economy*, 91 (3), 401–19

Diego-Fernández, Mateo (2008), 'Trade negotiations make strange bedfellows', *World Trade Review*, 7 (02), 423–53

Ehring, Lothar (2011), 'Article IV of the GATT: An Obsolete Provision or Still a Basis for Cultural Policy', in Inge Govaere, Reinhard Quick and Marco Bronckers (eds.), *Trade and Competition Law in the EU and Beyond* (Cheltenham: Edward Elgar), 96–118

Farhi, Emmanuel and Tirole, Jean (2012), 'Collective Moral Hazard, Maturity Mismatch and Systemic Bailouts', *American Economic Review*, 102 (1), 60–93

Foster, Caroline (2011), *Science and the Precautionary Principle in International Courts and Tribunals* (Cambridge: Cambridge University Press), 375

Francois, Joseph (1990), 'Trade in Nontradables: Proximity Requirements and the Pattern of Trade in Services' *Journal of Economic Integration*, 5 (1), 31–46

and Hoekman, Bernard (2010), 'Services Trade and Policy', *Journal of Economic Literature*, 48 (3), 642–92

Friedman, Thomas L. (2006), *The World Is Flat: The Globalized World in the Twenty-First Century* (Penguin London)

Galati, Gabriele and Moessner, Richhild (2012), 'Macroprudential Policy – A Literature Review', *Journal of Economic Surveys*, 27 (5), 846–78

Gari, Gabriel (2014), 'Capital Controls, GATS Disciplines and the Need for a More Coherent Global Economic Governance Structure', Queen Mary University of London, School of Law, Legal Studies Research Paper

Gennaioli, Nicola, Shleifer, Andrei and Vishny, Robert (2015), 'Neglected Risks: The Psychology of Financial Crises', *American Economic Review: Papers & Proceedings*, 105 (5), 310–314

Gersen, Jacob (2006), *Temporary Legislation*, University of Chicago, John M. Olin Law & Economics Working Paper No. 126, 1–44

Goodhart, Charles, Hartmann, Philipp and Llewellyn David T. (1998), *Financial Regulation – Why, How and Where Now?* (London and New York City: Routledge) 272

Grando, Michelle T. (2009), *Evidence, Proof and Fact-Finding in WTO Dispute Settlement* (Oxford: Oxford University Press)

Guiso, Luigi, Sapienza, Paola and Zingales, Luigi (2009), 'Cultural Biases in Economic Exchange?', *The Quarterly Journal of Economics*, 124 (3), 1095–131

Hoekman, Bernard M. and Mavroidis, P. C. (2015), 'Embracing Diversity: Plurilateral Agreements and Trade in Services', *World Trade Review*, 14 (1), 101–16

Horn, Henrik, Mavroidis, Petros C. and Sapir, André (2014), 'EU and U.S. Preferential Trade Agreements: Deepening or Widening of WTO Commitments?', in Kyle W. Bagwell and Petros C. Mavroidis (eds.), *Preferential Trade Agreements: A Law and Economics Analysis* (Cambridge: Cambridge University Press), 150–72

Hufbauer, Gary Clyde, Jensen, J. Bradford, and Stephenson, Sherry (2012), 'Framework for the International Services Agreement', Peterson Institute for International Economics – Policy Brief, 1–45

Irwin, Douglas A., Mavroidis, Petros C. and Sykes, Alan O. (2008), *The Genesis of the GATT (The American Law Institute Reporters Studies on WTO Law)* (Cambridge: Cambridge University Press)

Jackson, John H., Davey, William J. and Sykes, Alan O. (2013), *Legal Problems of International Economic Relations* (6th edn.) (St. Paul, MN: West), 1338

Jans, Jan H. (2000), 'Proportionality Revisited', *Legal Issues of Economic Integration*, 27 (3), 239–65

Jarreau, J. Steven (1999–2000), 'Interpreting the General Agreement on Trade in Services and the WTO Instruments Relevant to the International Trade of Financial Services: The Lawyer's Perspective', *North Carolina Journal of International Law & Commercial Regulation*, 25 (2), 1–74

Johnson, Simon and Schott, Jeffrey J. (2013), 'Financial Services in the Transatlantic Trade and Investment Partnership', Peterson Institute for International Economics – Policy Brief, 1–11

Kakabadse, Mario A. (1989), 'Trade in Services and the Uruguay Round', *The Georgia Journal of International and Comparative Law*, 19 (2), 384–91

Kampf, Roger (1997), 'Liberalisation of financial services in the GATS and domestic regulation', *International Trade Law & Regulation*, 5 (3), 155–66

Kelsey, Jane (2014), 'Memorandum on Leaked TISA Financial Text', 1–17, MIMEO

Kern, Steffen (2010), 'US Financial Market Reform – The Economics of the Dodd-Frank Act', *Duesche Bank Research – EU Monitor*, 23

Key, Sidney (2005), 'Financial Services', in Patrick F. J. Macrory, Arthur E. Appleton and Michael G. Plummer (eds.), *The World Trade Organization: Legal, Economic and Political Analysis* (I; New York: Springer), 955–88

Lane, Timothy, et al. (1999), 'IMF-Supported Programs in Indonesia, Korea and Thailand', *IMF Occasional Paper*, 1–82

Lang, Andrew and Conyers, Caitlin (2014), 'Financial Services in EU Trade Agreements', *Study for the ECON Committee of the European Parliament*, 1–47

Leroux, Eric H. (2002), 'Trade in Financial Services under the World Trade Organisation', *Journal of World Trade*, 36 (3), 413–42

Lewis, Michael (2014), *Flashboys – Cracking the Money Code* (London: Allen Lane) 274

Lim, Cheng Hoon, Krznar, Ivo, Lipinsky, Fabian, Otani, Akira and Wu, Xiaoyong (2013), 'The Macroprudential Framework: Policy Responsiveness and Institutional Arrangements', IMF Working Paper, WP/13/66, 1–38

Llewellyn, David (1999), 'The Economic Rationale for Financial Regulation', FSA Occasional Paper Series, 1–58

Marchetti, Juan A. (2008), 'Financial Services Liberalization in the WTO and PTAs', in Juan A. Marchetti and Martin Roy (eds.), *Opening Markets for Trade in Services* (Cambridge: Cambridge University Press), 300–39

(2011), 'The GATS Prudential Carve-Out', in Panagiotis Delimatsis and Nils Herger (eds.), *Financial Regulation at the Crossroads: Implications for Supervision, Institutional Design and Trade* (Alphen aan den Rijn: Kluwer Law International), 279–95

and Mavroidis, Petros C. (2011a), 'From Reluctant Participant to Key Player: EU and the negotiation of the GATS', in Inge Govaere, Reinhard Quick and Marco Bronckers (eds.), *Trade and Competition Law in the EU and Beyond* (Cheltenham: Edward Elgar), 48–95

(2011b), 'The Genesis of the GATS (General Agreement on Trade in Services)', *The European Journal of International Law*, 22 (3), 689–721

(2012), 'I Now Recognize You (and Only You) as Equal: An Anatomy of (Mutual) Recognition Agreements in the GATS', in Ioannis Lianos and Okeoghene Odudu (eds.), *Regulating Trade in Services in the EU and the WTO: Trust, Distrust and Economic Integration* (Cambridge: Cambridge University Press), 415–44

and Roy, Martin (2009), 'Services Liberalization in the WTO and in PTAs', in Juan A. Marchetti and Martin Roy (eds.), *Opening Markets for Trade in Services: Countries and Sectors in Bilateral and WTO Negotiations*, (Cambridge: Cambridge University Press), 61–112

Mattoo, Aaditya and Wunsch-Vincent, Sacha (2004), 'Pre-Empting Protectionism in Services: The GATS and Outsourcing', *Journal of International Economic Law*, 7 (4), 765–800

Mavroidis, Petros C. (2006), 'If I Don't Do It, Somebody Else Will (Or Won't)', *Journal of World Trade*, 40 (1), 187–214

(2012), *Trade in Goods* (2 edn.; Oxford: Oxford University Press)

(2013), 'Driftin' Too Far From Shore – Why the Test for Compliance with the TBT Agreement Developed by the WTO Appellate Body Is Wrong, and What Should the AB Have Done Instead', *World Trade Review*, 12 (03), 509–31

and Wu, Mark (2013), *The Law of the World Trade Organization: Documents, Cases & Analysis* (2nd edn.; St. Paul, MN: West), 1072

(2015), *Sealed with a Doubt – EU, Seals and the WTO*, MIMEO

(2016), *The Regulation of International Trade: GATT* (Vol. 1) (Cambridge, MA: MIT Press), 588.

McAllister Shepro, Mary (2013), 'Preserving National Regulatory Autonomy in Financial Services: The GATS' Prudential Carve-Out', MIMEO

Mishkin, Frederic S. (1999), 'Lessons from the Asian Crisis', *Journal of International Money and Finance*, 18, 709–23

Mitchell, Andrew D., Hawkins, Jennifer K. and Mishra, Neha (2016), 'Dear Prudence: Allowances under International Trade and Investment Law for Prudential Regulation in the Financial Services Sector', *Journal of International Economic Law*, 19, 787–820

Morgenson, Gretchen and Rosner, Joshua (2011), *Reckless Endangerments – How Outsized Ambition, Greed and Corruption Led to Economic Armageddon* (New York: Times Books) 331

Morrison, Peter (1998), 'WTO Financial Services Agreement: A Basis for Further Liberalisation in 2000?', *International Trade Law & Regulation*, 4 (5), 188–91

Nadakavukaren Schefer, Krista (1999), *International Trade in Financial Services: The NAFTA Provisions* (The Hague/Boston: Kluwer Law International)

Narlikar, Amrita (2003), *International Trade and Developing Countries: Bargaining Coalitions in GATT and WTO* (London: Routledge)

Nielson, Julia (2003), 'Labor Mobility in Regional Trade Agreements', in Aaditya Mattoo and Antonia Carzaniga (eds.), *Moving People to Deliver Services* (Washington, DC: World Bank and Oxford University Press), 93–110

Odell, John S (2010), 'Three Islands of Knowledge about Negotiation in International Organizations', *Journal of European Public Policy*, 17 (5), 619–32

Olson, Mancur (1965), *The Logic of Collective Action – Public Goods and the Theory of Groups* (Cambridge, MA: Harvard University Press) 178

Ortino, Federico (2005), 'From 'Non-Discrimination' to 'Reasonableness': A Paradigm Shift in International Economic Law?', *Jean Monnet Working Paper*, 59

Ostry, Jonathan D., et al. (2011), 'Managing Capital Inflows: What Tools to Use?', *IMF Staff Discussion Note*, 1–41

Paemen, Hugo and Bensch, Alexandra (1995), *From the GATT to the WTO – The European Community in the Uruguay Round* (Leuven: Leuven University Press), 293

Ramet, Sabrina P. and Ingebritsen, Christine (2002), *Coming in from the Cold War – Changes in the US-European Interaction Since 1980* (Lanham, MD: Rowman & Littlefield Publishers), 244

Reinhart, Carmen M. and Rogoff, Kenneth S. (2009), *This Time Is Different: Eight Centuries of Financial Folly* (Princeton: Princeton University Press), 512
  (2013) 'Banking Crises: An Equal Opportunity Menace', *Journal of Banking and Finance*, 37 (11), 4557–4573

Reyna, Jimmie V. (1993), *Services*, in Terence P. Stewart (ed.), *The GATT Uruguay Round: A Negotiating History (1986–1992)* (Deventer: Kluwer), 329

Romano, Roberta (2014), 'Regulating in the Dark and a Postscript Assessment of the Iron Law of Financial Regulation', *Hostra Law Review*, 43 (1), 25–69

Rosendorff, B. Peter and Milner, Helen V. (2001), 'The Optimal Design of International Trade Institutions: Uncertainty and Escape', *International Organization*, 55 (4), 829–57

Sapir, André (2011), 'European Integration at the Crossroads: A Review Essay on the 50th Anniversary of Bela Balassa's "Theory of Economic Integration"', *Journal of Economic Literature*, 49 (4), 1200–29

Sauvé, Pierre (2013), 'A Plurilateral Agenda for Services? Assessing the Case for a Trade in Services Agreement (TISA)', *NCCR Trade Regulation Working Paper* (1–24)

Scalia, Antonin (1989), 'Judicial Deference to Administrative Interpretations of Law', *Duke Law Journal*, 1989 (3), 511–21

Schinasi, Garry J. (2006), *Safeguarding Financial Stability – Theory and Practice* (Washington, DC: International Monetary Fund), 309

Shleifer, Andrei, and Vishny, Robert (2010) 'Unstable Banking', *Journal of Financial Economics* 97 (3), 306–18

Silber, William L. (2012), *Volcker – The Triumph of Persistence* (New York: Bloomsbury Press), 454

Simser, Jeffrey (1994–1995), 'Financial Services Under NAFTA: A Starting Point', *Banking & Finance Law Review*, 10

Singer, D. A. (2007), *Regulating Capital – Setting Standards for the International Financial System* (Ithaca and London: Cornell University Press), 163

Srinivasan, Thirukodikaval N. (2005), 'Nondiscrimination in GATT/WTO: Was There Anything to Begin With and Is There Anything Left?', *World Trade Review*, 4 (01), 69–95

Stephanou, Constantinos (2009), 'Including Financial Services in Preferential Trade Agreements – Lessons of International Experience for China', *World Bank Policy Research Working Paper*, (April 2009), 26

Stirling, Andrew (2001), 'On "Precautionary" and "Science Based" Approaches to Risk Assessment and Environmental Appraisal', in Andrew Stirling (ed.), *On Science and Precaution in the Management of Technological Risk* (Vol. II) (Seville: European Science and Technology Observatory), 36–93

Sunstein, Cass R. (1990), 'Law and Administration after "Chevron"', *Columbia Law Review*, 90 (8), 2071–120

Sykes, Alan O. (2006), *The WTO Agreement on Safeguards – A Commentary* (Oxford: Oxford University Press) 357

(2015), 'Economic "Necessity" in International Law', *American Journal of International Law*, 109 (2), 296–323

Tarullo, Daniel K. (2008), *Banking on Basel – The Future of International Financial Regulation* (Washington, DC: Peterson Institute of International Economics)

Tirole, Jean (2011), 'Illiquidity and All Its Friends', *Journal of Economic Literature*, 49 (2), 287–325

Trachtman, Joel P. (1996), 'Trade in Financial Services under GATS, NAFTA and the EC: A Regulatory Jurisdiction Analysis', *Columbia Journal of Transnational Law*, 34:1, 37–122

Trujillo, Samuel (2015), 'Demystifying the Prudential Carve-Out: A Proposal'. *Revista Con-Texto*, 43 (2015), 157–208

Ulltveit-Moe, Karen H., Vale, Bent, Grindaker, Morten H. and Skancke, Erling (2013), 'Competitiveness and regulation of Norwegian Banks', Staff Memo – Norges Bank, (18), 93

van Aaken, Anne and Kurtz, Jürgen (2009), 'Prudence or Discrimination?: Emergency Measures, the Global Financial Crisis and International Economic Law', *Journal of International Economic Law*, 12 (4), 859–94

Verdier, Pierre-Hugues (2013), 'The Political Economy of International Financial Regulation', *Indiana Law Journal*, 88 (4), 1405–74

Véron, Nicolas (2014), 'The G20 Financial Reform Agenda after Five Years', Bruegel Working Paper, (11), 9

Von Bogdandy, Armin and Windsor, Joseph (2008), 'Annex on Financial Services', in Rüdiger Wolfrum, Peter-Tobias Stoll and Clemens Feinäugle (eds.), *WTO – Trade in Services – Max Planck Commentaries on World Trade Law* (Leiden/Boston: Martinus Nijhoff), 618–39

Walter, Andrew (2008), *Governing Finance – East Asia's Adoption of International Standards* (Ithaca, NY: Cornell University Press), 256

Wang, Wei (2008), 'The Prudential Carve-Out', in Kern Alexander and Mads Andenas (eds.), *The World Trade Organization and Trade in Services* (Leiden/Boston: Martinus Nijhoff), 601–14

Weiss, Friedl and Kammel, Armin J. (eds.) (2015), *The Changing Landscape of Global Financial Governance and the Role of Soft Law* (Leiden/Boston: Brill Nijhoff), 424

Windsor, Joseph (2008), 'The WTO Committee on Trade in Financial Services: The Exercise of Public Authority within an Informational Forum', *German Law Journal*, 9 (11), 1805–32

Wolfe, Robert (2013), 'Letting the Sun Shine In at the WTO: How Transparency Brings the Trading System to Life', *WTO Staff Working Paper*, 43

Woodrow, R. Brian (1995), 'Insurance Services in the Uruguay Round Services Negotiations: An Overview and Assessment of the Final Agreement', *The Geneva Papers on Risk and Insurance*, 20 (74), 57–73

Xu, Yi-Chong and Moray Weller, Patrick (2004), *The Governance of World Trade: International Civil Servants and the GATT/WTO* (Cheltenham: Edward Elgar), 311

Yokoi-Arai, Mamiko (2008), 'GATS Prudential Carve Out in Financial Services and Its Relation with Prudential Regulation', *International and Comparative Law Quarterly*, 57, 613–48

Zaring, David (2012), 'Finding Legal Principle in Global Financial Regulation', *Virginia Journal of International Law*, 52 (3), 683–722

Zavvos, Georges (2013), 'Towards a European Banking Union – Legal and Policy Implications' (Speech delivered at the 22nd Annual Hyman Minsky Conference 'Building a Financial Structure for a More Stable and Equitable Economy', New York, 18 April), 23

INDEX

abus de droit principle, chapeau approach and, 180–2
adequate level of protection (ALOP)
  CETA level of prudential regulation and, 165–7
Adlung, Rudolf, 77–8
Admati, Arian, 57
adverse selection, gridlock problem and, 41–2
Akerlof, George A., 40–1
Annex on Financial Services of the GATS
  Argentina – Financial Services Panel findings and, 92–6
  Brussels Ministerial Conference and draft of, 203–8
  dispute resolution mechanisms in, 13–15, 226–7
  domestic regulation and, 212–15
  EU draft proposal for, 200–3
  financial services regulation and, 185–8
  'GATS-like' prudential carve-outs and, 117–20
  history of negotiations on, 195–9, 208–9
  PCO included in, 69–70, 194
  Uruguay Round negotiations on, 5–15
Argentina – Financial Services Panel, 1–3, 168–9
  domestic regulation and, 214
  evolutionary nature of prudential objectives and, 99–103
  exceptions provision and, 220, 221–4
  findings of, 96–103
  GATS-PCO and, 92–104, 225–6
  market access findings, 91–2
  Most Favoured Nation findings, 87–91, 103
  National Treatment findings in, 103
Article XIV, General Agreement on Trade in Services (GATS)
  Appellate Body interpretations of, 172
  Argentina – Financial Services Panel and, 92–104
  Brussels Ministerial Conference and, 203–4
  chapeau language, 116, 132–4, 143, 152–4, 169–70
  comparisons with Article XX, (GATT 1994), 183–4
  discriminatory behavior, 69–70, 172–3, 180
  necessity test, 72–3, 116, 212–15
  scheduling guidelines and, 74–6
  structure of provisions in, 184–5
  WTO case law and chapeau of, 171, 180–2
Article XX, General Agreement on Tariffs and Trade (GATT 1994)
  Appellate Body, interpretations of, 172
  chapeau language, 116, 152–4, 169–70
  comparisons with Article XIV, (GATS), 183–4
  discriminatory behavior, 69–70, 180
  necessity test, 72–3, 116
  WTO case law and chapeau of, 180–2
  WTO-plus obligations and, 188–91

247

248 INDEX

Ascher, Bernard, 7–8
ASEAN–Australia–New Zealand FTA, 140–1
ASEAN–Korea FTA, 146
Asian financial crisis (1997), financial regulation and, 44–8
asymmetric information
  CETA level of prudential regulation and, 165–7
  prudential regulation, 40–1
Australia
  negotiations on GATS PCO and, 195–9
Australia–New Zealand Regional Trade Agreement (ANZCERTA), 136–7

Bank for International Settlements (BIS), 21–2
Bankhaus Herstatt, 21–2
Banking Act (South Korea), 47–8
Banking Union, EU proposal for, 51–4
Bank of India, 58
Bank of Indonesia, 46–7
Bank of Korea Act, 47–8
Bank of Thailand, 45–6
Bank Recovery and Resolution Directive (BRRD) (EU), 53–4
bank runs, multiple equilibriums and, 35–6
Basel Committee on Banking Supervision (BCBS), 21–7, 46–7
  Australian PCO proposals and, 78–80
  capital and sector capital requirements, 57
  minimum margin requirements, non-centrally cleared derivatives, 59
  standards development and, 232–6
Basel III framework, 23–7, 54–5
  capital and sector capital requirements, 57
  loan-to-value (LTV) restrictions, 58
Bhagwati, Jagdish, 6–7
Brazil
  financial services agreements and, 9–10
  GATS PCO negotiations and, 199

Brazil – Retreaded Tyres Panel, chapeau approach and, 176–7
Brussels Ministerial Conference (1990), 203–8
burden of proof, PCO and, 68–73

Café au Lait group, 9–10
Cameron, Maxwell A., 122–3
Canada
  Brussels Ministerial Conference and, 203–8
  CETA prudential carve-out negotiations and, 161–7
  dispute settlement in PCO and, 208–9
  GATS PCO negotiations and, 197–8, 199
  NAFTA negotiations and, 122–3
capital conservation
  Basel III buffer for, 23–7
  EU directives for, 51–4
  macroprudential strategies, 60–2
capital requirements
  'Basel III' framework, 23–7
  BCBS establishment of, 21–7
  as macroprudential strategy, 57, 229–31
Capital Requirements Directive (CRD) (EU), 51–4
Cassidy, John, 48–51
Central Bank Act (Indonesia), 46–7
central counterparties (CCPs)
  BCBS framework for, 24–5
  Dodd-Frank regulations and, 50–1
  European Markets and Infrastructure Regulation and, 53–4
  macroprudential strategies and, 59–60
Central Securities Depositors (CSDs), EU regulation of, 53–4
CETA. *See* EU–Canada Comprehensive Economic and Trade Agreement (CETA)
chapeau approach
  comparison of GATS and GATT provision, 179–84

INDEX

in GATS, 116, 169–70
line of equilibrium and, 180–2
Malaysia–Australia FTA, 143
in prudential carve-outs, 116, 149–50
two-tier analysis and, 172
in WTO case law, 171–9, 180–2
Chevron doctrine, NAFTA-like PCOs and, 129–30
Chevron U.S.A., Inc. v. Natural Resources Defense Council, Inc. 467 U.S. 837 (1984), 129–30
China. *See* People's Republic of China
China – Audiovisuals panel, 88
China – Measures Affecting Electronic Payment Services, 73–4, 89
China – Publications and Audiovisual Products, 188–91
China – Rare Earths, 188–91
China – Raw Materials, 188–91, 219
Coalition of Services Industry (CSI), 7–8
'Code of Best Practices for Directors of Listed Companies' (Thailand), 45–6
Code of Liberalisation of Capital Movements (OECD), 61–2
Colombia–Mexico FTA, 120–30
commitment theory, preferential trade agreements and, 112–13
Committee on Regional Trade Agreements (CRTA, WTO), preferential trade agreements and, 107–8
Committee on Trade and Financial Services (CTFS, WTO)
 Australian proposal for a common understanding of 'prudential regulation,' 78–80
 Barbados communication on compatibility and, 81–2
 Ecuador statement on macroprudential regulation and GATS, 82–4
 'GATS 2000: Financial Services' communication, 80–1
 PCOs and, 73–84

competition, MFN status, *Argentina – Financial Services* Panel and, 87–91
confidence in market, prudential regulation and, 41
'Core Principles Methodology' (BCBS), 23
Cottier, Thomas, 69
countercyclical buffer
 Basel III capital requirements and, 23–7
 as macroprudential strategy, 57–8
counterparty credit risk, Basel III framework, 23–7
currency exchange
 in ASEAN–Korea FTA, 146
 in Japan–Thailand FTA, 145–6
 prudential carve-outs and, 59–60, 145–6

debt-to-income restrictions, 58
De Nicolò, Gianni, 36–8
deregulation, economic impact of, 209–11
derivatives markets
 FSB policies concerning, 32–3
 minimum margin requirements, non–centrally cleared derivatives, 59
developing countries, financial services negotiations and, 11–12, 200–3
Diamond, Douglas W., 35–6
disclosure requirements
 EU commitment to, 51–4
 macroprudential strategies and, 59–60
discrimination
 elimination of, in preferential trade agreements, 106–13
 in NAFTA case law, 124–6
 in prudential carve-outs, 116
dispute resolution
 Annex 13 B to CETA PCO and, 165–7
 Annex on Financial Services and, 13–15
 filter mechanisms in, 164–5, 226–7
 NAFTA provisions on, 123–4
 standard of review in, 71–3

250 INDEX

distributions, restrictions on, 58
Dodd-Frank Wall Street Reform and Consumer Protection Act (US), 48–51
domestic regulation. *See also* regulatory framework for financial services
  Argentina – Financial Services Panel findings and, 92–103
  in ASEAN–Australia–New Zealand FTA, 140–1
  Brussels Ministerial Conference draft and, 203–4
  in EFTA–Hong Kong, China FTA, 142–3
  in EFTA–third parties–like category of PCO, 132–4
  'GATS-like' prudential carve-outs and, 117–20
  GATS PCO interpretation and, 68–73, 195–9, 212–15
  Switzerland–China FTA, 144
  in TTIP PCO negotiations, 158–61
  WTO member comments on, 231
Dunkel, Arthur, 207–8
Dybvig, Philip H., 35–6
dynamic provisioning, 58

East African Community agreements, 137–8
EC – Sardines, 72–3
EC – Seal Products, 177–9
economic crisis of 2007–8
  EU financial regulation following, 51–4
  financial regulation following, 48–54, 209–11
  macroprudential strategies in aftermath of, 56–62
  PCO policies and, 224
  US financial regulation following, 48–51
economic necessity principle, 191–3
EFTA–Central America FTA, 133–4
EFTA–Colombia FTA, 132–3
EFTA–Hong Kong, China FTA, 142–3
EFTA–Korea FTA, 132–3

EFTA–Mexico FTA, 132–3
EFTA–Singapore FTA, 132–3
EFTA–third parties–like category of PCO, 132–4
EFTA–Ukraine FTA, 133–4
Egypt, GATS PCO negotiations and, 199
Ehring, Lothar, 217
Emergency Financing Mechanism, Asian financial crisis and, 44–8
escape clauses, PCOs and, 193
EU–Canada Comprehensive Economic and Trade Agreement (CETA)
  Annex 13 B to, 165–7
  filter mechanism in investment disputes on financial services in, 164–5
  guidelines contained in, 236–7
  prudential carve-out negotiations in, 161–7
EU–CARIFORUM States EPA, 139–40
EU–Central America FTA, 117–20
EU–Chile FTA, 117–20
EU–Colombia and Peru FTA, 143–4
EU–Korea FTA, 141–2
European Common Agricultural Policy, 203
European Communities – Approval and Marketing of Biotech Products Panel, 217–19
European Economic Area (EEA), 114
European Free Trade Association (EFTA), 114
  prudential carve-outs and, 136
European Markets and Infrastructure Regulation (EMIR), 53–4
European Union (EU)
  advocacy for financial services agreements by, 8–9, 10–13
  Brussels Ministerial Conference and, 204–8
  CETA prudential carve-out negotiations and, 161–7
  dispute settlement in PCO and, 208–9
  financial regulation following economic crisis of 2007–8, 51–4

INDEX 251

negotiations on GATS PCO and, 195–9
preferential trade agreements and, 110–11
prudential carve-outs in Association Agreements with, 134–5
trade in services agreements in, 108n8
in TTIP PCO negotiations, 158–61
exceptions provisions
Brussels Ministerial Conference and, 203–4
East African Community agreements, 137–8
in EFTA–third parties–like category of PCO, 132–4
EU–Colombia and Peru FTA, 143–4
EU–Korea FTA, 141–2
EU prudential carve-outs as, 134–5
GATS Article XIV, 61–2
GATS PCO and, 68–73, 117, 149–50, 219–24
GATT 1994 Article XX, 61–2
General Exceptions case law, chapeau approach, 171–9, 180–2
Malaysia–Australia FTA, 143
in North American Free Trade Agreement, 120–1, 124–30
Singapore–Australia FTA, 138–9
structure of GATS and GATT provisions, 184–5
Switzerland–China FTA, 144
US–Singapore FTA, 130–2
WTO-plus obligations and, 188–91

false positives, PCOs and, 4, 219–24, 225–6
Farhi, Emmanuel, 35n69
Federal Reserve, Dodd-Frank reforms for, 51
film quotas, Article IV of GATT on, 216–19
filter mechanism
CETA investment dispute provisions, 164–5
institutional balance in WTO and, 226–7

financial contagion, pecuniary externalities and, 36–8
Financial Sector Assessment Program (FSAP), 22
financial services
economic rationale for regulation of, 209–11
international cooperation on, 5, 16–33
multilateral trade agreements and, 5–10, 15
multiple equilibriums in, 35–6
NAFTA negotiations on regulation of, 122–4
negotiations on agreements, 10–13
outcomes of regulation of, 21
in preferential trade agreements, 111–13
US advocacy for trade in, 7–8
WTO Secretariat background note on, 75–6
Financial Services Committee (CETA), 161–7
Financial Services Committee (NAFTA), 123–4, 127
Financial Services Modernization Act 1999 (US), 48–51
Financial Stability Board (FSB)
development of, 30–3
implementation monitoring, 33
policy development and coordination, 32–3
systemically important financial institutions and, 60
vulnerabilities assessment, 31–2
Financial Stability Oversight Council (FSOC) (US), 51
Fireman's Fund Insurance Company v Mexico, 124–6, 128–9
foggy commitments, PCO and WTO member practices and, 77–8
foreign currency lending
caps on, 59–60
in Japan–Thailand FTA, 145–6
Francois, Joseph, 6–7
free trade agreements (FTA), prudential carve-outs in, 114–54

fumus boni iuris (likelihood of success on merits of the case), *Argentina - Financial Services* Panel findings and, 96

G20 Agenda Towards A More Stable and Resilient International Financial Architecture, 29–30
GATS PCO
  absence of requirements, 185–8
  chapeau approach and, 116
  contingencies and application of, 191–3
  delegations' positions in negotiations over, 197
  domestic regulation and, 68–73, 195–9, 212–15, 225–6
  Dunkel Draft of, 207–8
  economic rationale for, 209–11
  exceptions provisions and, 68–73, 149–50
  limitations of, 179–84
  negotiating history of, 195–9, 208–9
  periodic review in, 230–1
  trade agreements and, 1–3
  WTO case law and, 215–19
  WTO member comments on domestic legislation and, 231
General Agreement on Tariffs and Trade (GATT). *See also* Article XX, General Agreement on Tariffs and Trade (GATT 1994)
  Article IV, 216–19
  Article XIX, 191–3
  Article XXI, 191–3
  chapeau language in, 116, 169–70, 171–9
  exception provisions, 179–84
  policy objectives of exceptions, 184–5
General Agreement on Trade in Services (GATS). *See also* Article XIV, General Agreement on Trade in Services (GATS); GATS PCO
  Annex on Financial Services of, 13–15, 64
  Argentina - Financial Services Panel findings on, 92–104

  Article VI, 65–8, 212–15, 225–6, 232–6
  Article VII, 232–6
  Brussels Ministerial Conference draft of, 203–8
  capital controls in, 61–2
  CETA PCO provisions and, 163
  chapeau language in, 116, 169–70, 171–9
  Committee on Trade in Financial Services, 3
  comparison of NAFTA with, 126–30
  'GATS 2000: Financial Services' communication, 80–1
  history of negotiations, 3
  'non-application' clause in, 10–13
  preferential trade agreements in, 106–13
  progressive liberalisation *vs* right to regulate in, 194
  Second Protocol (Interim Agreement), 12–13, 15
  standards development and, 231–6
  structure of exception provisions, 184–5
  TiSA prudential carve-out negotiations and, 157–8
  transparency obligations in, 227–9
  Understanding on Commitments on Financial Services, 15, 207–8
Georgia, Republic of, EU Association Agreement with, 134–5
Glass-Steagall Act (US), 48–51
global systemically important banks (G-SIBs), 60
good faith principle, PCO interpretation and, 71–3, 219–24
Gramm-Leach-Bailey Act, 48–51
Grando, Michelle T., 2
gridlock problem, prudential regulation and, 41–2
Gross Domestic Product (GDP), financial services share of, 6–10
Group of 20 (G-20), 29–30
  central counterparties measures and, 59–60

INDEX 253

Group of Negotiations on Services (GNS), 11–12, 195–9
　Brussels Ministerial Conference draft and, 204–8

Hawes, David, 206n93
Hellwig, Martin, 57
high-frequency trading (HTF), European Markets and Infrastructure Regulation and, 53–4
high-quality liquid assets (HQLA), Liquidity Coverage Ratio (LCR), 26–7
Hoekman, Bernard, 6–7
Hong Kong–Chile FTA, 117–20
housing price bubble, United States, post-crisis financial regulation and, 48–51
Hungary, GATS PCO negotiations and, 199
hybrid prudential carve-outs
　ASEAN–Australia–New Zealand FTA, 140–1
　ASEAN–Korea FTA, 146
　Japan–Thailand FTA, 145–6
　Korea–Vietnam FTA, 147–8

'incomplete' agreements, PTAs in services as, 108–11
India
　financial services agreements and, 9–10
　GATS PCO negotiations and, 197–8
India – Quantitative Restrictions, 226–7
Indonesia, Asian financial crisis and, 46–7
Insurance Core Principles, 29
International Association of Insurance Supervisors (IAIS), 29, 78–80
International Centre for Settlement of Investment Disputes (ICSID), 164–5
international cooperation on financial services regulation, 5, 16–33
　capital controls and, 60–2
　institutions involved in, 20–33
　objectives of, 16–21
　standards development and, 232–6
International Monetary Fund (IMF)
　Asian financial crisis (1997) and, 44–8
　Financial Sector Assessment Program, 22
　recovery programs of, 42–4
International Organization of Securities Commissions (IOSCO), 27–8
　minimum margin requirements, non-centrally cleared derivatives, 59
'Inuit Community exception', 177–9
investment activities
　Annex 13 B to CETA PCO and, 165–7
　CETA filter mechanism in investment disputes on financial services and, 164–5
　NAFTA provisions on, 123–4
　restrictions on US commercial bank involvement in, 48–51

Japan
　Brussels Ministerial Conference and, 203–8
　dispute settlement in PCO and, 208–9
　GATS PCO negotiations and, 197–8
Japan–Mexico FTA, 139
Japan–Switzerland FTA, 117–20
Japan–Thailand FTA, 145–6
Jarreau, J. Steven, 10–13, 212–15
jurisdictional issues
　international cooperation on financial services regulation and, 16–21
　PCO and, 3
justiciability, Brussels Ministerial Conference negotiations and, 207–8

Kern, Steffen, 51
Key Attributes of Effective Resolution Regimes for Financial Institutions, 32–3

Korea–Vietnam FTA, 147–8
Krajewski, Markus, 69

lawfulness/unlawfulness, indicators of, CETA level of prudential regulation and, 165–7
Leroux, Eric, 68
Leverage Ratio, 54–5
  maximum leverage ratios, 57–8
leveraging regulations, Basel III framework, 23–7
lex specialis principle
  domestic regulation and, 212–15
  in NAFTA-like PCOs, 128
'likeness' principle, MFN status, *Argentina – Financial Services* Panel, 87–91
Liquidity Coverage Ratio (LCR), 26–7, 58
liquidity rules
  Basel III framework, 26–7
  EU directives, 51–4
loan-to-value (LTV) restrictions, 58

macroprudential policy
  in aftermath of economic crisis of 2008, 56–62
  capital controls, 60–2
  capital and sectoral capital requirements, 57
  central counterparties and, 59–60
  countercyclical capital buffers, 57–8
  debt-to-income restrictions, 58
  disclosure requirements, 59–60
  distribution restrictions, 58
  foreign currency lending caps, 59–60
  GATS PCO negotiations and, 200–3
  liquidity coverage ratio, 58
  loan-to-value restrictions, 58
  maximum leverage ratios, 57–8
  minimum margin requirements, non-centrally cleared derivatives, 59
  in NAFTA PCO, 126–30
  open currency positions, 59–60
  reserve requirements, 59–60
  systemically important financial institutions, 60

time varying/dynamic provisioning, 58
Malaysia
  Brussels Ministerial Conference draft and, 203–8
  GATS PCO negotiations and, 199
Malaysia–Australia FTA, 143
Marchetti, Juan A., 7–9
market access
  Argentina – Financial Services Panel findings on, 91–2
  CETA PCO negotiations, 161–7
  for financial services, NAFTA provision for, 123–4
  TiSA prudential carve-out negotiations and, 157–8
market discipline, Basel III framework, 23–7
market imperfections and failures, prudential regulation and, 39–40, 209–11, 229–31
Markets in Financial Instruments Directive (MiFID) (EU), 53–4
Markets in Financial Instruments Regulation (MiFIR) (EU), 53–4
Matoo, Aaditya, 76–8
maturity mismatch, multiple equilibriums and, 35–6
Mavroidis, Petros C., 7–9, 107, 112–13
maximum leverage ratios, as macroprudential strategy, 57–8
McAllister Shepro, Mary, 70–3
MERCOSUR
  Brazil – Retreaded Tyres, 176–7
  'GATS-like' prudential carve-outs in, 117–20
Mexico
  Brussels Ministerial Conference draft and, 204–8
  case law involving NAFTA and, 124–6
  NAFTA negotiations and, 110–11, 122–3
Mexico–Panama FTA, 117–20
microprudential strategies
  GATS PCO negotiations and, 200–3
  in NAFTA PCO, 126–30

MiFID II Package, 53-4
Milner, Helen V., 193
minimum margin requirements, non-centrally cleared derivatives, 59
minimum standards requirements, prudential carve-outs and, 158-61
Mitterrand, François, 8-9
Moldova, Republic of, EU Association Agreement with, 134-5
monitoring, economies of scale in, 40
moral hazard
  Asian financial crisis and, 44-8
  gridlock problem and, 41-2
  maturity mismatch and, 35n69
  prudential regulation and, 38-9
Most Favoured Nation (MFN)
  Argentina – Financial Services Panel findings on, 87-91
  CETA PCO negotiations, 161-7
  financial services negotiations and, 11-12, 75-6
Multilateral Memorandum of Understanding Concerning Consultation and Cooperation and the Exchange of Information (MMoU), 27-8
multiple equilibriums, prudential regulation and, 35-6
Mutual Recognition Agreements (MRAs), 233-4
  Annex on Financial Services and, 13-15
Mutual Recognition Agreements, Annex on Financial Services and, 13-15

naked short selling, 54n122
National Treatment
  in Australia-New Zealand (ANZCERTA), 136-7
  CETA PCO negotiations, 161-7
  GATS PCO negotiations and, 195-9
  in NAFTA case law, 124-6, 128-9
  in prudential carve-outs, 116, 149-50

TiSA prudential carve-out negotiations and, 157-8
necessity test
  chapeau in WTO case law and, 171-9
  EFTA-third parties-like category of PCO, 132-4
  in EU-Korea FTA, 141-2
  GATS PCO and, 217-19
  in NAFTA-like PCOs, 126-30
  in prudential carve-outs, 3, 72-3, 116, 149
negative listing approach
  CETA PCO negotiations, 161
  TiSA PCO negotiations, 157-8
net stable funding ratio (NSFR), 26-7
non-exhaustiveness, PCO strategies and, 75-6
North American Free Trade Agreement (NAFTA), 110-11
  Arbitral Tribunal of, 124-6
  Article 1407 (New Financial Services and Data Processing), 123-4
  Article 1415 (Investment Disputes in Financial Services), 123-4
  case law relating to, 124-6
  CETA PCO provisions and, 163
  Chevron doctrine and, 129-30
  comparison of GATS to, 126-30
  content and list of objectives, 115-16
  exceptions in, 120-1
  law and trade rules provisions in, 123-4
  negotiating history and rationale for, 122-3
  prudential carve-outs replication of, 120-30
  reasonableness test in, 198-9

Objectives and Principles of Securities Regulations, 27-8
'obligations of result' requirements, prudential carve-outs and, 158-61
open currency positions
  in Japan-Thailand FTA, 145-6
  limits on, 59-60

Organisation for Economic
   Cooperation and Development
   (OECD)
  Code of Liberalisation of Capital
   Movements, 61–2
  standards development and, 232–6
over-the-counter (OTC) derivatives
  central counterparties and, 59–60
  European Markets and
   Infrastructure Regulation and,
   53–4

Pacific Alliance FTA, 117–20
Panama–Central America FTA,
   120–30
Panama–Chinese Taipei FTA, 120–30
Panama–Peru FTA, 130–2
Pareto efficiency, pecuniary
   externalities, 36–8
path dependency, international
   cooperation on financial services
   regulation and, 18–20
pecuniary externalities, prudential
   regulation and, 36–8
peruculum in mora (danger in delay),
   Argentina – Financial Services
   Panel findings and, 96
Peru–Mexico FTA, 120–30
plurilateral agreement, TiSA prudential
   carve-out negotiations and, 156–8
Poland, GATS PCO negotiations and,
   199
precautionary principle, in economics,
   209–11
preferential trade agreements (PTAs)
  as exceptions in financial services,
   108–11
  financial services in, 111–13
  GATS provisions on, 106–13
  prudential carve-outs in, 3–4,
   114–54
  WTO-plus obligations and, 188–91
presumption of lawfulness, CETA level
   of prudential regulation and,
   165–7
*Principles for Sound Liquidity Risk
   Management and Supervision*,
   26–7

proportionality test
  GATS PCO and, 218
  in NAFTA-like PCOs, 126–30
protectionism, PCO and preemption
   of, 76–8
prudential carve-outs (PCOs). *See also*
   GATS PCO
  Argentina – Financial Services Panel
   findings on, 92–104
  ASEAN–Australia–New Zealand
   FTA, 140–1
  ASEAN–Korea FTA, 146
  Australia–New Zealand
   (ANZCERTA), 136–7
  Australian proposals for, 78–80
  Barbados communication on
   compatibility with the GATS and,
   81–2
  chapeau approach in, 116, 143,
   169–84
  in Committee on Trade and
   Financial Services (WTO), 73–84
  content and list of objectives,
   115–16, 148–9
  Dunkel Draft of, 207–8
  East African Community and, 137–8
  economic rationales for, 3
  EFTA–Hong Kong FTA, 142–3
  EFTA–third parties–like category of,
   132–4
  EU 2014 category of, 134–5
  EU–Canada Comprehensive
   Economic and Trade Agreement
   negotiations, 161–7
  EU–CARIFORUM States EPA,
   139–40
  EU–Colombia and Peru FTA, 143–4
  EU–Korea FTA, 141–2
  European Free Trade Association
   and, 136
  GATS-like category of, 117–20
  guidelines for, 236–7
  interpretive problems with, 3, 65–8
  Japan–Mexico FTA, 139
  Japan–Thailand FTA, 145–6
  Korea–Vietnam FTA, 147–8
  legal function of, 1–3
  Malaysia–Australia FTA, 143

NAFTA-like category of, 120–30
National Treatment principle in, 116
necessity test in, 3, 72–3, 116
reasonableness test in, 69–70, 116, 149
research on, 68–73
restrictiveness index, 152–4
scope of application, 115, 148
Singapore–Australia FTA, 138–9
standards development and, 117, 236
Switzerland–China FTA, 144
Trade in Services Agreements negotiations on, 156–8
in Trans-Atlantic Trade and Investment Partnership, 158–61
trends in preferential PCOs over time, 150
US post-2004 category, 130–2
prudential regulation
economics of, 34–5
filter mechanisms, 226–7
gridlock problem and, 41–2
importance of, 33–42
'lemons' and confidence and, 40–1
market imperfections and failures, 39–40
monitoring economies of scale, 40
moral hazard and, 38–9
multiple equilibriums and, 35–6
pecuniary externalities and, 36–8
periodic review and, 229–31
regulatory autonomy in other sectors and, 62–3
WTO Secretariat background note on, 75–6

rational choice theory, international cooperation on financial services regulation and, 18–20
'Really Good Friends of Services' (RGFS), 156–8
reasonableness test
CETA PCO provisions and, 163
EFTA–third parties–like category of PCO, 132–4
'GATS-like' prudential carve-outs, 119

GATS PCO negotiations and, 198–9
in prudential carve-outs, 69–70, 116, 149
scholarship concerning, 128–9
Regulation (EU) No 575/2013 (CRD IV), 51–4
Regulations on Banking Supervision of 1999 (South Korea), 47–8
Report of the Commission of Experts of the President of the United Nations General Assembly on Reforms of the International Monetary and Financial System, 1–3
reserve requirements, 59–60
restrictiveness index for PCOs, 152–4
retrocession services, trade in, 85–6
risk coverage for capital, Basel III framework, 23–7
Romano, Roberta, 230–1
Rosendorff, B. Peter, 193

safeguard schemes, economic necessity principle and, 191–3
sector capital requirements, 57
Securities and Exchange Committee (SEC) of Thailand, 45–6
self-executing standard of review, PCO interpretation and, 71–3
Self-Regulatory Organizations Consultative Committee, 27–8
shadow banking, FSB policies concerning, 32–3
shocks, multiple equilibriums and, 35–6
short selling, European Markets and Infrastructure Regulation and, 53–4
Silber, William L., 48–51
Singapore
Brussels Ministerial Conference draft and, 204–8
GATS PCO negotiations and, 199
Singapore–Australia FTA, 138–9, 225–6
single market for financial services, EU commitment to, 51–4

South Africa, GATS PCO negotiations and, 199
Southeast Asian Countries network (SEACEN), 200-3
  Brussels Ministerial Conference draft and, 203-8
  dispute settlement in PCO and, 208-9
South Korea, Asian financial crisis and, 47-8
Spain, dynamic provisioning in, 58
SPS Agreement (WTO Agreement on the Application of Sanitary and Phytosanitary Measures), 165-7, 209-11, 217-19
  PCO comparison with, 221-4
  periodic review in, 229-31
  WTO member comments on domestic legislation and, 231
standard of review, for PCO disputes, 71-3
standard of treatment, in EU prudential carve-outs, 134-5
standard setting organisations
  financial regulation and, 20-1, 231-6
  PCOs and, 117, 149-50
Standing Committee for the Assessment of Vulnerabilities (SCAV, FSB), 31-2
Standing Committee on Banking Regulations and Supervisory Practices, 21-2
Standing Committee on Standards Implementation (SCSI), 33
Stephanou, Constantinos, 112-13
Stirling, Andrew, 209-11
Stock Exchange of Thailand (SET), 45-6
subprime market in United States, financial crisis of 2007-8 and, 48-51
substantial sectoral coverage, in preferential trade agreements, 106-13
Sweden
  Brussels Ministerial Conference and, 203-8
  GATS PCO negotiations and, 198-9
Switzerland
  Brussels Ministerial Conference and, 203-4
  GATS PCO negotiations and, 199
Switzerland-China FTA, 144
Sykes, Alan O., 191-3
systemically important financial institutions (SIFIs), 26-7, 60
systemic banking crises, preceding events in, 35n68

taxation
  Argentina – Financial Services Panel and, 84-91
  retrocession services, trade in, 85-6
tax havens, retrocession services and, 85-6
technology, transnational trade in services and, 6-7
Thailand
  Asian financial crisis and, 45-6
  GATS PCO negotiations and, 198-9
Tier 1 Capital reform, 54-5
time inconsistencies, international cooperation on financial services regulation and, 16-21
time-varying provisioning, 58
Tirole, Jean, 35n69
Tomlin, Brian W., 122-3
Trachtman, Joel P., 126-30
Trade Act (1974) (US), 7-8
Trade in Services Agreements (TiSA), 109
  PCO negotiations in, 156-8
Trans-Atlantic Trade and Investment Partnership (TTIP), prudential carve-out negotiations, 158-61
transparency in financial services
  EU commitment to, 51-4
  in WTO agreements, 227-9
trust, preferential trade agreements and role of, 109-10

Ukraine, EU Association Agreement with, 134-5
Ukraine-Montenegro FTA, 133-4
Ulltveit-Moe, Karen H., 36-9

'Unintended Consequences of Remedial Measures taken to correct the Global Financial Crisis: Possible Implications for WTO Compliance', 81–2
United States
  advocacy for financial services agreements by, 7–8, 10–13
  Brussels Ministerial Conference draft and, 204–8
  on multilateral trade agreements and PCOs, 200–3
  negotiations on GATS PCO and, 195–9
  opposition to financial services agreements in, 11–12
  post-crisis financial regulation in, 48–51
  in TTIP PCO negotiations, 158–61
  WTO scrutiny of PCOs and, 200–3
Uruguay Round
  Annex on Financial Services and, 5–15
  financial services negotiations and, 10–13, 62–3
  US – *Gambling* Panel, 65, 70n18, 74–6, 224
    Article XIV GATS chapeau in, 171, 172–3
  US – *Gasoline* case, Article XX GATT chapeau in, 172
  US post-2004 PCO category, 130–2
  US – *Shrimp* case, Article XX GATT chapeau in, 174, 180–2
  US–Singapore FTA, 130–2

Verdier, Pierre-Hugues, 16–21
Vienna Convention on the Law of Treaties (VCLT)
  PCO interpretation and, 70–1
  scheduling guidelines and, 74–6
Volcker, Paul, 48–51
Volcker Rule, 48–51
vulnerability assessment, FSB SCAV, 31–2

Wethington, Olin L., 125–6
WikiLeaks, 157–8
Wolfe, Robert, 227–9
'Working Group on Financial Services including Insurance', 195–9
World Bank, Financial Sector Assessment Program, 22
World Trade Organization (WTO)
  Agreement on Safeguards, 191–3, 229–31
  Annex on Financial Services of GATS and, 215
  Committee on Trade and Financial Services, PCO discussion by, 73–84
  financial services negotiations and, 12–13
  GATS PCO and, 5, 65–8, 199, 200–3, 215–19, 225–6
  plurilateral agreements in Annex 4 of, 156–8
  preferential trade agreements and, 106–13
  Secretariat of, 74–6
  transparency obligations of, 227–9
WTO-plus obligations and, exceptions provisions and, 188–91
Wunsch-Vincent, Sacha, 76–8

Yeutter, Clayton, 7–8
Young, Kevin, 54–5